AF471185

Socrates in September

American University Studies

Series V
Philosophy
Vol. 53

PETER LANG
New York · Bern · Frankfurt am Main · Paris

Michael Jay Katz

Socrates in September

The Entanglements
of Complexity

PETER LANG
New York · Bern · Frankfurt am Main · Paris

Library of Congress Cataloging-in-Publication Data

Katz, Michael Jay
   Socrates in September.
      p. cm. — (American university studies. Series V,
Philosophy ; vol. 53)
      1. Complexity (Philosophy)   2. Simplicity
(Philosophy)   3. Science—Philosophy.   4. Philosophy.
   5. Socrates.   I. Title.   II. Series.
BI05.C473K384   1988,1991   110   88-12706
ISBN 0-8204-0652-X   CIP
ISSN 0739-6392

CIP-Titelaufnahme der Deutschen Bibliothek

Katz, Michael J.:
Socrates in September : the entanglements of complexity /
Michael Jay Katz.—New York; Bern; Frankfurt am Main;
Paris: Lang, 1988,1991
   (American university studies : Ser. 5, Philosophy ;
Vol. 53)
   ISBN 0-8204-0652-X
NE: American university studies / 05

The paper in this book meets the guidelines for permanence and durability
of the Committee on Production Guidelines for Book Longevity of the
Council on Library Resources.

DEDICATION

To my colleague
Raymond John Lasek

Contents

Contents

Acknowledgments

This is a companion to my volume *Socrates in October: Dialogues on Incondensable Complexity*.

I have become acquainted with Socrates through the translations of Plato that are collected in:

Hamilton, E. and Cairns, H. (eds.) (1961) *The Collected Dialogues of Plato, including the Letters* Bollingen Series LXXI, Princeton Univ. Press, Princeton.

especially:

Gorgias translated by W.D. Woodhead

Philebus translated by R. Hackforth *Socrates' Defense (Apology)* translated by H. Tredennick;

this last—Plato's *Socrates' Defense*—is one of the finest essays mankind has ever set in writing.

I have used the translation of Cicero's writings by Hubbell:

Hubbell, H.M. (transl.) (1949) *Cicero. II. De Inventione* Harvard Univ. Press, Cambridge MA.

the translations of Xenophon's writings by Marchant and Todd:

Marchant, E.C. (transl.) (1923) *Memorabilia and Oeconomicus* Harvard Univ. Press, Cambridge MA.

Todd, O.J. (transl.) (1923) *Symposium and Apology* Harvard Univ. Press, Cambridge, MA.

and the translations of Hesiod's writings by Evelyn-White:

Evelyn-White, H.G. (transl.) (1936) *Hesiod. The Homeric Hymns and Homerica* Harvard Univ. Press, Cambridge, MA.

As before, I have had the pleasure of seeing the Homeric landscape through the eyes of Richmond Lattimore:

Lattimore, R. (transl.) (1951) *The Iliad of Homer* Univ. Chicago Press, Chicago.

and of the poet Robert Fitzgerald:

Fitzgerald, R. (transl.) (1963) *Homer. The Odyssey* Anchor Books and Doubleday, New York.

Also, in the dialogue "September 21: PLATO,"I have quoted the entire Emily Dickinson poem:

Dickinson, E. How happy is the little stone. In: Williams, O. (ed.) (1955) *The New Pocket Anthology of American Verse* Washington Square, New York, p. 161.

Thanks be to poets—where would we be without them?

M.J. Katz

Prologue

A leaf that's red and brown,
Cold bare branches turning down,
September grades to fall—
And all.

On clear mornings, Socrates
Checks the weather indices,
Backporch meteorograph—
Wind-staff.

The brass barometer is taut;
Last night's moisture being caught
In ombrologic pipes—
Rain stripes.

"A light warm breakfast, I'd advise,
Against these graying autumn skies
With their cirro-stratus floats,"
He notes.

"I've monitored the gentle breeze
Through ancient atmospheric seas,
Mapped the clouds adagio—
Before snow.

"Now, this wisp of old wind here,
Peeking in the window mirror,
To brush and then to disappear—
You hear?

"It came from Homer's golden tongue
One spring—The world was very young
When he gently breathed that word
We've heard."

September 1: HERMIPPUS

EUDICUS: Hello, Socrates.

SOCRATES: Good morning, Eudicus—good morning, Apemantus. It is not often that I see a father and son sitting here together in the marketplace.

APEMANTUS: Ah, boys have their own concerns nowadays, Socrates.

EUDICUS: Boys? You will be calling me a boy when I am as old as Socrates.

APEMANTUS: True enough, you will always be a boy, Eudicus. Look at him, Socrates—he is not even fifty and already he wants to be old.

EUDICUS: Tell me, Socrates, did your father give you as much difficulty as this crusty old man gives to me?

SOCRATES: My father? Let me see, Eudicus . . . my father has been dead for thirty years now. But yes, I suppose that he did complain. He was a sculptor you know—a fine sculptor—but he was very particular about his work. He never approved of the modern trend toward life-like, animated figures; he always liked the stiff stylized gods and heroes.

EUDICUS: Do you mean like the statue of Heracles behind the Temple of Zeus?

SOCRATES: Exactly, Eudicus. Heracles is bent over at an unnatural angle; he is completely flat and symmetric (wrestling there with the sinuous river-god Achelous). An even clearer example is the famous Delian figure of Nike. You know the one, Eudicus; it has been copied many times. Nike's arms are perfectly symmetric triangles; her six wings are even, exact, and balanced; her long drapery flows in straight strong lines; and her knee bends at a smooth right angle.

EUDICUS: I prefer the realistic statues myself—they are warmer and more noble, they are like friends.

APEMANTUS: When you grow up, my son, your tastes will mature. Eventually, Eudicus, you will see that the *old* style is more noble: it is perfect, it is symmetric, and it is absolute. Remember: humans are only rough copies of the gods. Moreover, young man, the gods live apart, and they are *not* our friends. I agree with Sophroniscus: modern sculptors dilute the divinity of their figures. Modernists have acceded to the unbridled sensuality of the young—the unbridled sensuality of you emotional, headstrong children.

EUDICUS: Father, you only say that to be contrary.

APEMANTUS: Yes—contrary to your glib and ill-thought-out speeches.

EUDICUS: You see, Socrates? Will a father ever listen to his son?

APEMANTUS: Socrates, I knew your father Sophroniscus. He had solid values: he did not bend with every light breeze that passed through the populace. But I must say, Socrates, you were a bit of a disappointment to him. I remember that Sophroniscus went to great pains in order to secure for you the best instruction in gymnastics and music, in geometry, astronomy, and classic Greek thought.

SOCRATES: Yes he did, Apemantus.

APEMANTUS: Then he hopefully apprenticed you as a sculptor.

SOCRATES: True. I went to work with Phrynion (Echecrates's father), who was a student of Cresalius of Crete. (Cresalius carved those fine statues of amazons at Ephesus; he also made the well-known replica of Pericles. In *his* youth, Cresalius had learned his craft from Bupalus, the son of the famed Chian marble sculptor, Archermus.)

EUDICUS: Archermus, was he not also the father of the great sculptor Micciades?

APEMANTUS: No no, Eudicus—it is the other way around: Micciades was Archermus's father. You do not even attend to who is the father of whom—it is no wonder that you have no respect for your elders.

EUDICUS: Father—you are my elder and I respect you. In this you are more fortunate than me, because it appears that I will never receive the respect that you do; I will be dead before you will admit me to the class of elders.

SOCRATES: Eudicus, have more faith and patience. Somehow life manges to go on until we reach our goals. Remember Homer's verse in the *Odyssey*:

> How long runs a life's monologue?
> Until one's dream is found.
> (With patience, says the apologue,
> All hopes come betimes around.)
> Odysseus's faithful dog,
> Argos—the trusty hound
> Who'd hunted hare and jays
> Under gleaming skies
> In younger springtime days—
> Finally closed his eyes
> After twenty waiting years;
> After years of patient sighs,
> His lord, Odysseus, again appears.

HERMIPPUS: No, Socrates, you remember it awrong. As *I* recall, it goes:

> How long must life drag out
> Until our souls transfer?
> (If you wait, without a doubt
> The worst will soon occur.)
> Argos, thick and stout—
> Odysseus's lifeless cur
> Who'd hunted butterflies
> Under gloomy skies
> On sultry summer days—

> Now opened wide his eyes
> For after twenty years,
> His lord, in weak disguise,
> Has trod poor Argos's ears.

EUDICUS: Ah father, now here is someone who *truly* has no respect for his elders—Hermippus the one-eyed writer of Comedy. Hermippus has a stinging word for everyone, even for Homer.

HERMIPPUS: Bah! Respect for my *elders*? Young man I have no elders! People say that I am seventy-five, but each of those years seemed like two. So I am at least one hundred and fifty—and to tell the truth, it feels more like two hundred years. By now my teeth are gone and my mouth is sour continuously. I am so old that if I did not wash my ears with wine each morning, then I would not be able to hear a thing. (Of course that would be all the better, given all the foolish drivel you children are spilling out here in the marketplace.)

SOCRATES: Hermippus, I believe that you *will* live to be two hundred—you certainly seem to have been around here forever.

HERMIPPUS: Of course I have been around here forever: Where else should I be, Socrates? I am like the little old hermit under the hill—

> There was an old woman
> Lived under a hill,
> And if she's not gone
> She lives there still.

Besides, whether I have been here one hundred years or two hundred years—what is the difference?

SOCRATES: I will tell you the difference, you cranky old hermit: I estimate that after two hundred years we will no longer be able to see you.

HERMIPPUS: What kind of craziness are you talking now, Socrates?

SOCRATES: I am talking about you—you are like a piece of

dried beef preserved in vinegar. You never decay: all you do is shrivel a bit more every night. One day of course, you will be so thin that we will not be able to see you at all. But never fear, I do not doubt that your squeak will still remain, haunting us here in the marketplace, drifting about, badgering the pomposity out of windy speakers like me.

HERMIPPUS: Well, well, Socrates—it is good to see you with a little insight finally. But *your* portly figure need fear no shriveling.

SOCRATES: Perhaps when I get as old as you, my Comedic friend, then I too will be thin.

HERMIPPUS: Oh, you will? Undoubtedly that would pose problems: your overblown lungs would never fit in my skinny frame. If by some rare chance you became thin someday and if you managed to squeeze your windy lungs into a shrivelled chest and if you took a large breath, then you would go floating away over the clouds. For once people would be telling the truth when they exclaimed: "My, my, Socrates has been carried away by his own arguments."

EUDICUS: And is this just as people say that *Hermippus* is carried away by his own words?

HERMIPPUS: Which dogs say that?!

EUDICUS: Every youth has said that since my school days, you old rogue. Why, I remember the boys chanting your verse:

> Periwinkle Pericles
> Is itching now from more than fleas—
> His mistress, Aspasia, he can't please;
> So she takes up with Lysicles.

HERMIPPUS: Scurrilous runt! I never wrote that doggerel!

EUDICUS: Well, something that you *did* write must have inspired it.

HERMIPPUS: Socrates—this is the fate of an honest play-wright! We poor journeymen simply tell the truth, and then we are ridiculed and castigated by those who are so young that they need their parents to wipe their noses. It is a good thing that I have only one eye—if I was forced to see two of everyone, in this demented clamjafry, then I would despair and I would certainly kill myself.

SOCRATES: Hermippus, two eyes still give us only one vista.

HERMIPPUS: Yes yes, one *compound* vista—but your one view is much deeper than the picture that I can get with my one lone peephole.

SOCRATES: So, two eyes are better than one?

HERMIPPUS: Better? Of course they're better! Do you think that Zeus put us here with two eyes for no reason? Do you think that it was simply some whim of his that we have two eyes, two ears, two hands, two feet, two arms, two legs, two breasts, and two nostrils? By Athena, Socrates, you can certainly ask childish questions!

SOCRATES: Remember, Hermippus, I am younger than you.

HERMIPPUS: True enough, my child.

SOCRATES: And questions are a perogative of youth.

HERMIPPUS: Perogative? They are a curse, more truly.

APEMANTUS: Yes—they are definitely a curse.

SOCRATES: Nonetheless, Hermippus, you would concede that questioning comes with the territory. Would you not?

HERMIPPUS: It certainly does: the land of the young is littered with interminable questions and questions and questions.

SOCRATES: Then in deference to my age, you will permit me a few more questions?

HERMIPPUS: A few, Socrates? Come now, let us have a little forthright honesty here—you really mean vast oceans of questions, plains and seas and limitless expanses of questions. Do not be so modest, Socrates. You could ask questions day and night for weeks and weeks, and even then you would just be starting.

SOCRATES: Yes, I do enjoy questioning, Hermippus.

HERMIPPUS: Enjoy? It is a perverse pleasure—but it is all the same to me: What else does an old playwright have to do with his time but to spout answers to children's rambling musings. You are an insatiable pup who cannot stand silence:

> Two little dogs
> Sat by the fire
> Over a fender of coal-dust;
>
> Said one little dog
> To the other little dog,
> If you don't talk soon, then I must.

Zeus forbid that we have a bit of quiet, Socrates. But go ahead and yap, my young philosophical hound—already we have spent too much time on this prologue. If we have any hope of wading into the full drama, we should hurry before winter comes and the snows fall and my one good eye freezes right out of my head.

SOCRATES: Your one good eye? It is your one good eye that makes me wonder, Hermippus.

HERMIPPUS: Well I can understand *that*—it makes me wonder too, Socrates: I wonder what you are leading up to.

SOCRATES: You have said, my friend, that two eyes are better than one.

HERMIPPUS: Of course I said that, for they are.

SOCRATES: In what way are they better, Hermippus?

HERMIPPUS: Eudicus, do you hear him? And, Apemantus—you too are a witness. Socrates, my thick-headed friend, the gods gave men two eyes because two eyes are necessary. (Then of course, the immortal gods cursed me with just one. One eye! It is amazing that I can shoot an arrow at all; it is amazing that I can wrestle and that I can even reach for a cup.)

SOCRATES: You can still shoot an arrow?

HERMIPPUS: Yes by Zeus, I can.

SOCRATES: And wrestle?

HERMIPPUS: Do you think that I am a doddering old cripple?

SOCRATES: And you can reach for a cup and write with a stylus and drive a cart?

HERMIPPUS: Certainly, certainly! I can do anything you young men can do—and that is because I have kept my body in good trim. (Which is more than I can say for you, Socrates.)

SOCRATES: You can judge distances accurately?

HERMIPPUS: Yes.

SOCRATES: Can you cuff a dog before he steals a biscuit from the table?

HERMIPPUS: Do you have such a low opinion of me, Socrates? Would I hit a dog? Dogs are more well-mannered than our politicians—a dog would never bite someone who nutured him in youth. This is more than I can say for our leaders. But much as I have been tempted, I have never yet struck any of those arrogant demagogues of ours.

SOCRATES: So, you get about quite well in this life with one eye?

HERMIPPUS: Do I have two, Socrates? I was born with one good eye, I have lived all my life with one eye, and after seventy-five one-eyed years you would think that I could manage a few daily affairs myself with that one eye.

SOCRATES: Then, Hermippus, it took you seventy-five years to learn to use only one eye?

HERMIPPUS: Now, Socrates, would I have lived seventy-five years if they had all been spent learning to see? I cannot believe that I am hearing such thoughtless questioning from the one man who forever claims to use his mind.

SOCRATES: Then you lived a normal life even as a one-eyed youth?

HERMIPPUS: Ah, Socrates, I was not normal: I was better than normal. I was more daring than normal, I was wilder than normal—I jumped from rooftop to rooftop and I never missed one. (Well I must confess that our neighbor's court was too far to leap in one jump, but I managed to swing along the rafters and never to touch the ground.)

SOCRATES: That sounds like quite a bit of acrobatics for one eye.

HERMIPPUS: If that sounds strange, then your ears need some educating. I heard of a boy who, though totally blind, still jumped the roofs. His mother became so fearful and panic-stricken that she actually tethered him in the courtyard with a rope. It was totally useless of course, for he untied himself as soon as she left, and then he climbed off into the skies, toward the sounds of his friends.

SOCRATES: Ah, then he was "wrapped in the blanket sounds of trees."

HERMIPPUS: What? What is this you are saying, Socrates?

SOCRATES: Do you not recognize it, Hermippus?

HERMIPPUS: I am not sure.

SOCRATES: It is from your drama *Cloud Cities*:

> At night, there rolls a rippling breeze
> Of children's voices—floating vortices
> Wrapped in the blanket sounds of trees.

HERMIPPUS: I did not know anyone remembered that old play, Socrates . . . I barely do.

SOCRATES: A fine work, Hermippus.

HERMIPPUS: Then undoubtedly I plagiarized some better playwright—I'm just a scribbling scrivener, young man, spitting at those stupid things that rain down on all of us. I may not have two eyes, but I was born with two tongues—two pointed forks, like a snake—and Demagogues Beware! Tchah! Tchah! I tickle their fat guts with each point. Does old Pericles think that he can gambol about idly while the Lacedaemonians invade Attica? What a coward! And how can that churl Hyperbolus lie through his teeth time and time again? Or Cleon, a syncophant and a butcher—if let loose he would have put to death every single inhabitant of Mytilene! It's simply unbelievable. Don't these things infuriate you? They could drive you to attack the tyrants with your two bare hands.

SOCRATES: Well with two bare hands and two pointed tongues, you seem not to have suffered missing one small eye.

HERMIPPUS: I have told you, Socrates: I made do with what I had. Give me one foot and I will still run. Give me one hand and I will write; give me one ear and I will still hear. And, Socrates, even one tongue is enough with which to tell the truth.

SOCRATES: Then, Hermippus, do we really need two eyes, two ears, two hands, and two feet?

HERMIPPUS: What kind of a question is that? You sound like a four-year old—"Do we really need two eyes?"! Do you imagine that the gods have built a man casually, with two eyes, when one or three would do as well? Do you think that a one-armed man is any match for the one-two grasp of an Olympic wrestler? Socrates, go prattle to some child—don't bother me with such foolish toetalk and twaddle.

SOCRATES: Hermippus, are you saying that "two" is the best possible number of arms?

HERMIPPUS: Do you think otherwise?

SOCRATES: Well I am not certain, Hermippus, because I wonder about monkeys?

HERMIPPUS: Monkeys? What of them?

SOCRATES: Can they not use their feet like hands?

HERMIPPUS: Yes, I suupose that they can.

SOCRATES: And even their tails?

HERMIPPUS: Yes—those too.

SOCRATES: And is it not because of these extra "hands" that they can eat while climbing a tree or while swinging from branch to branch?

HERMIPPUS: Yes.

SOCRATES: Then are not three or four or five hands better than two hands?

HERMIPPUS: Certainly—if you wanted to clamber about the treetops, if you wished to swing from roof to roof, to jump from branch to branch, to scramble from fence to fence and from wall to wall. But that is for monkeys—it is not for men, Socrates.

SOCRATES: Are you not a man, Hermippus?

HERMIPPUS: What?! Apemantus, can you not prevail on this orator to stick with questions that require more intelligence than a horse?

APEMANTUS: Hermippus, you know quite well that I could as soon move Mount Olympos.

EUDICUS: Do not be petty, old men. Certainly Hermippus is a man, Socrates. What is your point?

SOCRATES: Well, Eudicus, one-eyed Hermippus has told me how he and his friends could not resist fence-walking and wall-climbing and rooftop-jumping and treebranch-scrambling, and I thought to myself: "Socrates, my puzzled friend, Hermippus is a man—perhaps men *would* be better off with more than two hands." Could this possibly be correct? Well, what do you think, Hermippus?

HERMIPPUS: I think that all of you children are like monkeys. Nonetheless when finally you do grow up, then you will be satisfied with the two hands bestowed upon you by the gods— and you will also appreciate your two legs, your two ears, and your two eyes.

SOCRATES: Oh? Then two eyes are better than one or three?

HERMIPPUS: By the gods, Socrates—can you remember nothing?! It is as if we were talking in a vast canyon: the same question bounces back again and again and again.

SOCRATES: Be patient, Hermippus, my mind has suffered much wear and tear in these last seventy years; I forget things easily.

HERMIPPUS: Socrates, things slip from you like sand between the fingers. Of course two eyes are best!

SOCRATES: Why is that?

HERMIPPUS: With two eyes you get the most accurate and the most detailed view of the world.

SOCRATES: Accurate? Are you saying that two eyes show you the truth?

HERMIPPUS: Of course they do, by the gods.

SOCRATES: How many thumbs do you have on your left hand, Hermippus?

HERMIPPUS: Ah—finally we are getting to some challenging problems, Socrates.

EUDICUS: Ignore his remarks, Socrates—he has one thumb on each hand.

SOCRATES: Thank you, Eudicus.

Now let me ask you, Eudicus: Did you ever attend any of Democritus's lectures on the soul?

EUDICUS: No, I have never heard him speak.

SOCRATES: That is too bad. I suppose that it is partly the fault of money. Democritus inherited considerable property; he *is* a wealthy man, and he is often abroad in Egypt; then, when he is in Athens, he talks only reluctantly. He believes in writing rather than in speaking. But if you ever have the opportunity to hear him, then definitely go. Democritus is wiser than the wise men, and quiet as he is today, history will remember him more than you or I. One day academies throughout the world will have fine marble statues of him in their sunny central courts.

I remember well one of his striking examples, when he talked about vision. Let me repeat his demonstration: Eudicus, hold out your right thumb in front of your eyes.

EUDICUS: Like this?

SOCRATES: Yes. And Hermippus, I need your help also—hold your tongue and put up your thumb.

HERMIPPUS: Put up my thumb? Soon you will ask me to stand on my head.

SOCRATES: Perhaps later—now, each of you hold up your other thumb behind the first, as far as your left hand will extend . . . Good.

EUDICUS: All right—now what?

SOCRATES: Concentrate on your near thumb. Now, Eudicus (still attending to your near thumb), how many thumbs do you see on your far hand?

HERMIPPUS: How many thumbs? Is he growing thumbs? (Or is the opposite happening? Are thumbs falling off his hand like unbalanced stones on a wall?)

SOCRATES: Quiet, Hermippus. Well, Eudicus, how many thumbs do you see on your far hand?

EUDICUS: If I focus on my near thumb, then I see two distinct thumbs on my far hand.

HERMIPPUS: Two?! Your mind is adled—I see one. There is only one thumb on each hand, and one there shall always be!

SOCRATES: And, Eudicus, if you close one eye?

EUDICUS: Then things change, Socrates: now I see only one thumb—clearly there is one thumb on each hand now.

SOCRATES: So, one eye gives a more accurate view of the world?

EUDICUS: It appears so.

HERMIPPUS: Rubbish!

SOCRATES: Rubbish? How many thumbs do you see on each hand?

HERMIPPUS: One.

SOCRATES: Hmm, your one eye seems to be better than Eudicus's two eyes . . . Now, Hermippus, you say that you can shoot an arrow accurately. How did you learn to shoot?

HERMIPPUS: I learned in the gymnastic academy with my friends, of course.

SOCRATES: And you follow the standard shooting form?

HERMIPPUS: The "standard form"?

SOCRATES: I mean your shooting stance: Do you stand erect?

HERMIPPUS: Yes.

SOCRATES: Do you set your left foot forward?

HERMIPPUS: Certainly.

SOCRATES: Do you hold the bow steady, the string taut, aiming patiently, almost like a statue?

HERMIPPUS: Yes.

SOCRATES: And all the while, you aim with one eye closed?

HERMIPPUS: With one eye closed? If I closed one eye, I would as likely hit Eudicus or Apemantus or you as the target. (Of course if I shot you, then I would not be subject to these interminable foolish questions.)

SOCRATES: But is this not standard shooting form, to aim with one eye closed?

HERMIPPUS: Of course—at least for those to whom the majestic gods, in their all-knowing glory, deigned to give two eyes.

SOCRATES: Oh? And why should an archer close one eye?

HERMIPPUS: How should I know, Socrates? It seems natural to me: I always have one eye closed.

EUDICUS: Hermippus, you know quite well that each of the two eyes gives a slightly different perspective, and in order to aim accurately one must concentrate on only *one* view. You close one eye to reduce the confusion.

HERMIPPUS: Do you expect me to know that? Do you think that a fish will ever know what it is like to have a shell on its back like a turtle? Can a dog know how an elephant feels with a trunk? How will a bird ever know what it is like to hug with arms? And do you imagine that a man will ever really know what it is like for a woman to give birth? So, Eudicus, how am I to know what a two-eyed man sees?

EUDICUS: Then you must take my word for it, Hermippus: to aim accurately, you must close one eye.

SOCRATES: Does this mean that two eyes are not as good as one?

EUDICUS: For archery, that is true.

HERMIPPUS: Hold your blather, Eudicus.

  Socrates, you Protean fish, you have slipped and slid and

slithered right off the edge of the sensible world. Two eyes are not as good as one? Do not be a fool. Listen here, Socrates, you have been to war, you know about injuries. Suppose that a man loses his hand or that he receives a blow to one side of the face— if he is a normal man, then he recovers. But where would I be if I tripped and put out my one eye on the edge of a cart? Where would I be if Eudicus carelessly dropped a stone on my head when I was sleeping? No matter what flummery you conjure up about visual images, you cannot deny the fact that two eyes provide a safeguard against accidents. Now, let us put an end to this impious chatter!

SOCRATES: So, Hermippus, two eyes are better because the second eye is a spare?

HERMIPPUS: Of course.

SOCRATES: Then would three eyes be better still?

HERMIPPUS: Three? I suppose that this would be better. But why stop there? Why not have four or five or six or seven eyes?

> One, two, three, four, five, six, seven—
> All good eyes will show us heaven.

Ah, but I should not get carried away—you seem satisfied with three. So now I ask you, Socrates: Where, pray tell, would you put another eye?

SOCRATES: A good question, old man. I imagine that the third eye should be far from the others; in this way any accident to one eye would be unlikely to involve the spare. I remember a little girl who thought that it would be useful to have an extra eye on the end of her finger—then she could peek around corners with no one seeing her. Of course she could never be a musician: playing the harp would undoubtedly be painful. And tapping her fingers might bring on headaches. On the other hand, these discomforts would be counterbalanced by her ability to see her back and to adjust her—

HERMIPPUS: Socrates, Socrates! When you open your mouth, the west wind rushes out, blowing every which way, knocking over trees, ripping the clothes from our bodies. If I did not have my feet firmly on the ground, my sandals would be blown off my feet and into the sausage stall over there. I suppose that in your roundabout gale-ridden fashion, you are trying to tell us that two is not the best number of eyes? Is this your point? If it is, then just say so and be done with it!

SOCRATES: I have no point; I am only asking questions, Hermippus. How does it look to you?

HERMIPPUS: How *can* it look to me? I have only one eye!

APEMANTUS: Socrates—although you have contrived a few lone examples where it *appears* that one eye might be better than two and where it *appears* that three eyes might be better than two, this is all wrong. The gods have given us two eyes: for that reason, two eyes *must* be best.

SOCRATES: Why is that, Apemantus?

APEMANTUS: I cannot say.

SOCRATES: You cannot say?

APEMANTUS: No—I cannot say.

SOCRATES: Does it not bother you that you cannot answer the question?

APEMANTUS: No, this does not concern me: I am a pious man, and I readily admit that the ways of the gods are beyond the comprehension of man. You and other young men, like my son Eudicus here, have the conceit that you can understand everything. Well, I am sorry to tell you, Socrates—you cannot. When you finally mature and when you acquire the calm long-term perspective of old age, then you will rest easier in a more modest role. Socrates, just accept the divine. Do not struggle so much.

SOCRATES: Apemantus, I am not destined to live as long as you or as long as Hermippus or Democritus. The autumn of my life is here, and I clearly see the winter ahead.

But, old friend, I am content. I have never enjoyed a full trust in absolute, simple, and divine truths—I have never had the wonderful calming faith that you have. I have never been warmed by pure and holy knowledge. I have lived my life by questions.

Nevertheless, I cannot complain because continual questioning has not been a bad lot. I have walked free and fresh through the marketplace everyday, and I have looked with my widest two eyes, listened with my tiniest two years, and felt with my softest two hands. And you know, Apemantus, I have not asked: Are these eyes and ears and hands the best eyes and ears and hands, the most perfect eyes and ears and hands, the correct eyes and ears and hands? These are *my* eyes, *my* ears, and *my* hands, and with them I have wrapped myself in the world, contentedly.

HERMIPPUS: Aha, you have finally given yourself away, my dear Socrates—you are a mystic. Do not try and fool us with your flimsy guise of rationality: you revel in the tangled and the unexplained complexities of the world. For you,

> Roses come and roses go,
> And violets begin to blow.
> Although you'll never really know
> Why they come or why they go—
> Still, your're just happy that it's so.

September 2: AESCHINES

SOCRATES: I am afraid that it is nonsense.

AESCHINES: Nonsense, Socrates?

SOCRATES: Yes, my friend—old Lysicles often spoke without thinking, and his most recent pronouncement is empty nonsense.

AESCHINES: Oh? Before you judge so hastily, Socrates, remember: Lysicles has been dead now for twenty-nine years. Do you not think that he has gained some wisdom as a shade? Spirits, I am told, hear Truths in the Land of the Dead.

SOCRATES: Apparently, Lysicles has become hard of hearing. (At least, the old world-worn politician part of Lysicles.) If the oracle has reported accurately, then old Lysicles continues to speak hastily not thoughtfully. "There must be a simple solution beyond mere restitution; a new constitution is the ideal resolution"—why, it is even terrible verse, Aeschines.

AESCHINES: Well, the oracle is aging and she is hard of hearing herself: she may have misheard Lysicles.

SOCRATES: She misheard doggerel?

AESCHINES: All right, Socrates—perhaps it *is* doggerel, but the sentiment is sound. Would you not admit that we do need fundamental political reform here in Athens?

SOCRATES: Yes we do.

AESCHINES: We have had enough of the elitist rulings—rulings with fancy, complex provisions, with unlimited conditions, and with piles of tangled requirements for every decision. Just give me the simple, the straightforward, and the everyday.

Lysicles had earthy common sense. He was a modest-born middle-class tradesman, and he had little formal education. In fact it was only through his wife, Aspasia's, backing that he became a member of the ruling council—

SOCRATES: Do you mean the Ecclesia?

AESCHINES: Of course I mean the Ecclesia—Aspasia pressured the other members of the Ecclesia into electing Lysicles.

SOCRATES: Do you know that I heard the name Aspasia just yesterday? Aeschines, have you ever heard the childish verse:

> Periwinkle Pericles
> Is itching now from more than fleas—
> His mistress, Aspasia, he can't please;
> So she takes up with Lysicles.

(It was attributed to one-eyed Hermippus.)

AESCHINES: Certainly I have heard that chant—every schoolchild knows that bit of doggerel. This must be the week for doggerel, Socrates.

SOCRATES: Yes, it *is* doggerel, young friend, for it does no justice whatsoever to Aspasia. She was a brilliant woman and a fine rhetorician. They called her the courtesan of Miletus, but she was sharp tongued and keen of mind. It is no wonder that Pericles made her his mistress.

AESCHINES: You know, Socrates, I am not always certain which stories about her are true and which are mere legends.

SOCRATES: I met her on a number of occasions, Aeschines; she was every bit as wise as her legends claim. When reasoning aloud she built her case with parallel upon parallel and with analogy after analogy. She would completely surround the issue. She would overlap all the edges until the true contention finally became unavoidable and then we would be forced to accept it. And when a problem was too difficult to attack directly, she tried the flanks. Aspasia never gave up.

AESCHINES: Undoubtedly some of her tenacity rubbed off on Lysicles, for that is precisely what the oracle tells us that

Lysicles is proposing. You see, the oligarchy here in Athens is making poor decisions, but we cannot simply throw up our hands in despair. We cannot give up. We must find some solutions. We must stay active. And if we cannot improve matters directly, then we must attack from the sides.

SOCRATES: There is no doubt that this is good advice, Aeschines. But your generous interpretation of the oracle is really Aeschines talking—it is not Lysicles speaking. Lysicles' pronouncement is too general to provide anything useful.

AESCHINES: It does not provide anything useful, Socrates? If nothing else, it has stimulated this conversation.

SOCRATES: Of course you are right, Aeschines. However, Lysicles has spoken too generally to provide anything other than the impetus for making our own sense of matters.

AESCHINES: You do not give him sufficient credit, Socrates. First, Lysicles speaks of recompense—he says that a repayment to the citizens for mistakes of the ruling few is not a lasting solution. Second, Lysicles speaks of substantive change—he proposes elemental reforms, namely, in the shape of a new constitution.

SOCRATES: Is that what Lysicles said?

AESCHINES: Certainly it is, Socrates.

SOCRATES: Oh? Then I must have misunderstood him, Aeschines—review his speech for me.

AESCHINES: The quotation is certainly brief and it is directly to the point:

> "There must be a simple solution beyond mere restitution—
> a new constitution is the ideal resolution."

This seems quite clear to me.

SOCRATES: As an old man, my friend, I must take my food in small bits. And I find this is a good plan for everything that I ingest, so let us do the same with Lysicles' wisdom.

AESCHINES: Fine, old man.

SOCRATES: Now, first Lysicles says: "There must be a simple solution." What does this statement mean?

AESCHINES: Socrates, we could not express anything more directly than: "There must be a simple solution." What is your difficulty? What do you not understand?

SOCRATES: I am puzzled.

AESCHINES: You often say that, Socrates.

SOCRATES: I am often puzzled, young friend.

AESCHINES: Clearly—and what puzzles you now?

SOCRATES: Does Lysicles mean: "There is a simple solution to our political problem, because all problems have simple solutions"? Or does he mean: "There is a simple solution to our political problem, because all *political* problems have simple solutions"? Or does Lysicles actually mean: "There is a simple solution to our political problem, because *our particular* political problem has a simple solution"?

AESCHINES: Socrates, I have listened to you long enough to have grown wary of statements with "all" in them—who can ever be certain of such absolutes?

SOCRATES: Yes, Aeschines—only the gods can trade in absolutes, in definitives, and in finalities.

AESCHINES: So, if we rule out absolutes, then the answer to your puzzlement is clear: we must imagine that Lysicles means only that there is a simple solution to our own particular political problem.

SOCRATES: Does this mean that Lysicles is saying: "There is a simple solution to our political problem, because our particular political problem has a simple solution"?

AESCHINES: Exactly.

SOCRATES: How does Lysicles know this?

AESCHINES: Lysicles knows that there is a simple solution, because he knows a particular solution. Specifically, the solution is "forge a new constitution."

SOCRATES: Ah, now I am learning how to understand Lysicles. You are telling me that he means:

> "Forge a new constitution" is a simple solution.
> We can forge a new constitution.
> Therefore, we can institute a simple solution.

AESCHINES: Of course, Socrates, that is just what Lysicles means.

SOCRATES: I see, Aeschines. So Lysicles misspoke.

AESCHINES: Misspoke? Absolutely not, Socrates—Lysicles said exactly what he meant.

SOCRATES: But, Aeschines, have we not agreed that Lysicles meant: "There *is* a simple solution"?

AESCHINES: Yes.

SOCRATES: And did not Lysicles say: "There *must be* a simple solution"?

AESCHINES: Is this what is bothering you, Socrates: the difference between "is" and "must be"? It is true that Lysicles said "must be" where he undoubtedly meant "is." But, old man, this is excessive hairsplitting. I cannot believe that you have reduced your argument to such petty distinctions. The content of the statement is important—the slight nuances of words only divert us from more serious understandings.

SOCRATES: Aeschines, unlike you I have the highest regard for words—

AESCHINES: I respect words, but I give them more latitude than you do. I allow words to have some color and some imprecision.

SOCRATES: Color and imprecision are wonderful, but precise speech is critical for sound logic. Each phrase, each word, and even each syllable is a model of our world. Everything that we say reflects a particular understanding that we use and that we promulgate. Those differences that you call "nuances" are differences that may at first glance appear only to be slight variants of the same meaning. Nonetheless, these colorings can at times carry us into widely different realms. With slightly variant words, we can step into completely disparate universes.

AESCHINES: This *sounds* grand, Socrates, but give me a real example.

SOCRATES: Fine. Consider Lysicles's declaration—here we have a good example. When trying to understand Lysicles, we are faced with two different possible statements.

1. There *is* a simple solution to our particular political problem.
2. There *must be* a simple solution to our particular political problem.

Let us examine the basic differences between these two positions.

AESCHINES: Very well.

SOCRATES: The first statement has two aspects to it. First, of course, it maintains that a solution exists.

AESCHINES: Obviously.

SOCRATES: Second, this assertion (namely, "a solution exists") is validated by a demonstrable example.

AESCHINES: What do you mean?

SOCRATES: Recall the logical formulation that we had discussed:

> "Forge a new constitution" is a simple solution.
> We can forge a new constitution.
> Therefore, we can institute a simple solution.

Now, if we have this set of logical clauses, then we can validate our first statement. The logical trio offers a specific example of the political solution. Thus, this set of three logically connected propositions can be used to prove our first statement—that is, by demonstration, it supports the statement: "There *is* a simple solution to our particular political problem."

AESCHINES: True, Socrates. But, you really have not helped

us much with all of your complex arguing. You see, old man, the very logical trio that you cherish as a proof of the first statement also proves our second statement. Consider the second proposal: "There *must be* a simple solution to our particular political problem." By offering a specific solution, the set of three logical clauses demonstrates that there *must be* a simple solution—just as it demonstrates that there *is* a simple solution.

SOCRATES: Oh? Do you think that the existence of a solution proves the second statement? "Existence" proves "must be" as well as "is"?

AESCHINES: Of course it does, Socrates. Do you not agree?

SOCRATES: I am not certain, Aeschines. Will you show me your reasoning?

AESCHINES: Gladly. How shall we begin?

SOCRATES: I suggest that we examine the general class of *must be* statements. These statements are of the form:

> A certain class of things (in this case, simple solutions to our particular political problem) must exist.

Now, would you agree that we would like to prove statements of this form?

AESCHINES: Yes.

SOCRATES: Then once again I am puzzled, Aeschines.

AESCHINES: That does not surprise me. Now what puzzles you, old man?

SOCRATES: I am puzzled by "proof." What does it mean "to prove a statement"?

AESCHINES: It means to show that the words are correct, that they are accurate.

SOCRATES: You say that by showing that the words are correct then a statement can be proved?

AESCHINES: Yes.

SOCRATES: Well, let me try out an example. If I say: "My foot is red," is that a valid statement?

AESCHINES: No—this is a cool day, and I can see (through your sandal) that your foot is pale this morning.

SOCRATES: That is strange: the statement "my foot is red" seems accurate to me. In fact, I suspect that we can "prove" it, using your definition of "proof."

AESCHINES: What are you talking about, Socrates?

SOCRATES: Listen: "my foot" is a correct phrase, is it not?

AESCHINES: I suppose so.

SOCRATES: And "red" is a correct word, is it not?

AESCHINES: What do you mean by "correct"?

SOCRATES: Aeschines, *you* introduced the criterion of "correct" into our discussion. You pointed out that to prove a statement, one must show that it is composed of correct or accurate words. What do *you* mean by correct?

AESCHINES: I would say that "correct" is quite straightforward. It means two things. First, a word or a phrase is correct if it makes sense standing by itself.

SOCRATES: Before you go any farther, give me an example in order that I may understand quite clearly what you mean.

AESCHINES: Certainly, Socrates, "my foot" makes sense standing by itself, but "my floot" makes no sense standing by itself.

SOCRATES: All right—go on.

AESCHINES: "Sensible when standing by itself" is the first half of "correct." And as a criterion for proving a statement, "correct" also has another meaning: a word or a phrase is correct if it makes sense when attached to the other words around it.

SOCRATES: Give me an example again.

AESCHINES: Well, "red" is correct when you surround it with "setting sun" or with "Theramenes' sails." In contrast, "red" is not correct when you surround it with "my foot" or with "those olive leaves."

SOCRATES: For "correct" to apply, a word must make sense in both ways?

AESCHINES: Yes. In "the setting sun is red" or in "Theramenes' sails are red," "red" is accurate in *both* senses. Thus, these sentences are fully correct. On the other hand, in "my foot is red" or in "those olive leaves are red," "red" is accurate when it stands alone, but it is not accurate in relation to its surrounding words. For this reason, "my foot is red" is not a truly correct statement: the words stand well alone, but they conflict when assembled together.

SOCRATES: I see. Now, Aeschines, yesterday after a hot bath, my foot *was* quite red. Yesterday the statement "my foot is red" was correct in all senses.

AESCHINES: That is foolish, Socrates. "My foot is red" cannot be said today for yesterday. "My foot is red" can only be said for today: "my foot *was* red" is what you really meant to say about yesterday.

SOCRATES: Very well, Aeschines: you have cleanly distinguished between "is" and "was." Now let us apply your reasoning to a clean distinction between "is" and "must be."

AESCHINES: Good.

SOCRATES: We both agree that the statement "my foot is red" is not correct and we both agree that the statement "my foot was red" is correct.

AESCHINES: Yes we do.

SOCRATES: How about the statement "my foot must be red"?

AESCHINES: "My foot must be red"? Well, now that we are being so careful about our words, I had best proceed slowly, step by step. In the way that we have been using "must be," I assume that what you mean is the following. Suppose that we have not looked down at your foot recently. We are talking of sundry things, when suddenly you say: "Hmm, Aeschines, my foot must be red." Is that the situation you imagine?

SOCRATES: Yes. Would that statement be correct?

AESCHINES: Feet are usually not red—so the statement must be incorrect.

SOCRATES: But, Aeschines, suppose that this conversation took place yesterday morning after my hot bath. Then would the statement be correct?

AESCHINES: Yes.

SOCRATES: Or suppose that I tightened my sandal excessively and that I felt the blood accumulating in my foot. Now might the statement "my foot must be red" be correct?

AESCHINES: Under those circumstances, it might be correct.

SOCRATES: Or what if I had just been visiting the scene-painter Agatharcus? You know how absent-minded he is; perhaps I suspected that he had spilled some red paint on my foot. Would I not be justified in proposing that my foot must be red?

AESCHINES: All right, Socrates, I admit that "my foot must be red" may be a correct statement under some unusual circumstances.

SOCRATES: Under some unusual circumstances? Let me see if we can be more specific and categorize those "unusual" circumstances.

AESCHINES: Fine.

SOCRATES: First, of course, we may have looked at my foot recently and in this way discovered that it is red.

AESCHINES: True.

SOCRATES: Second, we may *not* have looked at my foot recently. Nonetheless, some related information may suggest that my foot is actually red.

AESCHINES: Related information?

SOCRATES: I mean some indirect knowledge—some information such as that my sandal feels excessively tight or that I had just visited Agatharcus in the midst of his painting a red backdrop for the stage.

AESCHINES: I see.

SOCRATES: Do these two categories exhaust the situations in which "my foot must be red" is correct?

AESCHINES: I think that they do.

SOCRATES: Is my foot really red in all of these situations?

AESCHINES: No—you may have reasoned incorrectly. For instance, a tight sandal can produce a very white skin as well as a red skin. Or Agatharcus may have spilled white paint on you instead of red paint. (I am assuming that you still have not actually looked at your foot.)

SOCRATES: So, are you telling me that *is* statements require a demonstrated fact; whereas *must be* statements do not require a demonstrated fact?

AESCHINES: Yes—this one of the fundamental differences between these two types of statements.

SOCRATES: I see. But now you have left me puzzled again, Aeschines.

AESCHINES: Why are you puzzled, Socrates? Things seem quite clear to me.

SOCRATES: I am puzzled, because I cannot understand how to determine whether a statement with a "must be" in it—statements like "my foot must be red" and "there must be a simple solution to our particular political problem"—whether such statements are actually correct.

AESCHINES: If you recall, Socrates, I have already suggested some practical rules.

SOCRATES: Rules? Let me see: I remember that you said the words themselves must be correct.

AESCHINES: Yes, that is an important rule. Does that puzzle you?

SOCRATES: No—I understand *that* part of your test for correctness: the words themselves must be meaningful. However, I am puzzled by the second part of your test for correctness. You also said that the words need to fit appropriately with their surrounding words in order for the full statement to be correct.

AESCHINES: True.

SOCRATES: Does "red" fit appropriately with its surrounding words in the statement "my foot is red"?

AESCHINES: We can always make a simple test, Socrates. We look at your foot. If your foot is red, then we pronounce the statement to be correct—if your foot is not red, then we pronounce the statement to be incorrect.

SOCRATES: All right, you have shown me how to use this rule for *is* statements. How do we use this part of the test of correctness for *must be* statements? For example, how about the statement: "my foot must be red"? Does "red" fit appropriately with its surrounding words here?

AESCHINES: Socrates, perform the same test as before: simply look. If your foot is red, then the statement is correct—if your foot is not red, then the statement is incorrect.

SOCRATES: Ah your appearance belies your age, Aeschines.

AESCHINES: Are you saying that I am wise beyond my years, old man.

SOCRATES: No, I am saying that you are like me, Aeschines— you are becoming forgetful as you get older.

AESCHINES: Socrates, you are twenty years older than I am. If I am forgetful, then it is not due to my age. However, it may well be due to my worries over money—you know that things have been a bit tight for me recently. A sausage-maker's son does not inherit much wealth or property. If my father had only been a landowner, then I would be able to concentrate on philosophy and not let my finances distract me from the argu- ment. But anyways, what is it that you were saying?

SOCRATES: I was saying, Aeschines, that in your enthusiasm over your rules, you forgot your earlier inference. *Is* statements differ from *must be* statements specifically in whether we have actually demonstrated their validity.

AESCHINES: Of course—but what does this have to do with our rules?

SOCRATES: Listen a moment, Aeschines. For the statment "my foot is red" to be correct, you had decided that my foot must demonstrably be red. On the other hand, for the statement "my foot must be red" to be correct, you pointed out that my foot need not actually be red.

AESCHINES: True.

SOCRATES: Now, Aeschines, did you tell me that in order to decide whether a statement is fully correct, we need to decide whether the words are all accurate in context?

AESCHINES: Yes.

SOCRATES: Unfortunately, we do not have the test of an actual demonstration for *must be* statements as we have for *is* statements—*must be* statements need not accurately describe the world. So, tell me, my young friend: What other test shall we use? If we cannot always decide by looking at my foot, then how can we determine whether "my foot must be red" is a correct statement?

AESCHINES: Do you want one universal test?

SOCRATES: I would like one if there is one, Aeschines.

AESCHINES: All right. We decided that a *must be* statement is correct if it accurately describes the world—however, a *must be* statement is also correct if it is consistent with some other information in the world, regardless of our direct knowldege about the subject of the statement.

SOCRATES: Yes.

AESCHINES: Then it appears that the common criterion for all *must be* statements is our belief about its correctness. Thus, I would say that in all cases a *must be* statement is correct if it accurately describes our belief.

SOCRATES: And our belief need not coincide with reality? For "my foot must be red" to be a correct statement, my foot need not actually be red?

AESCHINES: Yes—as long as you truly believe that your foot

must be red, then the reality of the "foot situation" is not important.

SOCRATES: Let me see if I understand you: Do you propose that the correctness of a *must be* statement should be judged solely on the basis of its correlation with our beliefs?

AESCHINES: Exactly.

SOCRATES: I am afraid that still leaves me puzzled, Aeschines.

AESCHINES: Still puzzled? How can this be? We now have a simple and straightforward test for correctness. You know, Socrates, I am almost afraid to say anything to you at all: you seem to get puzzled by the slightest breeze; I hesitate to stir up the air with even the mildest answer to your questions.

SOCRATES: Perhaps it is the autumn weather, Aeschines—the hint of winter in the air makes everything feel uncertain to me.

AESCHINES: Socrates, you have always been this way, so do not blame the weather. Just face the problem squarely: What is bothering you now?

SOCRATES: Well, good friend, you know that I cannot wear new clothes.

AESCHINES: "Cannot," Socrates? Surely you do not mean "cannot"—you mean: "will not."

SOCRATES: I guess that you are correct, Aeschines—I will not wear new clothes. And you?

AESCHINES: I have nothing against new clothes. Appearance is important: new clothes make you feel good, and if you feel good, then you act well and you think nobly.

SOCRATES: I do not agree, Aeschines.

AESCHINES: That is your belief, Socrates—to which you are welcome—but I have my own beliefs about dress.

SOCRATES: Apparently our attitudes toward new clothes are individual.

AESCHINES: They definitely are, old man—that is the essence of a belief: a belief is an idea peculiar to a particular person.

SOCRATES: Then this is what puzzles me about *must be* statements.

AESCHINES: Ah—I wondered what you were getting at, Socrates.

SOCRATES: You see, Aeschines, you have told me that the correctness of a *must be* statement should be judged solely on the basis of its correlation with our beliefs. But I am puzzled: if men differ in their beliefs, then whose beliefs do we use to test a specific *must be* statement.

AESCHINES: Socrates, if you reflected a moment, then you would find that the answer is apparent.

SOCRATES: Good—tell it to me.

AESCHINES: It is the *speaker's* belief that is the critical test. If I say: "your foot must be red," then that statement is correct if and only if *I* believe it to be accurate. If you say: "my foot must be red," then that statement is correct if and only if *you* believe it to be accurate.

SOCRATES: I see. So, the correctness of a *must be* statement should be judged solely on the basis of its correlation with the speaker's belief?

AESCHINES: Exactly, Socrates.

SOCRATES: Well, let us try this test on Lysicles' *must be* statement. Lysicles said:
   "There must be a simple solution to our particular political problem." Is this a correct statement?

AESCHINES: It is correct if it accurately corresponds to his beliefs, Socrates.

SOCRATES: And does it accurately correspond to his beliefs, Aeschines?

AESCHINES: We would do best to ask Lysicles directly. However, Lysicles is dead and we have no oracles immediately available, so we must assume that Lysicles has not been trying to deceive us and that he actually believes what he says.

Therefore, "There must be a simple solution to our particular political problem" is undoubtedly correct.

SOCRATES: Why?

AESCHINES: "Why"?

SOCRATES: Yes—you have told me that Lysicles believed this statement. Now I am asking: Why did he believe this, Aeschines?

AESCHINES: I assume that he had a simple solution in mind, Socrates. Lysicles must have felt that it would be possible to institute appropriate reforms through a new constitution (perhaps by widening the participants in our democracy to all landowners, as Theramenes has advocated).

SOCRATES: Just a moment, Aeschines, you are moving too fast for me.

AESCHINES: I apologize, old friend. What is the difficulty?

SOCRATES: Did we not decide that the difference between *is* statements and *must be* statements is that *is* statements are validated by actual examples whereas *must be* statements are validated by personal beliefs?

AESCHINES: Yes.

SOCRATES: Then if Aeschines had in hand an actual example of a simple solution, should he not have said: "There *is* a simple solution" rather than "There *must be* a simple solution"?

AESCHINES: Well, I suppose so, Socrates.

SOCRATES: Why do you hesitate, Aeschines?

AESCHINES: To be honest, Socrates, it is possible that Lysicles was a bit sloppy in his speech. Lysicles may well have meant "is" when he mistakenly said "must be."

SOCRATES: Oh? This truly leaves me in a bewildered state. If your suggestion is correct, then what am I to make of the rest of his pronouncement? Is that sloppy also? Do you imagine that Lysicles may actually have meant "complex," when he mistakenly said "simple"? Or do you imagine that he may have said: "There must be a simple solution beyond mere restitution," when he actually meant to say: "There is no simple solution beyond mere restitution"? And now I wonder whether he has carelessly said: "a new constition is the ideal resolution," when a more precise statement would have been: "the old constitution is the ideal resolution"? Could he have mistakenly said: "beyond mere restitution," when he actually meant: "beyond mere revolution." And then—

AESCHINES: Stop a moment, Socrates. You have made your point: we must assume that Lysicles said what he meant—otherwise, we have no firm basis for discussion.

SOCRATES: All right, then you agree that Lysicles' statement: "There must be a simple solution" indicates exactly his personal belief?

AESCHINES: We have no choice but to accept this premise.

SOCRATES: And because we must assume that Lysicles spoke precisely and because his precise statement is a *must be* statement, then it cannot be based on any fully actualized example of this simple solution?

AESCHINES: Yes yes, Socrates, I agree: we must assume that this statement is correct on the basis of personal belief and not on the basis of any manifest example.

SOCRATES: So, we return to my earlier question: What is the basis for this personal belief of Lysicles?

AESCHINES: We have ruled out any specific demonstrated examples—a *must be* statement cannot be based on a specific example that applies in a particular case. Therefore, although he does not have the exact simple solution in hand, Lysicles must have other related information—he must have indirect information that leads him to infer that a simple solution exists.

SOCRATES: All right, Aeschines. Now tell me: What is that other related but indirect information?

AESCHINES: How can I know, Socrates? Lysicles is dead: I do not know what information he possessed, and it is probable that I will never know.

SOCRATES: Is there another possibility?

AESCHINES: Do you mean: Is it possible that we *will* know someday?

SOCRATES: No, I mean something else: Is it possible that Lysicles' belief is founded on something besides other related indirect information?

AESCHINES: Socrates, this sounds like one of your attempts to confuse matters.

SOCRATES: Have patience with me, young friend. Consider my foot again. Suppose that I come to you and I say: "My foot must be red." We have agreed that (if I am speaking precisely and if I am considering my words thoughtfully) this statement implies that I have not looked at my foot recently. Is that correct?

AESCHINES: Yes—it is a *must be* statement not an *is* statement.

SOCRATES: And for the "foot" statement to be correct, then I must actually believe that my foot is red?

AESCHINES: True.

SOCRATES: Good. Now, we have decided that one basis for this personal belief is other related information. For example, I might know that my sandal is tied too tightly or I might remember that paint had been spilled on my foot by Agatharcus.

AESCHINES: Yes.

SOCRATES: Is there yet another basis for this personal belief?

AESCHINES: I cannot imagine any other basis.

SOCRATES: How about innate desire?

AESCHINES: Innate desire?

SOCRATES: Yes—what if I hope very deeply that my foot is red?

AESCHINES: Well, that is a strange hope. But I suppose that a strong wish is consistent with the meaning of some *must be* statements. I can imagine that statements like "I must be present at the festival" or "The scenery must be painted red" or "Your wife must be allowed to purchase her own clothes," these statements may be made correct because of the strength of deeply rooted wishes.

SOCRATES: I think so too, Aeschines. Innate desire may shape our personal beliefs, and innate desire may give rise to correct *must be* statements.

AESCHINES: Just a moment: something is amiss here, Socrates. Through some slippery word tricks you have managed to slide us into a realm of human whim. I think that I have fallen into a trap by choosing examples about things clearly under human control. These examples—attending a feast, painting scenery, and buying finery—are situations over which we have control. Human situations *are* subject to human whims, and they can be under human control. Here, wishes can sometimes be transformed into facts.

But earlier you asked me for very general rules—for universal rules. In the wider realm, Socrates, many *must be* statements are completely independent of us. These statements *cannot* be based solely on innate desire. Some things are absolutely impossible, no matter how strongly we wish otherwise.

SOCRATES: They are?

AESCHINES: Of course they are. What if I proposed some impossible *must be* statements like: "The moon must be stationary in the sky" or "The world must speed through the Heavens like a bird" or "Man must be able to fly to the moon" or "Each star must be larger than the sun"? What if I claimed these to be true? Here strong wishes are insufficient to overcome the truths of the gods.

Moreover, I could say something simply nonsensical like: "Squares must be circles" or "The progress of time must be slowed if you run swiftly" or "Chickens must have teeth." Here strong wishes are just ridiculous distortions of reality. No, Socrates—desire is not a good basis for correct personal beliefs. I am afraid that innate desire cannot be invoked as the sole basis for any correct *must be* statements.

SOCRATES: Aeschines, you have studied natural philosophy;

so I must defer to you when it comes to determing what is actually impossible.

AESCHINES: Trust me, old man—these things are all impossible.

SOCRATES: I cannot judge your examples. I only know about everyday things—trees, houses, my feet, my hands—but these everyday things give me pause when it comes to impossibilities. For instance speaking of hands, do you remember the talk we had with Acumenus last spring?

AESCHINES: Acumenus the physician, Eryximachus's father?

SOCRATES: Yes.

AESCHINES: I have never talked with him personally, Socrates.

SOCRATES: Perhaps you were not with us that day.

AESCHINES: I was not. What did he say?

SOCRATES: He was relating a striking case that he had seen. A young woman was brought to him by her mother. It seems that this girl could not find a man to marry because of her hands.

AESCHINES: Her hands?

SOCRATES: Yes, her hands—when she became agitated, worried, or upset, her hands turned deep blue.

AESCHINES: Is this the truth?

SOCRATES: It is. And at these times, it was as if she were wearing blue gloves—there was a clearcut line separating the normal skin at her wrist from the strange blue skin of her hands. Then to compound this strange mystery, when the girl finally calmed down, her hands did not immediately become normal again. First they turned bright red (as if she had now put on a pair of red gloves), then they faded into a pale pink, and finally they became a normal skin tone again.

AESCHINES: First they turned blue, and then they turned red?

SOCRATES: Actually if I remember correctly, her hands first turned absolutely white, *then* they became blue, and the red followed the blue.

AESCHINES: That *is* quite strange, Socrates—I have never heard of anything like it.

SOCRATES: Apparently Acumenus had seen some variants of this condition before. For instance, he knew other young women whose hands turned pure white in cold weather—they turned white and then they progressed to bright blue and on to red. In any case, this particular young woman frightened off all suitors: they thought her bewitched.

AESCHINES: I can understand, Socrates. It seems like the gods were playing tricks with the poor girl. No normal person has those troubles.

SOCRATES: Acumenus did not feel there was some divine malevolence at work. In fact, this changing of the color of her hands reminded him of blushing; Acumenus wondered whether the girl's hands were blushing with emotion, just as one's face might change colors with emotion.

AESCHINES: It still seems abnormal to me, Socrates.

SOCRATES: It is strange perhaps, but "abnormal" is a tricky descriptor. Certainly though, we can call it "unusual."

You know, Aeschines, to me the strangest part of this story was how the girl's mother demonstrated the phenomenon to Acumenus. She said to her daughter: "Close your eyes and make your hands turn blue." And the girl did just that: she closed her eyes, and after a moment her hands—and only her hands—turned bright blue.

AESCHINES: The girl could *will* them to turn blue?

SOCRATES: Yes. Undoubtedly she had to think some agitating thoughts—but with sufficient desire, the young woman willed her hands blue. Later they turned red—so we might even say that she also wished her hands red.

AESCHINES: Ah, Socrates, I should have suspected that this medical tale had a devious point. I should have known that you were leading up to something. So someone can actually *wish* their hands or their feet red? I suppose that you will now claim that wishing or strong innate desire can be the basis for other seeming impossibilities, if they are phrased as *must be* statements.

SOCRATES: Well, Aeschines, Acumenus's example makes me wonder.

AESCHINES: No one can make me believe that this works for all *must be* statements. Wish all you want, Socrates, but a statement like: "Each star must be larger than the sun" remains ever a fiction. Stars are tiny points of light—that is reality and no strong desires on our part can change reality.

SOCRATES: As I have said, Aeschines, I do not know enough about astronomy to judge such matters. But when it comes to people, I have had much direct experience, and I have found repeatedly that *must be* statements are made and are sworn to and are acted on and are died for solely on the basis of strong innate wishes. There need be no specific examples, and there need be no other corraborative evidence. *Must be* statements can be correct from innate desire alone.

AESCHINES: On that, I must agree with you, Socrates.

SOCRATES: Then can it be that Lysicles has made his statement: "There must be a simple solution" on the basis of a strong innate wish?

AESCHINES: That is always a possibility—but there is no way of our knowing.

SOCRATES: Why not?

AESCHINES: Do you not agree that a strong innate wish is an individual and a personal matter?

SOCRATES: It certainly is.

AESCHINES: Therefore, to be certain about such an innate wish, we must question the wisher himself?

SOCRATES: True.

AESCHINES: In this case, the wisher is Lysicles?

SOCRATES: Yes.

AESCHINES: And Lysicles is dead?

SOCRATES: Yes.

AESCHINES: Then any further discussion will remain mere conjecture, Socrates—let us go and eat a midday meal.

SOCRATES: Aeschines, you were reasoning so well. Why abandon your argument precipitously? You are so near to its conclusion.

AESCHINES: What do you mean, Socrates?

SOCRATES: Did you not point out that in order to learn the basis of his *must be* statement, we must question the speaker?

AESCHINES: Yes.

SOCRATES: Then your next conclusion should be that we must question Lysicles.

AESCHINES: True.

SOCRATES: So do not be shy, Aeschines—question him.

AESCHINES: He is dead, Socrates.

SOCRATES: That is only a small obstacle. I have no doubt that we can conjure forth his shade.

AESCHINES: Are you a wizard or an oracle, Socrates? No wonder some men have accused you of defaming the gods and of corrupting the youth: you dare to invite the spirits of the dead to converse.

SOCRATES: Aeschines, I am not as bold as you suspect—in fact, I am only doing what your mother has done before me.

AESCHINES: My mother?! My mother is eighty-five years old. She is a frail and bent old lady who daily prays to the gods and who continues to revere the memory of my dear father. She is a pious, gentle old woman. What ever are you talking about?

SOCRATES: I am talking about my visit to your home last week.

AESCHINES: Socrates, you came for a sausage recipe.

SOCRATES: Precisely. You see, my wife (Xanthippe) became obsessed with sausage, and when none of the servants could buy sausages that were made to her satisfaction, she complained to no end. Your father was the preeminent sausage maker in Athens twenty years ago: so I went to consult your mother.

AESCHINES: Yes yes, Socrates—but what is this about my mother and witchcraft?

SOCRATES: Witchcraft? There was no witchcraft—I merely asked your mother to give me a good recipe for sausage.

AESCHINES: But Socrates, you said that my mother conjures forth the dead and—

SOCRATES: Patience, Aeschines—I am coming to that. When I arrived at your home, your mother was sitting in the courtyard, enjoying the morning sun.

AESCHINES: (As she does every morning, Socrates.)

SOCRATES: "Hello, madam," I said.
"Why, Socrates—hello," she began. "You know, young man, you still look like your mother." (She always tells me that I look like my mother, although they only knew each other in childhood.)
"I am an old man now, madam."
"Yes—and your mother would be an old woman now." Then we talked about the old days in Athens. Finally I said: "I need your help. Xanthippe has developed a craving for sausage, and she is unsatisfied with anything that our servants can find in the Agora. Can you remember a recipe for your husband's sausages? It would bring a bit of tranquility into my home."
"A recipe? One recipe? Why, there were dozens of recipes; there were scores of recipes! (You know that I used to make the sausage mixes myself.) In those days the finest nobility would come around weekly for our sausages—captains landing in Peiraeus made straight for our sausage stall; traders from the north always stopped by on their way home."
"Yes, your meats were quite special. Can you tell me the ingredients?"
"Oh," said your mother, "it is not only the ingredients that you must know: you must know exactly how to prepare them. Now let me see if I remember . . . The whole process was teamwork, Socrates. My husband chopped and mixed the meats; I added spices and a bit of grain and then I kneaded the

mix. Finally, my husband stuffed it into rolls. The steps are somewhat involved. Are you listening carefully, young man?''

"Quite—with my littlest and tiniest ears, madam.''

"Very well . . . now dear, I—''

" 'Dear?' ''

"Quiet, Socrates! You cannot expect me to remember this all myself—I must ask my husband to recount his part. Where was I? Ah yes, now what exactly did you do to start, dear? You prepared the sausage skins? Of course. Then I would make the first mash; the first mash was—let me see, spelt-grits. Yes yes, I cleaned the grains and I boiled them in the stock broth. (My husband kept a clear broth made from the meats, Socrates.) Next I added finely chopped leek—that is, the white part of the leek of course. I cooked the mash well and then I removed it to cool.

"And what did you do, dear? Oh yes, of course. The meat mix—you chopped the suet and the sliced meat together, then you pounded in pepper and eggs. How many? *Three*—three eggs. Anything else? Of course, of course we added ground herb, lovage. And I put the whole mix into the mash in a mortar with pine-kernels and with peppercorns, working it well—and I added just the right amount of stock broth.

"Then, Socrates, my husband stuffed the sausage skins and I boiled them. You know, you could eat the slices directly afterwards, although—yes dear, most customers grilled them lightly. And . . .''

And so she went on, Aeschines, talking to herself, shuttling between her activities and her husband's activities—with side comments to me. In the end she had recreated the entire process. (And I might add, that when I gave the recipe to my wife, we finally had a few days of calm at home. The sausages that she prepared exceeded even my fond memories of your father's wonderful product.)

AESCHINES: I am glad that it worked out so well for you, Socrates. But this is not an example of conjuring forth the dead:

my mother just used that absent-minded banter in order to jog her aging memory.

SOCRATES: You do not believe that she was actually talking to your father?

AESCHINES: Certainly not—my father has been dead for many years.

SOCRATES: And no part of him lives on?

AESCHINES: Not in this world—only in the plains of the Elysion Isle.

SOCRATES: I see. Let me ask you something, Aeschines: Do you enjoy Homer?

AESCHINES: What a question, Socrates! Homer must have been born of divine parents: all his words glow. His poetry is golden and wonderful. When listening to a Homeric rhapsode, I can close my eyes and see and feel every wind and every wave of the great Odyssean voyage. Do I enjoy Homer? I could not live without him.

SOCRATES: Do you feel that you know what Homer thought about Odysseus or about Telemakhos or about Laertes or about the two score suitors?

AESCHINES: Absolutely.

SOCRATES: Were these Homer's living thoughts?

AESCHINES: Certainly—they were not his dead thoughts.

SOCRATES: You have heard many Homeric discussions, Aeschines. You have heard rhapsodes and rhetoricians and philosophers cite passages from the *Odyssey* and the *Iliad*. These learned men often recite Homer's verse in order to support their contention that Homer felt this way about divination or that he believed certain things about chariot racing or that he had certain thoughts about various heroes.

AESCHINES: Of course, Socrates—that is a common procedure in discussing the great poets. We use their works to understand their thoughts.

SOCRATES: By "great poets," do you mean the great *dead* poets, Aeschines?

AESCHINES: Yes. Time tests all things, and great poetry is poetry that has endured beyond generations.

SOCRATES: So, we can still revive the thoughts of the dead poet. Would you say that this means the living thoughts of the dead poets?

AESCHINES: The *dead* thoughts of these poets are forever trapped beyond the grave.

SOCRATES: I see. Then would you say that some living part of these great poets lives on past their death in their poetry?

AESCHINES: Yes—their spirits and their minds and their living thoughts all persist in their poetry.

SOCRATES: Would you say that rhapsodes, rhetoricians, and philosophers can explore these ideas? Can we actually question the dead poets through their poetry?

AESCHINES: I suppose that is one way to describe poetic analysis.

SOCRATES: Is there some other description that you would offer?

AESCHINES: No, your description is fine.

SOCRATES: Rhapsodes, rhetoricians, and philosophers regularly question the dead?

AESCHINES: Dead *poets*, Socrates.

SOCRATES: We can only question dead *poets*, Aeschines?

AESCHINES: I would suppose so, but I am not certain, Socrates.

SOCRATES: Then let me help you. What is the difference between a poem and a memory?

AESCHINES: Why do you ask, Socrates?

SOCRATES: Rhapsodes, rhetoricians, and philosophers daily question the dead through poems. I claim that your mother was questioning the dead through memories. Perhaps poems are

types of memories—I was wondering if there is any real difference.

AESCHINES: Socrates, you ask a strange question. Allow me
a moment to think . . . It seems to me that a poem is a more
communal thing than a memory: we all have access to a poem;
whereas a memory lies hidden in one person's soul.

SOCRATES: Memories are personal and poems are communal?
Then would you agree that it is through memories personally—
and through poems communally—that the dead live on forever in
this mortal land of ours?

AESCHINES: Yes—I suppose that this is true.

SOCRATES: So would you now agree that your mother was
actually speaking with your father last week? Was she not
talking with him, Aeschines, in the personal poetry of her soul?

AESCHINES: Perhaps, perhaps. I presume, Socrates, that you
propose we can speak with Lysicles in the same way?

SOCRATES: We can try.

AESCHINES: Very well, let us try. What is it that you would
ask Lysicles?

SOCRATES: Let us ask Lysicles about his beliefs. Lysicles has
said: "There must be a simple solution." I would like to know:
Has he said this because he stongly *wishes* that there must be a
simple solution? Or does Lysicles know something else that he
has not yet told us?

AESCHINES: Then go ahead and ask him, Socrates.

SOCRATES: "Lysicles, why do you think that there must be a
simple solution?"

AESCHINES: I am afraid that the murmur of the marketplace
has drowned out his answer, Socrates. What did he say?

SOCRATES: He said, Aeschines, that simple solutions are the
best solutions.

AESCHINES: He did? That is not a satisfying answer, Socrates.
Simple solutions may well be the best solutions, but there is no
reason for us always to expect to achieve the best solutions.

SOCRATES: True.

AESCHINES: Let me ask him a question: "Lysicles, you say that simple solutions are the best solutions. Do you have some independent reason to imagine that we can always achieve the best solutions—or is it just that you strongly wish always to achieve the best solutions?"

SOCRATES: A good question . . . Hmm, did you hear his answer this time, Aeschines?

AESCHINES: No, I heard nothing. What did he say?

SOCRATES: Lysicles—the young part of Lysicles—said that he is an incurable optimist. He believes firmly that we should always strive to do our best. And he says that we should always assume that we will succeed.

AESCHINES: So, Lysicles has told us that there must be a simple solution, because he deeply wishes for there to be a simple solution.

SOCRATES: That is how it appears, Aeschines.

AESCHINES: But, Socrates, this contradicts one of your elemental principles: often, you have pointed out that the world has pockets of incondensable complexity—thus some problems have no simple solutions.

SOCRATES: Yes, and that is especially true in the political arena, in relation to just such problems as Lysicles addresses. When there are many individuals involved, it is hard for one simple rule or one simple plan to satisfy them all. Mankind has a myriad of diverse and independent natures. Who can predict all the streams of thought, the courses of action, and the nuances of whim that will appear in a crowd? For multitudes, throngs, scrums, scrunges, and squashes, most solutions will be complex.

AESCHINES: Well, our Lysicles is definitely speaking in the arena of scrums and squashes, Socrates. "There must be a simple solution to our particular political problem," he said. But as Lysicles has told us himself, he is just a dreamer. No wonder you declared his proposal to be nonsense.

SOCRATES: Aeschines, you misunderstood me. Lysicles pronouncement was:

> There must be a simple solution
>   beyond mere restitution—
> A new constitution
>   is the ideal resolution.

and this is nonsense. It is nonsense, because it is dogmatic and at the same time it is vague and insubstantial. Initially, you championed this pronouncement by imbuing the vacuous words with your own particular concrete substance. *You* gave the words their meaning. Remember, someone else—someone like Critias, for instance—could easily have refuted Lysicles by using other interpretations of these same empty generalities. So here in this doggerel we see old Lysicles the airy platitudinist.

AESCHINES: Yes, Socrates—I am afraid that you have convinced me.

SOCRATES: But just a moment, Aeschines, do not be discouraged—that is only one part of Lysicles. That is old Lysicles the platitudinist; it is Lysicles the politician—it is not young Lysicles the dreamer. And, Aeschines, I cannot fault Lysicles the dreamer, I cannot reproach him, I cannot chide him. I can only stand with him and hold his arm and smile.

AESCHINES: You would hold hands with a man who spins out dreams?

SOCRATES: Yes, I would hold his hand or just sit at his feet and look up at him. This young Lysicles—Lysicles the dreamer—hopes for simple solutions. Sometimes he will find them. Many times he will not. But this Lysicles is filled with a divine spirit, and he aspires to simplicity, regardless of the strange complexities cast in his way by the whims of Nature. Simple is pure and it is godly, and Lysicles the dreamer sleeps a pure and godly sleep.

You know, my good sausage-maker's son, there are two Lysicleses: an old world-worn political Lysicles and a young bright-eyed dreaming Lysicles. And I would wager that the young Lysicles now sleeps the clean, calm peace of a new baby. That little baby's world is bright and true and golden and pure: in a word, it is simple. The baby colors are clear and absolute, the baby tastes are warm and good, the baby smells are clean and fresh, and the baby sounds are bright and glowing. A baby's sun bakes and basks his world in bold, bright, simple joys.

Young Lysicles the dreamer dreams in this baby world, and he will not give up his dream. The baby world is the world of the Olympian gods, and our highest aspiration is to return someday to that divine glowing garden of our baby days. They are days at the edge of the world. They are days when once we rocked in the warm arms of our fathers, who were the great gold gods of our first born days.

September 7: SOPHRON
(Part I)

PLATO: Socrates, I would like you to meet my friend Sophron, the poet.

SOCRATES: It is a great pleasure to meet you, Sophron.

SOPHRON: Likewise, Socrates.

PLATO: I was just visiting Sophron, and I persuaded him to come back with me in order to take a rest from the uncomfortable political climate at home. Sophron comes from Syracuse—

SOPHRON: From Syracuse in Sicily—

PLATO: Where the tyrant Dionysius (who, as you know, took control of the city four years ago) has plunged the area into a myriad of petty intrigues and divided allegiances.

SOPHRON: There are secret societies, payments for protection, and lists of the favored and the disfavored merchants. The city is fragmented into tiny fiefdoms.

PLATO: There are accusations of disloyalty, curt summary trials, banishments, and deaths—a vague unease hangs over everyone like an evil miasm.

SOPHRON: Yes, it is a sad, tense life in Syracuse. You know, Socrates, it was not until I got far asea and finally began to breath the fresh salt air that I realized what a cloud I had been living under.

PLATO: There was an ill fog in his soul.

SOPHRON: But already I am feeling revived; I am happy to be here in the bright Athenian sunshine of this autumn day.

SOCRATES: Well then, sit and be refreshed, friend.

PLATO: Gifts . . .

SOCRATES: Gifts, Plato?

PLATO: Gifts, old teacher of mine—Great Gifts: Sophron's verses are wonderful presents to us all, and I am hoping that the change of climate—

SOPHRON: The new scenery, the rejuvenating atomospherics—

PLATO: Yes, the restorative weathers—I hope that these will stimulate him to create even more fine poetry.

SOCRATES: That would be a fine use of our old Athenian countryside. But I wonder: Can you write from a distance, Sophron?

SOPHRON: What do you mean?

SOCRATES: Those lines of yours that I know best, Sophron, are all mixed in with the day to day lives of your compatriots.

PLATO: Yes, Sophron—with your friends and with your folk—

SOCRATES: With the people of Syracuse in their homes, in the market, and in the surrounding farms. Do you not need to immerse yourself in their affairs in order to recreate them in verse?

SOPHRON: To tell the truth, I am not certain, Socrates—we will see. But the undercurrents of bad feeling had begun to take their toll on me. Now, though, I take heart from Aesop's old saying: "A crust of bread chewed in peace is far better than a rich banquet gobbled in anxiety." A wise man was that old Aesop, a wise man.

SOCRATES: Sophron, do you believe that there really was such a person as Aesop?

SOPHRON: Certainly—why would you ever doubt it?

SOCRATES: Some say that he is just a legendary figure—

PLATO: A mythic man—

SOCRATES: Around whom animal fables have been collected.

SOPHRON: Socrates, some say that Homer never existed.

PLATO: Homer, Socrates!

SOPHRON: Of course there was an Aesop: too many details of his life have been remembered for there to be any doubt.

PLATO: That is right, Socrates—too many details.

SOPHRON: Why, there are men alive today whose grand-fathers' grandfathers personally witnessed the payment that the Delphians gave to Iadmon.

PLATO: Iadmon, who himself was the grandson of the Iadmon who was Aesop's original master.

SOPHRON: We have all heard a great many stories about that payment, Socrates. You will recall that Aesop was born in Thrace—

PLATO: Or Lydia.

SOPHRON: Well some also say Phrygia.

SOCRATES: (I had heard that it was Samos.)

PLATO: Samos? That is no more likely than Attica, Socrates.

SOCRATES: Actually, Plato, some have said that Aesop *was* born in Attica (in Athens, specifically); others have said that it was Sardis or Aethiopia.

SOPHRON: I believe that it was Thrace, good friends. Anyways, in his youth Aesop moved to Thessaly—

PLATO: To Lydia—

SOCRATES: I had heard that it was Samos.

SOPHRON: Samos? Samos was later, Socrates. Aesop was taken as a slave by Iadmon of Samos—

PLATO: Iadmon of Thessaly, Sophron—

SOCRATES: I had heard that it was Phocis.

SOPHRON: No no, gentlemen—Phocis (at Delphi) was where Aesop eventually met his death.

PLATO: True, but Iadmon was a landowner in Thessaly.

SOCRATES: I thought that it was Phocis.

SOPHRON: Actually, it was Iadmon of Samos. And there, after perhaps ten years of servitude to Iadmon, Aesop was given his freedom.

PLATO: Yes, his freedom.

SOCRATES: Ah—his freedom.

SOPRON: And it was on Samos, the most fertile island of all the Aegean, famed for its sweet vineyards, renowned for its rich grains, celebrated for its carob groves, that Aesop passed his time recounting stories.

PLATO: Animal tales—

SOPHRON: Creature stories, beastie fables—remembered from his youth, I suspect.

PLATO: A youth passed in Lydia—

SOPHRON: (Actually, it was in Thrace, Plato.) But Iadmon's lands were on the island of Samos, outside its capital city, Samos. Iadmon's estate was beyond the walls, across from the promontory of Mycale, past the rich slopes of Mount Astypalaea, and off where the great Temple of Hera—

PLATO: Ah, the magnificent Temple of Hera—

SOPHRON: With its thick gleaming columns, the Temple of Hera was but a crisp edge, a finely etched architecture, on the horizon as seen from Iadmon's lands. There sat Aesop by the vineyards, spinning fables. Of course he did not speak in verse.

PLATO: Not in verse—

SOPHRON: Not in verse, no—he talked in the common speech of everyday man, and the stories were so simple that they just floated by.

PLATO: Like clouds—

SOPHRON: Like light, wispy, almost unnoticed clouds, Plato.

PLATO: Gentle tales.

SOPHRON: Most definitely gentle, Plato. And it was not until one of the neighboring landowners was accused of theft and defended by, of all people, Aesop, that the townsfolk began to take notice of him. Aesop's presentation in court was humble and simple.

PLATO: It was simple and straightforward.

SOPHRON: Exactly. The defense was simple and straightforward, and he supported it with common fables. It was such a contrast to the usual stilted and convoluted speeches, the interminable "wherefores," "whichsays," "whysos," and "willfuls"—

PLATO: The "heresos," the "highsets," the "happenstances," and the "hierarchies"—

SOPHRON: The overblown jangling accusations, and the pointy "I-thou-accuse" style. Aesop was so strikingly plain that he overwhelmed the listeners. He became a sensation. Soon, he was called to Croesus's court at Sardis in Lydia, where he dined with Solon and he met the Seven Sages of Greece. He travelled to Athens—

PLATO: Yes, here to Athens.

SOPHRON: Then he returned to Samos. Eventually, he was asked by Croesus to go to Delphi, in Phocis, in order to deliver a large sum of money. When he arrived, he refused to give the money to anyone other than the chief priest, in accord with Croesus's specific charge. It was just about this time of year, Socrates; it was mid-September, during the feast of Demeter—

PLATO: It was during the Eleusian mysteries and the secret worships, when emotions were highly charged—

SOPHRON: And when the chief priest was in seclusion—he was absolutely alone—for two weeks. So, misunderstanding Aesop's motives, the local guards thought that he wanted the money himself, and angrily they killed Aesop.

PLATO: They killed him, and they took the money.

SOPHRON: The guards took the money, and the money was distributed among the populace. But a drought and a pestilence followed the next summer, and it returned during the six summers thereafter.

PLATO: It lasted seven lean years, Socrates, seven lean dry years.

SOPHRON: And the Delphians eventually had to make their peace with the gods—

PLATO: With the austere and pious gods and godlings of Olympos.

SOPHRON: They made their peace with the gods by paying a large compensation to the grandson of Iadmon (the grandson was also named Iadmon), in lieu of any other known family of the old fable-teller Aesop.

PLATO: Old Aesop left no family.

SOPHRON: True. Aesop lived to be sixty-two years old—

PLATO: Sixty-two or sixty-three sun-soaked years.

SOPHRON: And before his ill-fated trip to Delphi, he spent most of his elder years in the countryside of Samos, living on the estate of his old master Iadmon. It was there that Pythagoras—

SOCRATES: Pythagoras?

SOPHRON: Pythagoras.

PLATO: When just a boy—

SOPHRON: When he was just a boy of less than ten years, he heard old Aesop talk. Eighty years later Pythagoras said: "Aesop was the white-haired grandfather of all us boys. He himself was the grandfather earth; he spoke like a vineyard, and he smiled like the warm Samian sun."

PLATO: Yes, Socrates, he smiled like the warm and gentle Samian sun.

September 7: SOPHRON
(Part II)

SOCRATES: Sophron, you mentioned Aesop's old saying: "A crust of bread chewed in peace is far better than a rich banquet gobbled in anxiety."

SOPHRON: Yes, Socrates.

SOCRATES: Was Aesop correct?

SOPHRON: *I* think so. What do you think?

SOCRATES: Well, Sophron, this brief saying sounds good—

PLATO: It does.

SOCRATES: But, friends, there is always more to learn from Aesop. Shall we study this saying a bit more closely?

SOPHRON: Very well. How shall we begin?

SOCRATES: I like to begin with questions, so let me ask you, Sophron: Do you think that Aesop meant exactly what he said?

SOPHRON: Certainly—why do you ask?

SOCRATES: I ask, Sophron, because of Plato's ears.

SOPHRON: His ears?

PLATO: My ears?

SOCRATES: Yes—your wayward whiffling ears, my friend.

PLATO: Now, Sophron, I ask you is this any way for a teacher to speak to his pupil? Wayward and whiffling? Socrates, you disrepectful old codger, out with it. What is really on your mind? I doubt whether you want to talk about my ears. What are you really thinking about?

SOCRATES: Ah, my young Plato, it is music to which I refer.

PLATO: Music?

SOCRATES: Yes—music. Were you not telling me about the music of Orthagoras just yesterday?

SOPHRON: That is rather esoteric knowledge, Plato: Orthagoras was the founder of the famed Sicyon dynasty, centuries ago. Do you know something about Sicyon music?

PLATO: No no, Sophron—Socrates is speaking of Orthagoras of Thebes, Orthagoras the flute player. He is a contemporary wizard of music; there is probably none more agile with the interplay of song and flute.

SOCRATES: Plato, you are quite a champion of Orthagoras. To hear you speak, he is like a priest in the mystical cult of wind instruments.

PLATO: Yes—he is the high priest of beautiful, rolling, Olympian sounds.

SOCRATES: So you have said many times, my good Plato. But what of Pronomus? Think back to last week for a moment. After you heard Pronomus play, did you not tell me that he is incomparable?

PLATO: I certainly did. (Pronomus was one of Alicbiades's teachers, Sophron.) Pronomus is a great musician; he is a superb flautist—he plays the aulos. And, Sophron, what a musical athlete he is. He can roll and riffle—

SOPHRON: Roll and riffle?

PLATO: Yes—Pronomus can roll and riffle a cascade of notes so effortlessly that it slips by you before you notice. Sometimes he will even make a song echo back on itself, as if there were two flutes playing together at once. He is a master, an absolute master.

SOCRATES: Well, Plato, you are certainly enchanted by Pronomus and his aulos flute—

PLATO: Enchanted, thrilled, and ecstatic.

SOCRATES: But, young man, recently (I do not recall the exact occasion) you told me that the pan-pipes are the ideal musical instrument. Did you not say something like: "Through the pan pipes, we approach the true voice of divinity, the pure sounds of Olympos"?

PLATO: Absolutely, Socrates—there is nothing like the sound of the pan-pipes. Their crystalline purity and clarity give us a glimpse of the gods.

SOCRATES: I see. Now, Plato, do I not remember that earlier this summer you were enraptured by the cithara?

PLATO: Certainly, I had just heard Connus play. (Connus, the son of Metrobius, was Socrates's old music teacher, Sophron.) It was heavenly.

SOCRATES: Plato, my child—what am I to make of you? On one day it is the cithara, on another day it is the pan-pipes or perhaps it is the aulos—and first Connus is the finest musician, then Lamprus is the best, and now Pronomus is unsurpassed.

PLATO: Hold on a moment, Socrates—Lamprus is not in the class of Connus and Pronomus.

SOCRATES: Be that as it may, Plato, I cannot keep up with your musical whims.

PLATO: Whims?

SOPHRON: Whims?

PLATO: Socrates, these are not whims—these are serious and deeply felt beliefs.

SOCRATES: Perhaps they are serious and perhaps they are deeply felt, but I call them "whims" because they are not beliefs that I can predict. I can only sit back and say: "Well, well—I wonder which instrument and which musician has permeated young Plato's soul today?"

PLATO: When you introduce the idea of prediction, then I think of Rules—

SOCRATES: I do too, Plato.

PLATO: But I can give you no Rules for these matters,

Socrates. My musical beliefs and feelings are dictated by my innermost spirit; they do not follow some rhetorician's logic.

SOCRATES: I understand, Plato. In fact, that is precisely why I invoke your musical passions when Sophron is examining Aesop's saying.

SOPHRON: Oh? I was wondering what this had to do with analyzing Aesop, Socrates.

SOCRATES: There is a principle of analysis to be discovered here.

SOPHRON: There is?

SOCRATES: There is—and it is simply this. With Plato's feelings about music, we find no independent logic. There is nothing to take away from the man himself. One cannot reach deep into Plato's bowels and extract a set of predictive decrees that can sit quiet, clean, and sure, alone and outside of our Plato.

SOPHRON: How do you know, Socrates?

SOCRATES: Well listen, Sophron: Now, tell me, Plato, do you have some Rule that I can use to predict your musical preference for tomorrow?

PLATO: I have already told you that there are no simple Rules, Socrates.

SOCRATES: So, your feelings simply well up from some chaotic, bubbling pot of emotions?

PLATO: The origin of my feelings is complex, but it is not as chaotic as you make it sound, Socrates. Remember: although it is difficult to predict my feelings, there is an underlying continuity and organization, and that continuity and that organization are called "Plato." I am the connecting link. Through me there is a coherence and a continuity to the feelings. Of course this does not change the fact that my feelings are a particularly intricate business; they cannot be summarized in some short and pithy formulas. There are no simple Rules.

SOCRATES: So, Plato, you feel that there is some underlying coherence to your feelings?

PLATO: Undoubtedly. That is why they are the feelings of Plato that we are discussing and not the feelings of Socrates or of Sopron.

SOCRATES: Then, do you, Plato, have access to information about these feelings?

PLATO: Of course—*I* know how I feel. But I am afraid that Socrates and Sophron can only guess about Plato.

SOPHRON: I see.

SOCRATES: So, Sophron, it seems that in order to determine what Plato feels on any particular day, we will not be able to refer to some written set of Rules that we can store in our pockets. Instead, we must carry Plato himself about with us— then we can always ask him when we are in doubt.

SOPHRON: That exercise would keep me thin; carrying Plato everywhere on my back would be quite a chore.

SOCRATES: It might be physically exhausting, but with Plato at least you have that option. However, with Aesop we are in a more difficult position.

SOPHRON: Socrates, it is good to hear the name Aesop again. I feared that you had forgotten about the old gentleman.

SOCRATES: I will never forget about him, Sophron. However, we have lost the physical man himself. To discover his feelings, we cannot carry him around and question him when we need a bit of enlightening, as we could with Plato. We can only hope to understand him through the bits and pieces, the fragments and shards that have been passed to us. Fortunately, the world did manage to cart away a few flakes and slivers of old Aesop.

SOPHRON: A few scraps and shreds, a few wisps and rags—

PLATO: Some collops and parings, some tatters and tiles.

SOCRATES: Yes, we have hints and bits. Thus, we must now resort to logic, and this is a very poor substitute for the real Aesop. We must take his words as exactly as possible; we must set them into our logical argumentation—artificial though that is—for this is our only hope of making any sense of Aesop, who is now the shade of a once wonderful man.

SOPHRON: I see. And all of this wandering speech, Socrates, means that you hope to define Aesop's words with great precision? You hope to find his exact meaning?

SOCRATES: Well, Sophron, the answer to that is both "yes"and "no."

SOPHRON: How can something be both "yes" and "no" at the same time, Socrates?

SOCRATES: You ask a good question, Sophron—and it deserves a good question in return: When we met earlier, did you not say that it was good to meet me?

SOPHRON: I did, Socrates.

SOCRATES: What did you mean by "good"?

SOPHRON: "Good"? Well, let me see. I suppose that I meant I was happy to see you in person.

SOCRATES: Did you mean anything else?

SOPHRON: Yes—I imagined that in talking with you I would learn something new and that I would see the world a bit differently.

SOCRATES: Now I ask you, Sophron: Does the word "good," in its usual sense, mean "happy to see someone"?

SOPHRON: No.

SOCRATES: Or does the word "good" mean "to learn something new"?

SOPHRON: No.

SOCRATES: Or does it normally mean "to see the world a bit differently"?

SOPHRON: No.

SOCRATES: Then, if we were to analyze precisely the meaning of your statement "It is good to meet you, Socrates" and if we used conventional understandings of the word "good," then we might miss some of your real meaning?

SOPHRON: Yes, I suppose that we should.

PLATO: Definitely we should, Sophron.

SOCRATES: And I too suppose that we should, Sophron. Of course we are fortunate. Are we not, Plato?

PLATO: Do you mean that we are fortunate in the blue sky above us and that we are fortunate with the warm air around us, old man?

SOCRATES: Yes—and also in the fine companionship here with us, Plato. Specifically, we are fortunate in having Sophron at our side. Thus, we are not dependent on any careful logical definitions in order to understand his sentences—the sentences passed down to us by word of mouth. We have the real Sophron at hand to question directly, when we wish to understand precisely his meanings. With the living Sophron at my side, I can hope to understand his real meanings. Is that not true?

SOPHRON: Yes.

SOCRATES: And so, my young friend, when you ask: "Do you hope, through logic and thoughtfulness, to define Aesop's *words* with great precision?" then I answer "yes." But when you ask: "Do you hope, through logic and thoughtfulness, to define Aesop's *ideas and meanings* with great precision?" then I answer "no."

SOPHRON: Socrates, if there is no hope in understanding Aesop without Aesop himself, why should we bother with this logic? Why analyze at all? Why ask such questions?

PLATO: Sophron, our Socrates lives to question.

SOPHRON: But if the answers are unattainable, then why bother to ask these questions?

SOCRATES: Why bother? A life unexamined is a life not worth living, Sophron—and that does not apply only to one's own life, it applies to others' lives as well.

PLATO: To Aesop's life, Sophron.

SOCRATES: Yes—to Aesop's life especially. Of course we can learn much about ourselves from *every* other person's life, but some lives are particularly rich windows. Those lives—the wonderful, inspired lives like that of Aesop—are exceptional.

Now, how do we go about this, Sophron? We work from principles, and principle number one is: Examine a life from inside its own soul. To see a life, look from within. The elemental question is: What does a man see in his own particular life? What does he see from the inside, through his own eyes? I would love to ask that of Aesop—

SOPHRON: You have missed your chance, Socrates.

PLATO: Yes, old man, you missed your chance.

SOCRATES: Granted that we may no longer understand completely old Aesop, still we must try. I do not have the man, so I must content myself with his potshards, with the potshards of Aesop.

SOPHRON: And how do you use these potshards?

SOCRATES: I rework them with the only tools that I have: I use careful, methodical, logical analyses. I question patiently, precisely, and carefully. I take small, regular steps, and then (if necessary) I retrace my steps. In general, Sophron, I follow a rather tiresome and orderly plan. I use what Rules and Regulations and Rigorous Definitions I can.

SOPHRON: Forgive me for agreeing, Socrates, but your program does sound bland and tedious.

SOCRATES: True—but without Rules and Regulations and Rigorous Definitions, then we are in the land of intuitive decisions. With no orderly analyses and no repetitive operations, we are at the mercy of whim and of caprice, and in that land we cannot hope to gain reproducible understandings.

SOPHRON: I am feeling a bit lost, Socrates. I presume that all of this philosophizing has come from: "A crust of bread chewed in peace is far better than a rich banquet gobbled in anxiety." But we have still not begun to talk directly about this old saying.

SOCRATES: Aesop's saying is still in sight, Sophron.

PLATO: Yes. Aesop is on the horizon.

SOPHRON: Is he? Now I understand why people say that Socrates can see vast landscapes in a tiny garden plot. Your horizons are far and wide, old man. In fact, we seem to have travelled to far off lands. Can we still return to Aesop here in Athens?

SOCRATES: Certainly, Sophron, we were just about to meet Aesop and to try see precisely what his words mean.

SOPHRON: All right—then what is next?

SOCRATES: Well, let us begin by understanding the edges of Aesop's saying.

SOPHRON: Which edges?

SOCRATES: How about the *absolute* edges. For instance: Is a crust of bread *always* better than a banquet?

SOPHRON: Always? No, not to the starving man—a man who truly needs food must be given more than a crust of bread in order to survive.

SOCRATES: Then was Aesop wrong?

SOPHRON: No, Socrates—remember: we agreed to assume that Aesop meant *exactly* what he said. Aesop qualified both "crust of bread" and "banquet." He did not say that a crust of bread is *always* better than a banquet. Aesop said only that a crust of bread is *sometimes* better than a banquet.

SOCRATES: So, Aesop was not comparing all crusts of bread with all banquets?

SOPHRON: Correct—he was comparing crusts of bread with banquets only on certain occasions.

SOCRATES: I see. And when are these special occasions?

SOPHRON: Clearly, Socrates, the special occasions for a crust of bread are peaceful times. Aesop says that relaxing and restful meals are better than hurried and harried meals, regardless of the content of the meal.

SOCRATES: Is that exactly what he said?

SOPHRON: Yes, that is what he meant.

SOCRATES: Let us be careful, Sophron: we agreed to pay attention to exactly what Aesop said. Did we not?

SOPHRON: Yes we did.

SOCRATES: As I recall, Sophron, the exact saying was: "A crust of bread chewed in peace is far better than a rich banquet gobbled in anxiety." This statement is a comparison, is it not?

SOPHRON: Yes.

SOCRATES: And it compares crusts of bread and banquets?

SOPHRON: Not all crusts of bread, Socrates, and not all banquets.

SOCRATES: Ah yes—"crusts of bread chewed in peace" are compared to "banquets gobbled in anxiety."

SOPHRON: Exactly.

SOCRATES: Now, Sophron, answer me this: Suppose that you are trying to decide which is better, honey or water jugs—how would you go about it?

SOPHRON: Honey or water jugs?

PLATO: Honey or water jugs, Socrates?

SOCRATES: Yes—honey or water jugs.

SOPHRON: I am not certain that you can compare them, Socrates: they are completely different things.

SOCRATES: They certainly are different. Would you say that they cannot be compared?

SOPHRON: I am afraid that I do not see how we can judge them, at least not with some common method.

SOCRATES: What do you mean?

SOPHRON: Well, consider use. Each item has a different use. Honey is used for eating, and water jugs are used for holding liquids. Or consider sensation. Each item appeals to a difference sense. Honey is judged by our taste, whereas water jugs are judged either by our eye or by our touch.

SOCRATES: I see. Would you say that we cannot compare things that are different?

SOPHRON: Well, we cannot compare things that are so totally different.

SOCRATES: Then this leaves me puzzled about Aesop. In Aesop's saying, he is attempting to compare different things. How can you accept his judgement?

SOPHRON: Socrates, Aesop is comparing food: he compares a crust of bread with a banquet.

SOCRATES: True—but he is comparing a crust of bread chewed peacefully with a banquet gobbled under duress.

SOPHRON: Of course there are some differences. Nonetheless, these two things still have much in common. For example, we use the same sensation—namely, taste—in both situations. Also, we use the same inner perception to evaluate peacefulness and stress.

SOCRATES: We use the common sensation, taste, to make part of the judgement—

PLATO: Yes, we use a common sensation.

SOCRATES: And for the other part of the judgement, we must compare peacefulness and stress. Is there a common sensation for these?

SOPHRON: Yes, there is some one place within our soul where both feelings are judged. Just as there is one place (our tongue) where all tastes are judged in common. It is true that Aesop's saying compares different things, but these things are compared by single judges. Aesop's saying requires comparing food using taste as an individual common judge, and Aesop's saying also requires comparing emotional states using an "emotional evaluator" as an individual common judge.

SOCRATES: We seem to have made much progress here, Sophron. Let me see if I can repeat your criteria for comparing different things.

SOPHRON: All right.

SOCRATES: We begin with two apparently different items, and

we partition the items into traits, traits like taste or color or emotional aura.

SOPHRON: Correct.

SOCRATES: Hmm, I can already imagine some problems here, Sophron. How do we decide which particular traits to identify?

SOPHRON: What do you mean, Socrates?

SOCRATES: Well—you might attend either to taste or to color or to emotion.

SOPHRON: True.

SOCRATES: Is there a universal way to partition items? Or does the partitioning depend on the particular common judges that we have in hand?

SOPHRON: I do not follow you, Socrates.

SOCRATES: Did you say that in order to compare different things, we must use individual common judges?

SOPHRON: Yes.

PLATO: Single common judges, Socrates.

SOCRATES: Is it your contention, Sophron, that if two traits cannot be evaluated by a single common judge, then they cannot be compared?

SOPHRON: Yes.

SOCRATES: I would like to understand thoroughly this stance, Sophron. Would you go so far as to say this: If two traits cannot be evaluated by an individual common judge, then there is nothing whatever that we can say about them?

SOPHRON: That is a rather extreme statement, Socrates. I would not say *nothing*. Instead, I would say: if two traits cannot be evaluated by a single common judge, then we can make no useful comparison.

SOCRATES: I see. So, when comparing objects, is it only useful to identify traits that can be evaluated by individual common judges?

SOPHRON: That is correct.

SOCRATES: All right. Now when making comparisons, do we judge each of these features separately?

SOPHRON: Exactly. We make separate and independent decisions. Each judgement implies a single common judge. Each individual common judge represents an autonomous judgement.

SOCRATES: I think that I understand you better now, Sophron. But I am still puzzled about the honey and the water jugs.

SOPHRON: Oh? Why is that?

SOCRATES: Sophron, did you not tell me that honey and water jugs were too different to compare together?

SOPHRON: Yes.

SOCRATES: Let us be precise, here: Do you mean that honey and water jugs are impossible to compare, or do you mean that they are very difficult to compare?

SOPHRON: What do *you* mean, Socrates?

PLATO: Yes, Socrates, you yourself had best be precise.

SOCRATES: Well, gentlemen, by "impossible," I mean that you cannot imagine any situation in which you would compare the items. Whereas, by "very difficult," I mean that there are some situations in which you might actually make a comparison.

SOPHRON: Socrates, someone with a good imagination can dream up almost any possible situation. Let us limit this to practical situations.

PLATO: Be practical, Socrates—discuss a real situation.

SOCRATES: Very well. Suppose that I were in the market-place—

SOPHRON: As you really are.

SOCRATES: Yes. And suppose that I have only a limited amount of money—

SOPHRON: As you do—

PLATO: Quite a limited amount of money.

SOCRATES: So, I cannot afford to buy both honey *and* water jugs. Now, I am at a potter's stall, and I decide to buy a water jug; it is something that I can definitely use. Suddenly, I look next door. I see a pot of honey, and it is something that I also want. But here I am, caught trying to compare honey and water jugs. You admit, Sophron, that this is a practical, realistic situation? Is it not something that we can easily imagine actually occurring?

SOPHRON: Yes.

SOCRATES: Well then, how am I to proceed?

SOPHRON: How?

SOCRATES: Yes—how?

SOPHRON: I suppose that you will proceed the way that anyone proceeds, you will follow your intuitive feelings.

SOCRATES: Intuition? Sophron, we are sliding backwards. Remember, my poetic friend, intuitive feelings are only useful when we have the intuitor right here before us.

SOPHRON: Fine. We have the intuitor before us—he is you, Socrates.

SOCRATES: Yes—for the moment, I am here. But I may not always be at your side. (I am seventy years old, Sophron.) To be safe, we should discover Rules and Regulations and Rigorous Definitions; in this way, you will have something that you can carry about with you long after I am gone.

SOPHRON: And how will we find these Rules?

SOCRATES: I think that earlier we were close: you had provided us with a set of rules for comparing disparate things. Perhaps they will help with honey and water jugs. If I remember properly, you suggested this: we begin with two apparently different items. Next we partition the items into traits, like taste or color or emotional aura. To decide on the correct partitioning, you proposed that we use the individual common judges that we have in hand. Finally, you pointed out that we should apply each of the judges separately, evaluating each trait independently.

SOPHRON: Exactly.

SOCRATES: So, let us try your rules on honey and water jugs.

Now, how do these two compare? First, we partition "honey" and "water jug" into traits—traits that share a common individual judge.

SOPHRON: Good.

SOCRATES: And what might those traits be?

SOPHRON: I see that you really do hold to a tedious program, Socrates.

SOCRATES: I am afraid that it is necessary at times.

SOPHRON: Very well, Socrates. Where were we?

SOCRATES: What traits will we pick for honey and water jugs?

SOPHRON: Well, we cannot choose the traits "taste" or "functional utility" (like carrying water)—

SOCRATES: Just a moment, Sophron. Why can we not use taste?

SOPHRON: Taste? Socrates, we need traits that are features of *both* honey and water jugs: taste is not a trait of a water jug.

SOCRATES: It is not? Did you not nibble pieces of broken pottery when you were a child?

SOPHRON: Yes, but—

SOCRATES: But what, Sophron?

SOPHRON: Taste is not a trait that is *relevant* for a water jug.

SOCRATES: Relevance? This is a new addition, Sophron. When you first gave me your rules, there was no requirement that the traits had to be relevant to anything.

SOPHRON: Relevance was implied, Socrates.

SOCRATES: What do you mean?

SOPHRON: Clearly it is not enough for us to divide each object into *any* traits that can be judged by a single common evaluator. Otherwise, we could pick traits haphazardly, and often we would find ourselves in our present dilemma. It is true that water jugs have a taste, and it is also true that taste is a common trait between honey and water jugs. Nonetheless, taste is not a relevant trait for our discussion.

SOCRATES: I see. Well, Sophron, we have been using a general principle: operate by explicit rules wherever possible. And it seems that we need an additional rule here. So, give me the rule for relevance. How can we decide which traits are relevant and which traits are irrelevant?

SOPHRON: Hmm . . . all right, Socrates, here is what I suggest. We are concerned with comparisons; specifically, we have two things to contrast and to judge. Thus, relevant traits are those traits that are useful in making the specific comparison at hand.

SOCRATES: Ah, "useful" you say?

SOPHRON: Yes—that is the heart of the matter: relevant traits are useful traits.

SOCRATES: And the taste of the water jug is not a useful trait?

SOPHRON: Correct.

SOCRATES: Why not, Sophron?

SOPHRON: This is simple, Socrates. Taste is an incidental trait of a water jug. You see, no one uses a water jug as food; no one chews water jugs for pure enjoyment. Taste for a water jug is like color for honey. (No one paints with honey.) Pleasing or displeasing as such incidental traits may be, they are extra, superfluous, and nonessential. They are incidental; thus, they are irrelevant.

SOCRATES: I am beginning to understand your point, Sophron. Let me ask you a little more to be absolutely certain that it is clear. Do you know any beekeepers?

SOPHRON: Yes I do.

SOCRATES: Have you seen them judging honey in the marketplaces?

SOPHRON: I certainly have.

SOCRATES: Do they judge the honey by taste?

SOPHRON: Sometimes.

SOCRATES: Sometimes?

SOPHRON: Well, they know the honeys so well that they can usually rely on appearance alone.

PLATO: Yes. Commonly the lighter the color, the finer the honey. Is that not so?

SOPHRON: True.

SOCRATES: Honey from young hives is light and clear and sweet?

SOPHRON: So I am told.

SOCRATES: Whereas honey from old hives is inferior in quality?

SOPHRON: Yes—it is thicker, and it has tinges of unpleasant taste.

SOCRATES: And honey from old hives is darker?

SOPHRON: It is.

PLATO: Yes, the colors can be quite revealing. For instance, honey from white clover is light greenish-white, and honey from heather is rich golden-yellow. Moreover, reddish honey is always disagreeable; it is even mildly poisonous.

SOCRATES: Then would you not say, Sophron, that color is a useful trait for honey?

SOPHRON: So it seems.

PLATO: Yes—from color, you can infer taste.

SOCRATES: So, Sophron, when you said that the color of honey is an incidental trait—an irrelevant trait—were you mistaken?

SOPHRON: Well, Socrates—I admit that I was not thinking of an experienced beekeeper, I was only thinking of an average housewife in the marketplace.

SOCRATES: I see. And when you said that the taste of a water jug was an irrelevant trait, then you were not thinking of the child who likes to nibble on pottery?

SOPHRON: Exactly.

SOCRATES: Nor were you thinking of old Lasicus?

SOPHRON: Lasicus?

PLATO: Ah, Socrates, I wondered when you would bring him up.

Lasicus is an old codger, Sophron; he is well-known in the Athenian Agora. Lasicus hobbles about every day, rain or shine, nodding to everyone but rarely speaking. And, Sophron, his habit is to chew on an old piece of pottery; he is always rooting about among the shards behind the stalls.

SOPHRON: Then, Socrates, you are right: I was not thinking of old Lasicus.

SOCRATES: Would you agree that the color of honey is a relevant trait to beekeepers?

SOPHRON: Yes.

SOCRATES: Would you agree that the taste of a water jug is relevant to Lasicus?

SOPHRON: I suppose that it is.

SOCRATES: Earlier, Sophron, you said that "relevance" means "usefulness." Now it appears that "relevance" means more: it means "usefulness to a particular specified person."

SOPHRON: I guess that it does. (You speak very precisely, Socrates.)

SOCRATES: It is because I am a very lazy man, Sophron.

SOPHRON: What does laziness have to do with precision and with exact rules?

SOCRATES: You see, Sophron, I would as soon hum as sing.

SOPHRON: You would?

SOCRATES: Yes—and also I would love to let my tongue float along, rolling out all manner of fine-sounding sentences. Without precise rules, I am afraid that this is exactly what would happen.

Listen a moment, Sophron: "Comparisons stem from the active coincidence of sense impressions." "To compare and to contrast is to merge the essential natures of images." "Commonality commodes the cores of objects." What do these fine-sounding statements mean?

SOPHRON: I do not know.

SOCRATES: I do not know either, Sophron—but the lazy part of me would happily accept them. At heart I am a lazy man. It is only through the discipline of constant testing—of questioning everything—that I can goad myself into some meager semblance of truth. Moreover, I have a device for ensuring this constant testing. I attempt to be ever more precise and always to be formulaic: Make exact rules, I say to all lazy men like myself.

SOPHRON: I think that you are too hard on yourself, Socrates.

SOCRATES: One cannot be too hard on oneself: one can only be too easy on oneself. But I do not mean to lecture; we should return to the fine Rules that you have been formulating, Sophron. Let me see if I can remember your precise definition of how to compare two disparate objects.

SOPHRON: All right.

SOCRATES: We begin with two apparently different items. Next, we partition the items into appropriate traits, like taste or color or emotional aura.

SOPHRON: Correct.

SOCRATES: And we recognize appropriate traits by two criteria. First, we use the individual common judges that we have in hand. Second, we attend only to those traits that are relevant— that is, we pay attention to those traits that are actually useful to the particular person making the judgement.

SOPHRON: Exactly, Socrates.

SOCRATES: (And you also pointed out that we should apply each of the relevant judges separately, evaluating each trait independently.)

SOPHRON: True.

SOCRATES: Well, Sophron, have we succeeded? Do we have a complete set of rules for judging different things? Do we have the Rules and Regulations and Rigorous Definitions for comparing dissimilars?

SOPHRON: I think so, Socrates.

SOCRATES: Good. Then let us try again and test these rules on our honey and our water jugs.

SOPHRON: Very well.

SOCRATES: Now, here I stand between the beekeeper's stall and the potter's stall. My eye goes back and forth. Honey or water jug? Which shall I choose? . . .

PLATO: Well, we are waiting, old man.

SOCRATES: It is a dilemma. Now, Plato, I turn to my friend Sophron, and he tells me: "It is a difficult decision, Socrates, but I can help with my Universal Rules of Comparison. First, partition the objects into separate traits, traits that can be compared with a single common judge but traits that also are useful to you, Socrates."

So, Sophron, I look at the honey and then at the water jugs. Taste is a common trait, but in relation to the water jug it is useful to Lasicus and not to me. Color is a common trait, but in relation to honey it is useful to the beekeeper and not to me. (Is this acceptable, Sophron?)

SOPHRON: Yes—this is fine reasoning so far.

SOCRATES: Good. Now, I need a common trait for honey and for water jugs; in addition, this trait must be useful for Socrates, in relation both to honey and to water jugs.

SOPHRON: True.

SOCRATES: Do you have any suggestions?

SOPHRON: How about happiness?

SOCRATES: Happiness? Is this a trait of honey and of water jugs?

SOPHRON: I mean the ability to make Socrates happy.

SOCRATES: And what common feature of honey and of water jugs will make me happy?

SOPHRON: It depends on what use you wish to put these objects to.

SOCRATES: I would like to eat the honey, and I would like to carry water in the jug.

SOPHRON: Then we are stuck, Socrates: I see nothing in common between eating and carrying water. The situation seems to fall into your category of "impossible comparisons."

SOCRATES: Oh? By "impossible," do you mean that it cannot be carried out?

SOPHRON: Correct.

SOCRATES: Well, Sophron, let us jump forward a bit to the afternoon of the same day.

SOPHRON: If you wish.

SOCRATES: I have returned home from the marketplace, and Xanthippe (my wife) says: "Ah, Socrates, I see that you have spent all our money."

"Yes dear," I reply.

"And what bargain did you obtain?"

"A water jug."

"A water jug?" she says. "I thought that you were supposed to bring us back some honey!"

(Xanthippe is extraordinarily fond of honey, you see, Sophron.)

SOPHRON: I see, Socrates. This is entertaining, but what does it have to do with "impossibility"?

SOCRATES: I bought a water jug, Sophron.

SOPHRON: Obviously—and?

SOCRATES: And—I made a choice in the marketplace. Evidently I made some sort of comparison between honey and water jugs. Therefore, it was not impossible to make a comparison between these items. This is proof by demonstration.

SOPHRON: "Proof by demonstration"?

SOCRATES: Yes—proof by demonstration. Do you know Euclides?

PLATO: Euclides comes from Megara Hyblaea, near you, Sophron.

SOPHRON: He is from Megara? No, I do not think that I have never heard of him.

SOCRATES: He is a thin little man—a student of ours. Once, he gave a very clever demonstration that has become rather well-known here.

PLATO: Yes. You see, Sophron, Hippias—(But do you know Hippias, Sophron?)

SOPHRON: I have heard that he is an eloquent speaker, who is also quite fond of himself.

PLATO: That is Hippias. Anyways, Hippias had just argued that it is impossible for something to be both in motion and not in motion at the same time.

SOCRATES: Euclides then asked whether something in motion appears to be in motion.

PLATO: Certainly it does, said Hippias.

SOCRATES: Does something at rest appear to be at rest?

PLATO: Yes.

SOCRATES: Then is it impossible for something to appear to be in motion and to appear to be at rest at the same time?

PLATO: Obviously, said Hippias.

SOCRATES: And "appearance" means "how it looks to some observer"?

PLATO: Of course, said Hippias.

SOCRATES: Now, if I rock back and forth, then am I in motion? asked Euclides,

PLATO: You are.

SOCRATES: And if I rock back and forth with my hand held rigidly before my eyes, then does my hand appear to you to be in motion?

PLATO: Yes, said Hippias.

SOCRATES: But, Hippias, I find that if I focus only on my hand then it does not seem to be moving—instead, it appears to me to be at rest.

Now, to me it appears that my hand is at rest. To you, it

appears that my hand is in motion. Therefore, the same thing appears simultaneously to be at rest and to be in motion.

PLATO: But, said Hippias, that demonstration relies on appearances only.

SOCRATES: True, replied Euclides, and earlier you agreed that the appearance of motion and the appearance of rest are sufficient tests of this supposed "imppossibility." But in any case, Hippias, appearances are clear demonstrations. Thus, my point remains proven unequivocally: it is proof by demonstration.

PLATO: Oh? responded Hippias. Perhaps—but then again perhaps not, Euclides. In any event, you have cheated by invoking two different observers: one observer (namely, you) is moving, and the other observer (namely, me) is at rest.

SOCRATES: True, again, Hippias. But I ask you: Who is to say which observer is correct? In fact, I consider it possible that they may both be correct. Certainly they are both equivalent.

PLATO: Exactly, Socrates.

SOPHRON: What did Hippias reply to that, Plato?

PLATO: Oh he dismissed Euclides's comments. Hippias proclaimed that no matter what verbal jousting and quibbling was presented, two opposite viewpoints cannot be right simultaneously. Hippias said that two different observers cannot hold different perspectives that are equally acceptable. There is always a best frame of reference, said Hippias.

SOPHRON: You must admit: it is logical that only one thing can be correct at a time.

SOCRATES: Logical? No, Sophron, that is not logical: that is intuitive. Logic does not preclude simultaneous contradictions, only our human need for simplicity dictates this supposed "Rule." In fact, Euclides's demonstration suggests that this rule may sometimes mislead us.

PLATO: Proof by demonstration is a very compelling argument, Sophron. (You may even have heard how our friend Antisthenes has taken it to the extreme; he claims that only those things exist that can be demonstrated palpably. Antisthenes once said: "A human exists, because a human can be seen. Humanness does not exist, because humanness cannot be seen.")

SOPHRON: That sounds like mere wordplay to me.

All right, for the moment let us accept "proof by demonstration." I suppose, then, that this means that honey and water jugs can somehow be compared on the same terms: you demonstrated that this is possible by actually making the comparison in some fashion. But, Socrates, it is *you* who made the comparison, so it is *you* who must tell us what common, standard, and individual judge you used for those two very different objects.

SOCRATES: Sophron, I see that I can escape you no longer. I must confess the truth.

SOPHRON: Good—please unburden yourself. What is the answer?

SOCRATES: The truth is that I do not know how I made the judgement.

SOPRHON: Socrates, does that end our discussion? If *you* do not know, then who does?

SOCRATES: My confession is not over, Sophron.

SOPHRON: There is more?

SOCRATES: Yes. You see, Sophron, after all my preaching about exact phrasing, I have been a bit sloppy here. In truth I should I have said: "I do not *yet* know how I made that judgement." For, good friend, I intend to find out.

SOPHRON: I appreciate your doggedness, Socrates. But how do you plan on discovering that which you do not know but which only you can know?

SOCRATES: I am a man of few tools and few talents. I only know of one way to discover things—it is by questioning.

SOPHRON: And whom will you question?

SOCRATES: Obviously I must question myself.

SOPHRON: Then I and the gods wish you well, Socrates. Please proceed—I will just sit here quietly.

SOCRATES: Very well, Sophron:

Now, Socrates, you claim to have chosen a water jug instead of a pot of honey. Is this correct?

Yes.

Does this mean that you made a comparison between honey and water jugs?

I do not know.

Is there some other possibility?

Well, I could have chosen blindly.

Blindly? What do you mean?

"Blindly" means arbitrarily. Perhaps I said to myself in the marketplace: "If the potter moves his left hand next, then I will buy the water jug. On the other hand, if he moves his right hand next, then I will buy the honey."

If this was the case—if you acted blindly and arbitrarily—then does this mean that you made no comparison, Socrates?

Well I contend that arbitrary decisions are the weakest of comparisons; they are so weak that they can (for all intents and purposes) be called comparisonless.

This is an interesting idea. Let me see if I understand you, Socrates: Would you say that in your "arbitrary decision situation" the potter's left hand symbolized the water jug whereas the potter's right hand symbolized the honey?

Yes.

And a movement of one of the objects (as symbolized by a movement of one of the potter's hands) was chosen to be the deciding factor in your judgement?

Correct.

Then in a sense, the potter's hands represent certain "critical distinguishing traits" between these two objects?

Yes, you could say that.

All right. Now, what was the judge in this situation?

The judge? My eyes were the judge because I watched the potter's hands.

Your eyes were the common judge for comparing water jugs and honey?

Yes.

Your final decision used distinguishing traits, and it stemmed from a common judge?

Yes.

Come now, Socrates, you are trying to deceive me.

What do you mean?

Earlier, old friend, you told me that in this situation—a situation that you called an "arbitrary decision situation"—there is no comparison made. Did you not say: "arbitrary decisions are comparisonless"?

Yes I did say that.

But now you tell me that you have made a comparison using critical traits and a common judge. Does this not sound exactly like the standard type of comparison, as outlined by Sophron's Rules? How does this "arbitrary decision situation" differ from making a standard comparison?

I think that you have twisted my words, old man.

I have only asked you questions, my friend. Were you not free to give whatever answer you saw fit?

Perhaps—but an arbitrary decision differs from the type of critical and discerning comparisons about which you and Sophron were talking. Nonetheless, you have led us to the position that arbitrary decisions are indistinguishable from discerning comparisons. And I do not believe that.

Ah, then your logic was wrong?

(It is *our logic,* my friend.) But I think that we have analyzed this correctly so far.

Now, now—you cannot have it both ways. On the one hand, you say that you believe that arbitrary decisions differ from discerning comparisons. On the other hand, you tell me that arbitrary decisions fulfil Sophron's criteria for discerning comparisons. Which is it: "yes" or "no"?

Socrates, it is neither "yes" nor "no"—

SOPHRON: Socrates, you are a most perplexing man. You even seem to be able to confuse yourself. Than man over there is beginning to laugh—

PLATO: (That man is Eudicus, Sophron.)

SOPHRON: Yes, Eudicus is laughing at the tangles that you create even when talking to yourself. You are getting lost in some sort of word jungle. Step back a moment onto a clearer path, Socrates; get to the essence of the matter.

SOCRATES: Sophron, Sophron, you interrupted me in the middle of a sentence. I was saying:

Now, now—you cannot have it both ways, old man. On the one hand, you say you believe that arbitrary decisions differ from discerning comparisons. On the other hand, you tell me that arbitrary decisions fulfil Sophron's criteria for discerning comparisons. Which is it, "yes" or "no"?

Socrates, it is neither "yes" nor "no," because arbitrary decisions do not completely fulfil Sophron's criteria.

They do not? Which criterion is not met?

If you recall, Sophron proposed three major Rules.

1. Begin with two apparently different items.
2. Partition the items into traits, traits like taste or color or emotional aura, using two criteria:
   a. Use the individual common judges that we have at hand.
   b. Use traits that are useful to the particular person making the judgement.
3. Make a comparison by applying each of the relevant judges separately, evaluating each trait independently.

True—and how do these Rules differ from arbitrary decisions?

Well, Socrates, let me answer you with a question: What trait did we choose on which to base our comparison?

Do you mean when we compared honey and water jugs?

Yes.

In our arbitrary comparison, we arbitrarily assigned a water jug to the potter's right hand and a pot of honey to the potter's left hand. The traits were "right hand" and "left hand."

Now, Socrates, exactly what do you mean by "we arbitrarily assigned"?

I mean that we made this decision for no particular reason.

I see. Does "for no particular reason" mean that you could have made exactly the opposite assignment? Could water jugs be assigned to the potter's left hand and honey to the potter's right hand?

Certainly they could—

SOPHRON: Excuse me for interupting again, Socrates. In your original example, water jugs *were* assigned to the potter's left hand and honey to the potter's right hand—you had it backwards just now.

SOCRATES: Ah, then this makes the point all the more clearly. As I was saying:

Socrates, if the two traits (that is, "left hand" and "right hand") could be assigned to either object, then it appears that they are attached quite weakly to the objects. Would you agree that these traits are tied to the object in such a loose way as to be transient and ephemeral?

Absolutely.

The next time that we look at a honey pot or a water jug, could the assignment of these traits easily be reversed?

Yes.

So, these traits have no enduring character?

True.

Now, as a general statement: Is a characterization of an object useful if it can only be used one time and then may or may not be applicable ever again?

No.

So, our arbitrary traits are not useful?

No, they are not.

Then, Socrates, this is exactly where arbitrary decisions fail to meet Sophron's Rules for Discerning Comparisons. You said that arbitrary decisions are comparisonless. Instead, I would say that arbitrary decisions are true comparisons but that they stem from useless traits.

Arbitrary decisions are based on a partitioning into useless traits?

Precisely.

And this, Sophron, is my discovery: arbitrary decisions are

comparisons, but they are very weak comparisons, and they are certainly not *discerning* comparisons.

PLATO: They are the weakest comparisons; they are undiscerning comparisons.

SOPHRON: Very interesting, Socrates. Nonetheless, old man, our original question was different. We wondered on what basis one could compare two completely disparate objects—objects as different as honey and water jugs. Now, if I understand you correctly, you claim that there is a whole spectrum of comparisons available to us. But for very different objects (objects like honey and water jugs), you can only use the weakest comparisons, and the weakest of comparisons are "arbitrary decisions."

SOCRATES: Well I would qualify your statement, Sophron.

It is always possible that someday we may discover how to identify more useful comparative traits among honey and water jugs. In that case, we could move farther along the spectrum of decisions: we could abandon the weak arbitrary decisions, and we could use stronger discerning comparisons. In this complex world, there is always the possibility of movement along the decision spectrum.

However, whether we use relevant or irrelevant traits, we can always find *some* traits; whether we have weak or strong comparisons, we can always make *some* comparisons. Comparisons do not depend on the usefulness of the traits—they only require that we identify certain traits that can be evaluated by an individual common judge.

SOPHRON: If the traits are not relevant or useful, then how can the decisions be relevant or useful?

SOCRATES: The decisions may not be the *best* decisions, Sophron, but decisions they will be nonetheless. Did I not come home with a water jug?

SOPHRON: You did—but it did not satisfy Xanthippe.

SOCRATES: I am afraid that Xanthippe is difficult to satisfy, Sophron.

SOPHRON: Did the decision satisfy anyone?

SOCRATES: It satisfied the potter, to whom I paid my money.

It also satisfied me. At first I was in a state of indecision, but after the purchase, I had moved on. It was an active step, and it allowed me to move on to other things. In fact after the decision, I was happy with the water jug.

SOPHRON: Socrates, purchasing the *honey* would also have satisfied a merchant, and it too would have been an active step.

SOCRATES: True. And after the decision, undoubtedly I myself would have been happy with the honey. This is separate from ''absoluteness'' and from ''bestness'': if my decision is arbitrary, then I have no guarantee that it is the *best* decision—there may well be other good decisions. However, at the very least I made a decision, and that *is* better than no decision at all.

SOPHRON: So, even a weak decision is something substantive.

SOCRATES: Yes. Action is better than promises, and in this world of very complex situations—

PLATO: In this world with its pockets of incondensable complexity—

SOCRATES: It is not always possible to guarantee that particular actions are the *best* actions. Remember, Sophron, the perfect, the absolute, and the simple actions—

PLATO: The perfect, the absolute, and the simple actions—the divine actions—

SOCRATES: The divine actions are actions where the act and the end are guaranteed in advance. Hold these actions apart from the imperfect, the conditional, and the complex actions—

PLATO: The imperfect, the conditional, and the complex actions—the mortal actions—

SOCRATES: The mortal actions are actions where the act and the end are not both ensured in advance: in a complex world, we must sometimes accept partial success, and we must be content. The mortal's lot is not divine. Our task, Sophron, is merely to try and to try and not to give in. This means that we must act, but it does not mean that we will always succeed.

September 9: CORISCUS

CORISCUS: Socrates, what is the flower for?

SOCRATES: Hello, Coriscus. I like the blue color of this weed, and I picked it to carry about with me this morning. These flowers stay opened only in the morning—they awake well before breakfast, but they fall asleep again in the afternoon sun.

CORISCUS: Those flowers grow everywhere nowadays, along all the roadsides. The gods have set us upon a beautiful autumn, Socrates; there is a blue sea along the waysides.

I notice that some of the poor peddlers here in the marketplace actually sell these weeds, these Succory flowers—although I do not know why anyone would buy something that he could as easily pick himself.

SOCRATES: Why would anyone buy them? Well, this *is* a wonderful plant; it is such a pure blue. (But you know, Coriscus, I have always called these flowers Chicory.)

CORISCUS: Yes, I have heard that name also. Of course Succory (or Chicory) is a wonderful plant—and not only for its color; it is good for salads in the spring—

SOCRATES: And for vegetable stews in the fall.

CORISCUS: In the winter, many people peel the roots and roast them and eat them.

SOCRATES: And if you grind up the roasted root, then it can be boiled into a fine warm drink.

CORISCUS: But in spite of all its uses, anyone can have the plant for the asking. You yourself casually picked a flower this morning. How can stall-keepers and costermongers be so brazen as to sell Succory? Why, you might as well sell air or water or dirt or stone.

SOCRATES: "Costermongers," my friend?

CORISCUS: Yes—costermongers—men who sell vegetables and such things from little stalls, men who wander about bartering their wares.

SOCRATES: I have never heard that word before.

CORISCUS: It is a real word, Socrates; I did not invent it.

SOCRATES: Very well, Coriscus, I believe you.

CORISCUS: Anyways, these costermongers unblushingly hawk roadside weeds.

SOCRATES: You must admit, Coriscus, that they certainly are beautiful weeds.

CORISCUS: True enough, old friend.

SOCRATES: It was quite thoughtful of the gods to have lined the roadways with Chicory. Undoubtedly it was the doing of my favorite god, Pan. Pan is always fiddling with the flowers and the trees. He cannot resist—this godling Pan—he is the shepherd god, the woodland god, long-haired and unkempt. Every snowy crest, every mountain peak, and every rock cliff is his home. He rambles and ambles here and there, through the close thickets. First he is lured by soft streams; then he presses on among the rocks. He scans the flocks and the high mountains and the birds and the meadows. And, Coriscus, he loves every field and roadside cluster of plants, and very kindly, he lines them all with every sort of flower imaginable. But Chicory is his especial favorite.

CORISCUS: That is a nice tale, Socrates, but it is not an act of kindness that we have here. Pan (or whoever) had no choice but to put the Succory out along the roadsides.

SOCRATES: He had no choice? What do you mean, Coriscus?

CORISCUS: I mean what I say, old philosopher: Pan could do nothing else. Here, let me prove it to you, Socrates.

SOCRATES: By all means, young friend.

CORISCUS: Now, is it not true that the field lands of the countryside either lie along roadways or they do not?

SOCRATES: That is true.

CORISCUS: And Succory is found in all field lands?

SOCRATES: No—Chicory grows in airy fields and in open meadows; it has a predilection for sunny areas.

CORISCUS: But within the sunny areas, the range of the plant is extensive?

SOCRATES: Yes.

CORISCUS: This widespread range—would you say that it occurs because the plant likes all sunny areas equally?

SOCRATES: Undoubtedly.

CORISCUS: And because roadways are cleared areas, they are almost always sunny?

SOCRATES: Yes.

CORISCUS: Then it stands to reason that we should find Succory lining all the roadsides (as well as filling all the sunny non-roadside areas).

SOCRATES: This is your proof, Coriscus?

CORISCUS: It is.

SOCRATES: What does it prove?

CORISCUS: It proves that Succory must of necessity be found along all the roadways. It proves that there was no special kindness of the gods in this; there was no thoughtful design. It proves that there was no planning. Given the disposition of the plant (which I admit, may originally have been a gift of some god), we *must* find Succory by all the roads.

SOCRATES: I see, Coriscus. However, your reasoning leaves me somewhat puzzled.

CORISCUS: Oh? Why is that?

SOCRATES: Let me ask you to consider a related situation. Do you remember the story of Pan and Selene, the Moon goddess?

CORISCUS: If I recall properly, Pan fell in love with Selene (as he fell in love with every nymph and goddess that he ever met) and as usual, the goddess was not equally enamoured of him.

SOCRATES: True.

CORISCUS: Then there was some trick that Pan played, using a fleece—was there not?

SOCRATES: Exactly. You see, Selene completely ignored Pan. She would not talk to him; she would not look at him. But Selene, goddess of the white moon, loved all pure white things—white rocks, white flowers, and especially the soft white fleece of young sheep. So, Pan lured her into a cave with a trail of the finest white fleece.

CORISCUS: Oh yes, now I remember.

SOCRATES: However, Selene was wary; she was a goddess wise in the signs of the woodlands. Therefore, Pan had to hide carefully all tracks and all traces of himself. As he went, he walked backwards, and with his hands he smoothed out the broken grass blades. Pan unbent twigs, he carefully replaced all the bits of dirt that he had knocked aside inadvertently, and he ruffled the fleece as if the gentle evening breezes had simply laid them out in the woods. In the end, he did so fine a job that his route looked like one created by Nature herself, and Selene was fooled.

CORISCUS: Very well, Socrates. But you said that this was to be a *related* story. I fail to see how it fits in with my logical proof, my proof of the unplanned haunts of the Succory plant.

SOCRATES: Be patient, Coriscus.

Let us review the machinations of Pan: to Selene, the final route—the trail of pure white fleece—appeared completely natural. Did it not?

CORISCUS: Apparently it did—it certainly deceived Selene.

SOCRATES: It might well have been a natural trail?

CORISCUS: Well—the fleece were quite unusual.

SOCRATES: But they fooled Selene, a wise and natural goddess?

CORISCUS: So we are told.

SOCRATES: Why was she deceived?

CORISCUS: Clearly it was because Pan had in all other ways arranged things completely naturally.

SOCRATES: And this took effort on Pan's part?

CORISCUS: It did.

SOCRATES: It took planning? It was by design?

CORISCUS: Definitely.

SOCRATES: Then would you say that the natural appearance of something does not necessarily rule out the work of a planner behind the scenes? Would you agree that the hand of a designer cannot always be distinguished from the course of Nature?

CORISCUS: I suppose that is true.

SOCRATES: So, your argument that Pan need not be invoked to explain the arrangement of Chicory flowers does not appear to be a good proof. Could we perhaps have been deceived, like Selene? Could Pan have actually been involved? I suspect, Coriscus, that you did not prove anything at all. In fact, I am convinced that Pan has designed the beautiful meadowlands and the fields and the roadsides. I believe that Pan has filled them all with Blue Sailors.

CORISCUS: With "blue sailors"?

SOCRATES: (Sometimes Chicory is called "blue sailors," Coriscus.)

CORISCUS: Well, Socrates, I admit that what you say sounds correct. But sound can differ from sense, and I suspect that actually you are wrong.

SOCRATES: Why, Coriscus?

CORISCUS: You are arguing in the messy realm of gods and flowers and sheep and dusty fields. In these areas, it is easy to turn logic in any direction that you wish. To see an argument clearly, we must stick with the purest logic, like mathematics.

SOCRATES: Can you do that here?

CORISCUS: Certainly—you can say anything with mathematics. Now, let me cast my essential argument in geometric terms: consider four-sided figures.

SOCRATES: All right.

CORISCUS: Would you agree that a pure four-sided figure is either a square or a rectangle or an irregular figure, like a parallelogram?

SOCRATES: Yes.

CORISCUS: And if we restrict ourselves to the regular figures, then pure four-sided figures are either squares or rectangles?

SOCRATES: Yes.

CORISCUS: Good. Suppose that I draw one and only one pure regular four-sided figure in the dust at my feet, but suppose that you cannot see it. Here, I will actually draw it behind this rock. Can you see it?

SOCRATES: No.

CORISCUS: Very well. Tell me, Socrates: What is this figure?

SOCRATES: I do not know.

CORISCUS: You do not know?

SOCRATES: No—I cannot see it.

CORISCUS: It is either a square or a rectangle.

SOCRATES: So I had surmised.

CORISCUS: I will help you out: the figure has four equal sides. What is it?

SOCRATES: I still do not know.

CORISCUS: Come now, Socrates—it is a square.

SOCRATES: All right, I will take your word for it.

CORISCUS: You sound dissatisfied. What is the problem, Socrates?

SOCRATES: Perhaps you have deceived me.

CORISCUS: Socrates, I am an honest man.

SOCRATES: Let me see the figure.

CORISCUS: Certainly, step over here . . . There. Is that not a square?

SOCRATES: It looks rectangular to me.

CORISCUS: Rectangular?

SOCRATES: Coriscus, do you see the side near the rock? That edge of the figure looks longer than the adjacent side.

CORISCUS: Oh. Well, Socrates, I just scribbled the figure hastily; clearly it is meant to be a square.

SOCRATES: I was not sure of that, Coriscus.

CORISCUS: Take my word for it, Socrates: it is a square.

SOCRATES: Frankly, Coriscus, I would be hard pressed to tell you whether this figure is a square or a rectangle. But grant that it is a square, how does this exemplify your reasoning about Pan and the Chicory?

CORISCUS: It is very simple, Socrates. Either the roadside arrangement of flowers has been organized by Pan or it has not been organized by him. We see (from simple mathematical logic) that if a thing is not A, then it must be B. Either a figure is a square or it is a rectangle. In the case of the Succory, the natural disposition of the plant is a perfectly good explanation for its arrangement in the world. Therefore, we can choose between the two logical alternatives, and Pan has not been involved. There is no escape from this elemental logic, Socrates—I am afraid that you cannot twist and slip out of it.

SOCRATES: Let me understand you, Coriscus. Do you maintain that mathematical logic states that either something is clearly A or else it is clearly B? Does the logic demand two clean alternatives?

CORISCUS: Obviously.

SOCRATES: Does this logic demand clearly defined objects like your square-rectangle here in the dust?

CORISCUS: (That is a square, Socrates.)

SOCRATES: Does this logic demand unequivocal clear causes, as with the fleecy trail of sheepskins—the trail that appeared to be completely natural but that was, in fact, designed by Pan?

CORISCUS: Socrates—these examples of yours suffer from the imperfections of our everyday world. Mathematical logic is pure; it has no imperfections.

SOCRATES: So, Coriscus, our world has imperfections?

CORISCUS: Of course it has! All manner of quirks and variations creep into this poor mortal world of ours: it is messy, dusty, dirty, and imperfect.

SOCRATES: Hmm, this puts a question in my mind, Coriscus.

CORISCUS: What is that?

SOCRATES: Do you speak Egyptian?

CORISCUS: Egyptian? No.

SOCRATES: Have you ever been to Egypt?

CORISCUS: I have.

SOCRATES: Did you speak Greek there?

CORISCUS: I spoke Greek to my companion, who (fortunately) spoke Egyptian quite well. It is not possible to make sense of anything in a foreign land unless you speak their language.

SOCRATES: So, you must speak the appropriate language of the land, in order to make sense of things in that land?

CORISCUS: Certainly.

SOCRATES: Now, Coriscus, you have told me that our land— our whole mortal earth—is a land of imperfections, variations, entanglements, and strangeness.

CORISCUS: Unfortunately that is true.

SOCRATES: Now, Coriscus, I would call this messiness "complexity"; in fact, I would call it "incondensable complexity."

CORISCUS: Fine—you are free to call it what you like.

SOCRATES: Good. Now, in the land of incondensable complexity (as in any land), we must speak the appropriate language in order to make the appropriate sense of our surroundings. But pure logic, my young friend, is the language of some other land. Pure logic is the language of the land of perfections, homogeneities, and simplicity. This otherworldly land is the land of mathematics. It is a divine land, but it has its own natural language, and it has its own natural logic. *That* is the logic of which you have been speaking. To live in our world, however, we must have recourse to our own natural language and this means we need our own logic—the logic of complexity.

CORISCUS: Oh? And our "logic"—the "logic of complexity"—is different from mathematical logic?

SOCRATES: Yes, it is. For instance, in our real and incondensably complex world, true, pure, and clear alternatives are rare. Instead, it is common to find things that are not cleanly either A or B. In the mortal world, many things (perhaps most things) are largely A or largely B—but at the same time they are also somewhat A *and* B. Moreover, in the real world the hand of a designer cannot always be inferred from the design: many roads lead to the same end, and from a priori considerations we cannot predict which road was actually taken.

CORISCUS: This does not seem like logic to me, Socrates: it seems like a mess of confusion.

SOCRATES: I agree that these are not the same rules that apply to simple and clean mathematics; nonetheless, we can still use orderly and methodical reasoning.

CORISCUS: Perhaps—but I do not see how they will help us to understand Succory flowers.

SOCRATES: Let me stop you for a moment, Coriscus.

CORISCUS: Very well.

SOCRATES: In our land—in our mortal land, in the land of incondensable complexity, in the human realm of our day to day lives—logical reasoning begins with another question. It is a question that does not start the logic in the mathematical realm.

CORISCUS: Oh? And what is that question?

SOCRATES: The first question, Coriscus, is whether we want to understand these flowers at all.

CORISCUS: What do you mean?

SOCRATES: I mean this: perhaps we do not need to understand everything.

CORISCUS: What? Do you forget that you are a philosopher?

SOCRATES: Coriscus, even the philosopher in me enjoys just looking at Chicory flowers.

CORISCUS: Very well, Socrates—look at them all you wish. If you recall, I was only pointing out that Succory is free to be looked at and enjoyed. Nature (or if you prefer, Pan) has set the flowers out for all of us to enjoy, and frankly, it is a bit insulting that stall-keepers actually charge money for the plants.

SOCRATES: But, Coriscus, they are such beautiful plants.

CORISCUS: Yes yes, Socrates—of course the Succory flowers are beautiful. But think of it: these peddlers have the cheek and the effrontery to charge money for a commodity that you and I would buy only out of the most shameful laziness.

SOCRATES: And?

CORISCUS: And?! My good man, does it not make your blood bubble and boil to see this, to be confronted by such gall? Are you not insulted?

SOCRATES: No, Coriscus, I am not.

CORISCUS: Well I am.

SOCRATES: I can see that you are; as Odysseus says to good King Alkinoos—

> We mortals, the races built of dust
> And earth, are quick to flare unjust
> In anger or in rage or lust.

CORISCUS: Well in this case, Socrates, I am angry with just cause.

SOCRATES: Perhaps, perhaps.

All right then, come along, Coriscus—let us find one of your scurrilous costermongers and reprimand him.

CORISCUS: Very well.

SOCRATES: Ah here is a low gentleman indeed: not only is he selling Chicory, he is selling honey too.

CORISCUS: Honey? What is wrong with selling honey?

SOCRATES: Why, Coriscus, I am surprised at you. Do not tell me that you are so lazy as to leave beekeeping to others? Should you not be raising bees yourself?

CORISCUS: Go easy with your sarcasm, Socrates. Just speak to this stall-keeper here.

SOCRATES: All right, Coriscus.

Good morning, sir—I see that you are selling Chicory.

STALLMAN: Yes I am.

SOCRATES: Are the flowers fresh?

STALLMAN: They certainly are; I picked these bunches just this morning.

SOCRATES: They are very pretty.

STALLMAN: There is nothing quite as blue, I would say. But of course, you can use them for things other than decoration. Chicory cures the warts. Chicory also keeps your skin fair. And if you eat the leaves in salads, then your bowels remain comfortable and regular. "There is nothing quite as blue, but nothing quite as good for you," they say.

Here, my friends, the bunches are cheap—I have plenty. I am practically giving them away. It is a good time to choose some fresh ones, gentlemen, before the housewives descend. For these fresh clean bunches, you need pay only two drachmas each.

CORISCUS: Two drachmas! That is outrageous—I could just as easily have picked those plants myself, for nothing!

STALLMAN: Now now, gentlemen—I carefully chose these

flowers this morning. I picked them far from people and animals; they are clearly the best that you could buy. And you fine gentlemen have better things to do with your time than to wander about the countryside dirtying your clothes and wasting your time rooting among the fields.

CORISCUS: But two drachmas! That is robbery.

SOCRATES: I think the flowers are quite fine. My wife Xanthippe will undoubtedly find a good use for a bunch—but I have only five obols. Tell me, sir, do you have a small bunch of Chicory, one that you would part with for five obols?

STALLMAN: Five obols? Let me see . . . Yes here is a small bunch—it is really worth at least a drachma, but I will give it to you for five obols, for the sake of your wife.

SOCRATES: Ah thank you very much.

CORISCUS: Socrates, I cannot believe that you actually bought these weeds from him—and you got a pitifully small bunch!

SOCRATES: It *is* rather tiny, Coriscus: I will just have to pick some more to add to it . . . There is a good patch of Chicory on that little hillock, I can see them clearly from here. Come along with me.

CORISCUS: Socrates, first you pay good money for a little pile of weeds; now you are picking more for nothing. I do not understand you.

SOCRATES: I cannot help myself, Coriscus. Chicory is a like a little blue eye on a spindly green stalk, and the fields of bright blue Chicory flowing away forever, these give me a happy vision. Well, not a vision—they give me a happy feeling. They remind me of Homer's verse in the *Odyssey*:

> And then Athena, the grey-eyed one,
> Arose with grace, and back she went
> To Olympos, beneath a golden sun,
> To the mountain embattlement
>
> Where no chill, no wet raindrops,
> No errant snowflake finds its way,
> Instead sun shines on white cloudtops
> With skies so blue and fresh each day

Like vast fields of star-blue flowers
Stretching endless, bright and clean
Across the heavens' lofty towers—
There, where all the gods convene.

Why, for a mere five obols, Coriscus, I can carry a bit of Heaven about with me.

September 14: PHERECYDES

SOCRATES: Good morning, Pherecydes.

PHERECYDES: Ah, good morning, Socrates.

SOCRATES: May I sit down here?

PHERECYDES: Of course, of course—the sun is warm, the day is young. Tell me what news you have heard, my friend.

SOCRATES: Nothing new has happened since yesterday, old man.

PHERECYDES: Well then, tell me this: What new philosophical devilment have you been up to, Socrates?

SOCRATES: I am still worn out from my long discussion with Archytas. Instead of my talking, I would rather hear a tale from you.

PHERECYDES: From me? All I know are the old myths—the children's tales. You need something new and fresh to keep your mind keen, Socrates. Otherwise you will become an old man like me, and you will find yourself constantly musing and dozing and nodding off in the sun, dreaming of home and of other places and of long ago times.

SOCRATES: I am already an old man, Pherecydes.

PHERECYDES: Oh? You think that seventy years is old? Let me tell you, Socrates, wait until you become eighty—*then* you will be old.

SOCRATES: I doubt that I will live to see eighty years.

PHERECYDES: Then you will never grow old, Socrates.

SOCRATES: That is fine with me, Pherecydes . . . So, old man, tell me a story.

PHERECYDES: As I have said, I know no special stories. However, before you came I was remembering Artemis and Endymion and the Cairn Caves. Just a little earlier, you see, a fine young woman walked by here. She was tall and self-confident, and she put me in mind of Artemis, in a story that I had heard from old Creon.

SOCRATES: Prince Creon of Thebes, son of Menoeceus?

PHERECYDES: A prince? Our Creon? Certainly not! Why, do you not remember him, Socrates? He was poor and tired, and he was quite thin. We always brought him some bit of food—bread or meat or something—in exchange for a story. He sat in the main marketplace on Leros everyday. And do you remember how he was always licking his lips with his long thin tongue? That is how I still picture him, although he is long since dead. Now do you know whom I mean?

SOCRATES: I never met him, Pherecydes—I have not been to Leros.

PHERECYDES: Never, Socrates? You know that I spent all my happy lazy youth on Leros.

SOCRATES: I know.

PHERECYDES: It is a shame that you never got to Leros, my young friend. It is a delightful sleepy little copy of the island of Rhodes.

SOCRATES: Of Rhodes?

PHERECYDES: Yes, of Rhodes—but there are probably less than a thousand people living on all of Leros. The entire island is forested, with gently rolling hills and fine valleys, valleys that produce the most delicious fruits and vegetables—figs and pomegranates and oranges. On the sloping hills, carob trees grow abundantly. And wine? The Lerosian vines grow only the sweetest of grapes, and of course Lerosian grains make the richest of breads. Ah, it is a heavenly land. And everyone— every single householder—is a sailor. The winds come out of the West for nine months of the year (they blow away the summer heat), and it is only an afternoon's easy sail to the Carian coast. A fine place for a little boy to grow up.

SOCRATES: And you knew Creon there?,

PHERECYDES: How could I not, Socrates?

SOCRATES: Ah yes, how could you not.

PHERECYDES: Everyone knew Creon.

SOCRATES: They did?

PHERECYDES: Of course they did. He was a fixture in the marketplace; he was there every afternoon. I do not know what he had done in his younger years; when I knew him, he slept in the Temple of Artemis (in a small chamber in the back). He wore the same old grey tunic every day, warm weather or cool, and most often he was barefoot. You know the magic of the barefoot, Socrates.

SOCRATES: I do not think that I do, Pherecydes.

PHERECYDES: Oh? I am surprised, Socrates: Do you not remember what my mother used to say?

SOCRATES: Your mother? No, I never had the opportunity to meet her; I was never on Leros you know.

PHERECYDES: Ah, you missed a fine woman, Socrates, a fine woman.

SOCRATES: Undoubtedly, Pherecydes—and what was it that she said?

PHERECYDES: Why, she said many things, young man, many things. Anyone on Leros will tell you *that*. Lerosians often turned to my mother when they wanted to hear things. As she said to me: "Pherecydes, my lovely lad, some people are born to talk, others are born to listen." I am a listener, Socrates; I think that you must be a born talker.

SOCRATES: I guess that I am.

PHERECYDES: There is no guessing about it: if we asked around the marketplace here, we would find unanimous agreement.

SOCRATES: Was Creon a born talker?

PHERECYDES: Of course he was. What else could you think, Socrates? Do you not remember how people would collect to hear his dry voice unravelling some story or another?

SOCRATES: I am afraid that I never heard Creon speak; I was never on Leros.

PHERECYDES: Ah more is the pity, Socrates . . .

SOCRATES: Yes? . . . Pherecydes?

PHERECYDES: What is the problem, Socrates?

SOCRATES: You had stopped talking and you closed your eyes; I wondered whether everything was all right.

PHERECYDES: Of course, of course—can an old man not have a moment of rest?

SOCRATES: I am sorry, Pherecydes; please continue with your story.

PHERECYDES: Very well. Let me see now, where was I? Oh yes, I think that it was a scop that always set Creon to telling this story. You see—

SOCRATES: Just a moment, Pherecydes—a "scop"?

PHERECYDES: Yes yes, Socrates—a scop! Can you not sit more quietly. We will never get the story unfolded—let alone get it neatly refolded again—if you insist on telling it your way. Do you think that you know it better than Creon, who heard it from his father who actually saw it happen?

SOCRATES: I am sorry, Pherecydes; I will be more patient.

PHERECYDES: Oh I do not blame you for wanting to tell it also, for wanting to be a part of the excitment, for wanting to walk back through those warm historic days. But Artemis is the tall, pale, dreamy goddess of the countryside—and Artemis, you will recall, is originally from Leros. Therefore, who should know her better than a thin old man from Leros?

Well, Socrates, I do not mean to embarass you. But perhaps you should just admit that while Pan may be a friend of yours, Artemis belongs to Leros—does she not? (Now, now—do not make a long speech, my friend; just answer "yes" or "no.")

SOCRATES: A long speech? You leave me speechless, Pherecydes.

PHERECYDES: Socrates, I am too old to leave you anywhere. It is Creon who is still speechless, so if you will refrain from talk a moment then I will allow him to continue.

SOCRATES: Please do.

PHERECYDES: Very well.

Once there was a scop, a pererrating scop, and—

SOCRATES: A "scop"? A "pererrating scop"?

PHERECYDES: A scop, Socrates, a scop! Do you not know what a scop is?

SOCRATES: No.

PHERECYDES: You spent some years in the Athenian Lyceum, did you not?

SOCRATES: It was not called the Lyceum then, Pherecydes— but yes, my gymnasium was eventually transformed into the Lyceum.

PHERECYDES: And you never learned the word "scop"?

SOCRATES: I am afraid not.

PHERECYDES: I should charge you for this education, my young friend: a pererrating scop is a wandering bard.

SOCRATES: I see—so, it began with a wandering bard?

PHERECYDES: Yes, it began with a young wandering bard; he had been a shepherd in the back hills of Leros. As with all boys, he spent his evenings listening to the old men recite verses and myths. Soon he too was repeating the stories. Endymion was his name.

Endymion had a strange manner. He never really listened to you; instead, he just began to talk and then he completely lost track of his surroundings. Do you remember Thadenos, Socrates?

SOCRATES: No, I do not recall the name.

PHERECYDES: You do not? He was certainly a well known character on Leros.

SOCRATES: I have never been to Leros, my friend.

PHERECYDES: Then that explains it, Socrates.

Thadenos was completely deaf. He was undistractible. A wall once collapsed behind him as he was drinking a cup of wine, and Thadenos did not spill a drop.

Endymion was like that too: if someone else began to talk, Endymion was unaware—he kept on reciting. If there was a laugh or a cough or a rude comment, it floated right by Endymion. People could walk away until there was no audience left, but no matter, Endymion chanted on and on. It might begin to rain or a strong wind could rush down among the listeners, but Endymion continued talking. A lamb began to bleat or a branch suddenly fell, yet Endymion's stories rolled ever forward. And these stories themselves—why, they were filled with new and startling details: strange animals wandered into the classic legends; unusual conversations took place. As my mother said to me once: "Pherecydes, every bush hides a new bird, every rock covers a bizarre insect." She said that many times—perhaps you remember?

SOCRATES: No I do not, Pherecydes.

PHERECYDES: Then your memory is weakening, Socrates. Anyways it was not long before Endymion's sheep herds regularly were spread too wide afield. Animals became lost, and too many young lambs were injured. Meilon (the owner of the flocks) finally got fed up with this absent-minded behavior, and he dismissed Endymion. So, Endymion became a pererrating scop . . .

SOCRATES: Yes?

PHERECYDES: Yes, Socrates—he became a pererrating scop . . .

SOCRATES: I see. Is that the end of the tale?

PHERECYDES: Certainly not, Socrates, we have not even introduced Artemis yet.

SOCRATES: Oh? Artemis had a role?

PHERECYDES: Socrates, your youthful exuberance is bubbling up again. Be patient, young friend: Artemis will appear soon enough.

SOCRATES: Very well. What happened next?

PHERECYDES: Now let me ask you, Socrates: Have you ever had a big dream?

SOCRATES: I am not certain that I follow you, Pherecydes. What is a "big dream"?

PHERECYDES: A big dream is a dream that is strange but vivid. It is mythic. It is otherworldly. And it remains etched behind your eyes even after you have awakened. The feelings remain clear and overwhelming. Do you remember what Homer tells us in the *Odyssey:*

> Ivory dreams scintillate,
> Bright cobwebs of no earthly weight.
>
> (For ghostly dreams, two doors await:
> An ivory portal and a wooden gate.
>
> Now, floating through the ivory door
> Are mirages with no solid core.
>
> But marching through the gates of wood
> Come truths, if mortals only understood.)

SOCRATES: I remember that passage. But I must confess that I never connected it with what you have called "big dreams"— I thought of the verses a bit differently than the way in which you have presented them.

PHERECYDES: That is your trouble, Socrates: you think of *everything* a bit differently.

SOCRATES: Tell me, Pherecydes: What has this Homeric poetry to do with overwhelming mythic dreams—with your "big dreams."

PHERECYDES: Endymion had a big dream one night, Socrates.

SOCRATES: He did?

PHERECYDES: He most certainly did. He dreamed that he was

lying on his back in a lake. Was he in a boat? Was he on a raft, or was he merely floating wild and free? It was warm. The water was cool, and it flowed and raced past him. The water rolled over him. The tides flowed and raced over his arms, but he was not wet. A deep gentle hum filled the air—many voices blended in low harmony, and a cosmic tapping beat on hollow logs. Then, all of a sudden there was a woman. She was tall and strong, and she was thin and long. A blue robe draped her shoulders. She had a bow, and a noble dog trailed at her back. "How can this woman walk alongside me on the water?" he wondered. Somehow she was pulling him along with her. Why, it was *she* who sped his raft through the waves. He was overcome by a sensuous empty feel: it was as if he was falling, he was falling deeply and happily through space. And then . . .

SOCRATES: Yes? And then?

PHERECYDES: I am afraid that it is just: "and then" *nothing*.

SOCRATES: Nothing?

PHERECYDES: Nothing—Endymion awoke, and the feelings were strong and the images were vivid. But he was awake, and Endymion found himself in our real, clay world. Of course you know what he did then, Socrates.

SOCRATES: No I do not think that I know, Pherecydes.

PHERECYDES: Of course you do, Socrates! Think, young man—you must have done it a thousand times. Have you not awakened from a wondrous dream and then desparately tried to crawl back again? You close your eyes, knowing how futile the effort. But after such a dream, Socrates, can you just open your eyes to the bland, impure, dismagic of our daily earth?

SOCRATES: "Impure dismagic"?

PHERECYDES: These dreams—the big, magic, mythic dreams—are an immersion in pure golden joy, young man.

SOCRATES: Yes by the gods, they are, Pherecydes.

PHERECYDES: Exactly, Socrates—it is by the good gifts of the gods that we taste these dreams. And what god gave to Endymion his joy? It was Artemis: passing by the sleeping scop, she gently brushed her robes over his cool forehead, and suddenly he was filled with a mythic, magical, big dream. She left as light as she came. And when Endymion awoke, he remained overwhelmed—but the dream was, of course, lost.

Dawn came. The morning passed. The afternoon dragged on, and finally night arrived. Endymion lay upon his blanket. Late at night he fell asleep, and he slept the sleep of the dreamless. Another dawn, another day, and another ordinary night—and these, then, were followed by days and days and weeks and weeks and months and months of the same. You know, Socrates, my mother used to say: "Pherecydes, never chase a dream." Perhaps you heard her say this? She repeated it often.

SOCRATES: I never had the opportunity to meet your mother, Pherecydes.

PHERECYDES: She said this, and she said many other wise things, Socrates. But it is obvious that she lived long after Endymion, because Endymion did not follow her advice. Endymion did exactly the opposite: he set off to recapture the Artemis dream.

Perhaps, thought Endymion, he had dreamed of some actual place—divine, holy, and magical as it was. Where is that lake with the flowing, racing tides? Where is that land with a deep gentle hum filling the air, with many voices blending in low harmony, and with a cosmic beat tapping on hollow logs? Where is the tall, strong woman, thin and long, with a blue robe draped over her shoulders, with a bow, and with a noble dog trailing at her back? It was certainly not on Leros. Or do you imagine that there was some hidden area on that tiny island? Do you think, Socrates, that Endymion did not know every bit of the Lerosian lands? . . . Well, Socrates, what do you think?

SOCRATES: No, Pherecydes—I am certain that the regions of which Endymion dreamt were not to be found on Leros.

PHERECYDES: Oh? You have been to our fine island? Then you must know the Cairn Caves.

SOCRATES: I was never on Leros, my friend.

PHERECYDES: But did you not say, just now, that Artemis's magical realm was not to be found on Leros?

SOCRATES: Yes, that is what I said: I presumed that this land was not to be found anywhere on our mortal earth.

PHERECYDES: Is that what you presumed? But Socrates, Endymion found it on Leros.

SOCRATES: I did not know that, Pherecydes.

PHERECYDES: Then you still have much to learn, my young friend. Of course, at first Endymion left the island in search of the dream land. He begged a ride to Caria with an old sailing master. From there, he pererrated, scopping and barding as he went. Who knows what adventures he had? Certainly I do not. Perhaps you have heard some of them, Socrates.

SOCRATES: No, old man.

PHERECYDES: Neither have I, Socrates. However, I *do* know that one day, ten or fifteen years later, Endymion returned. He was very thin—too thin. Some said that he had wasted away from worry or from lack of sleep; others said that he had been ravaged by a disease. He was weak and unwell. He was like a dried, shrivelled reed. No one could believe that he was still less than forty years old—he looked as if he had been worn by six or seven tiring decades. His hair was greying and thin, his skin was wrinkled, and his nails were yellow.

Creon's father saw Endymion when he first came ashore, and Creon's father did not recognize Endymion: no one did. It was only that Endymion *was* Endymion, the shepherd, the wandering bard, the pererrating scop, come home again. Endymion knew this—and so, eventually, everyone else believed it too.

SOCRATES: Had he found the Artemis dream?

PHERECYDES: No, Socrates—he had not found even the slightest hint of it, anywhere.

SOCRATES: And why had he come home, my friend?

PHERECYDES: Why do any of us come home, Socrates?

SOCRATES: We come home for comfort, old man.

PHERECYDES: Do you think that is why Endymion returned?

SOCRATES: Undoubtedly. Endymion was tired and discouraged and disspirited. When all else is gone, we return to our home, to our mother's arms.

PHERECYDES: Oh? Is that what you think, Socrates? Well, Endymion had no home; he had no mother. He may have been the child of a slave—or perhaps his parents were killed—in any case, he had no family.

SOCRATES: Even so, Pherecydes, the haunts of our youth are absorbed unconsciously and they become built into our souls. Our memories are our homes.

PHERECYDES: Well this may be true for you or for me, Socrates. But it did not hold for Endymion.

SOCRATES: How could this not work for *any* man, Pherecydes? Do we not *all* feel at ease when we return home?

PHERECYDES: Yes, we may all feel at ease when we return home. Endymion, too, would probably have felt at ease when he returned home. But, Socrates, Endymion did not know that he had returned home. To Endymion, Leros seemed to be just one more mild island. The Lerosians were merely familiar faces—reminiscent of faces he had seen elsewhere. And where had he seen them before? He did not know; he could not remember. Endymion barely looked about him. He stepped sad and blank through the town, and he walked out toward the hills. He walked through the afternoon, and he walked through the evening. Late at night, he came upon the Cairn Caves. Do you remember them, Socrates? They are low and cool, and they are surprisingly dry for mountainside caves.

SOCRATES: I cannot picture them, Pherecydes—I have never been to Leros.

PHERECYDES: Ah, my young friend, you should go there sometime. Do you know that I spent my happy lazy youth on Leros?

SOCRATES: Yes I know.

PHERECYDES: Leros—what a delightful, sleepy little copy of

Rhodes. But you know, there are probably less than a thousand people living on all of Leros. The entire island is forested, with gently rolling hills and fine valleys, and away back inland—in the mountainsides—are the famed Cairn Caves. I hear that they are not much frequented nowadays.

Did Endymion recognize those caves? He must have visited there, years before when he wandered the island talking to himself, telling stories for his own ears. Creon certainly thought that Endymion knew where he was. I remember that Creon licked his lips with his quick tongue, he pushed aside his thin messy hair, and he said: "Endymion was finally home." But, Socrates, I myself am not certain that Endymion knew where he was even then . . . Ah, but who can ever truly know what Endymion thought? . . .

SOCRATES: Pherecydes?

PHERECYDES: Yes?

SOCRATES: Are you all right? . . . Is that all? Is that the entire tale?

PHERECYDES: No—why do you ask?

SOCRATES: You had stopped talking, and you closed your eyes, old friend.

PHERECYDES: Old men need to rest, Socrates—and Endymion was feeling very old. When he reached the caves, he was tired. He walked in to the smallest cave (it was just a dry, gray hollow), he lay down on a pile of leaves inside the mouth, and he closed his eyes. He was worn out; immediately, he fell asleep, and he slept and slept.

Endymion slept for two days. And on the night of the second day, kind and holy Artemis stepped by. She swept past the cave, tall and lean and majestic. A blue tunic draped her divine form. She carried a bow, and a dog trailed behind. Artemis knew why Endymion slept there, she knew of his pererrations. Artemis came to the cave, and she stepped inside. She looked down at the dried and wrinkled figure of a man, curled on the floor like an old baby reed. She stood a moment, and then she tore a strip from her tunic. Artemis tore a thin piece of blue robe, one finger long and two fingers wide.

Artemis tore the strip, and she bent down. Gently, she laid the cloth on the brow of the sleeping Endymion. She softly kissed his head, she touched a finger to his closed eyes, and she turned and she swept away. And Endymion never awoke, but he dreamt:

Endymion dreamed that he was lying on his back in a lake. Was he in a boat? Was he on a raft, or was he floating free? It was warm. The water was cool, and it flowed and it raced past him. The water rolled over his arms. The tides raced by him, but he was not wet. A deep gentle hum filled the air. Many voices blended in low harmony, and a cosmic tapping beat on hollow logs. Then, suddenly there was a woman. She was tall and strong, and she was thin and long. A blue robe draped her shoulders. She had a bow, and a noble dog trailed at her back. "How can this woman walk alongside me through the water?" he wondered. Somehow, she was pulling him along. Why, it was *she* who sped his raft through the waves. He was overcome by a sensuous empty feel: it was as if he was falling, he was falling wonderfully through space.

September 16: PROTARCHUS
(Part I)

SOCRATES: Protarchus, reconsider what you have been saying: the two ideas are incompatible.

PROTARCHUS: Pleasure and reasoning are not mutually exclusive, Socrates.

SOCRATES: No, they are not completely separate—

PROTARCHUS: Exactly.

SOCRATES: But they are quite different, and if we are focusing our lives on one or the other then we should decide between them. We must take a stand.

PROTARCHUS: Not necessarily.

SOCRATES: No?

PROTARCHUS: No—consider the philosopher Socrates. Would you agree that Socrates is the archetype of a man who puts intellectual reasoning before all other goals?

SOCRATES: I certainly value reasoning, my friend.

PROTARCHUS: Why?

SOCRATES: It is what I believe.

PROTARCHUS: Is it also what makes you happy?

SOCRATES: Well, it makes me content.

PROTARCHUS: Then what you believe makes you happy?

SOCRATES: In this case.

PROTARCHUS: And is not happiness the result of pleasures?

SOCRATES: Sometimes.

PROTARCHUS: Sometimes? Well, Socrates, reasoning is a pleasure, is it not?

SOCRATES: For me it is often a pleasure.

PROTARCHUS: Exactly—pleasure is fully compatible with reasoning. It is as I have said all along: chasing after thoughtful understandings is the same as chasing after pleasure.

SOCRATES: I see: reasoning equals pleasure. Then let me ask you a question, Protarchus.

PROTARCHUS: Ask anything, Socrates.

SOCRATES: Do you believe that if I fasted and that if I became a bit thinner then I would be healthier?

PROTARCHUS: Definitely. You would walk faster, you would feel livelier, and you would breath more easily if you had a smaller stomach.

SOCRATES: I agree; unfortunately I become cranky and unhappy when I do not eat.

PROTARCHUS: It is the same with everyone: hungry, long-suffering Odysseus pointed out to Alkinoos (king of the great sea-faring Phaeacians, on the island of Scheria):

> The brazen Belly calls like a dog unfed
> Shouting: "Remember me! Eat meat—eat bread!"

SOCRATES: Yes, a fast would be no pleasure, although you and I both believe that fasting would be good for my health. It appears, then, that all beliefs are not pleasures.

PROTARCHUS: True, beliefs are not always pleasures.

SOCRATES: Now, Protarchus, this belief is based on my reasoning; so, reasoning does not always lead to pleasure. And let us look at the other side of the question. Consider a related pleasure—eating bread with honey each morning. I must confess, Protarchus, I love honey.

PROTARCHUS: I do too, Socrates; honey is the elixir of the gods.

SOCRATES: It would make me happy, Protarchus—but I firmly

believe such a breakfast to be an indulgent intemperance. This pleasure is contrary to my belief.

PROTARCHUS: Well you are too hard on yourself, Socrates. You are an extremist: you eat only the simplest and most tasteless foods—plain groats and rough bread, water and bland corn cakes—

SOCRATES: And olives and figs.

PROTARCHUS: And a few olives and figs—you know, old man, it would not hurt you to eat some meat and wine, some cakes and fine bread and honey.

SOCRATES: It is true that I am very fond of honey, my friend.

PROTARCHUS: Then there is no reason not to have it for breakfast every morning.

SOCRATES: It is better as a rare treat: a taste of honey is better than ten pots.

PROTARCHUS: Of course, Socrates, every child learns that principle. One time (I must have been seven or eight years old), my mother left me alone when she went to the marketplace with all the servants. Philebus and I took out the honey pots and we ate and ate until we were sick. For a while, honey actually became distasteful—I remember that for weeks afterwards I had absolutely no desire for honey.

SOCRATES: Then eating honey was both a pleasure and a pain?

PROTARCHUS: But it was not both a pleasure and a pain simultaneously.

SOCRATES: Nonetheless, the same action could be *either* a pleasure or a pain?

PROTARCHUS: Yes.

SOCRATES: Could it be something else? Could it be something other than a pleasure or a pain?

PROTARCHUS: Socrates, that is contrary to all your cherished logical reasoning. Either a thing must be a pleasure or it must not—and if it is not a pleasure, then it must be a pain.

SOCRATES: What about rest?

PROTARCHUS: Rest, Socrates? Rest?

SOCRATES: Yes, rest—inactivity, quietude.

PROTARCHUS: Rest is a pleasure: when I am tired, then there is nothing better than rest. There is no greater pleasure than having:

> The light gray goddess materialize
> To rain gentle sleep upon my eyes.

SOCRATES: And when you are not tired?

PROTARCHUS: Sleep when I am not tired?

SOCRATES: We are speaking of "rest," Protarchus. Do you remember last month's spontaneous speech by Hippias, when he talked about the derivation of herbal names?

PROTARCHUS: I certainly do. Hippias talked for hours; I could not believe how he rambled on and on and on. Each time that he finished with the name of one crazed and useless plant, I hoped against hope that it was the last. But, no—on he went to the next plant. Hippias must have memorized the names of two hundred obscure herbs.

SOCRATES: And we sat there at rest?

PROTARCHUS: We did—but I cannot imagine how we managed. (Do you remember that I had to restrain Philebus from throwing a stone?)

PHILEBUS: (That was Antisthenes, Protarchus.)

PROTARCHUS: In any case, we were all thoroughly bored and irritated.

SOCRATES: So, that particular rest was painful?

PROTARCHUS: Of course it was—but Socrates we have already decided that the same act (such as eating honey or resting) can sometimes be a pleasure and at other times be a pain. Why belabor the point?

SOCRATES: Patience, Protarchus—old men reason slowly. I am just managing to get a hold of "rest." Will you tear it from my hands before I have gotten a good grasp?

PROTARCHUS: Ah Socrates, undoubtedly you eat poorly in order to look older, then you can request our sympathy. You are probably a malnourished twenty-nine years old rather than the seventy doddering years to which you lay claim.

SOCRATES: You may be right, Protarchus—but in that case you might at least show some sympathy for my ill-health.

PROTARCHUS: Very well, Socrates, I concede that, whatever may be the cause, you are unable to reason at a normal pace. Let us get on with your argument before the winter comes.

SOCRATES: Thank you, Protarchus. I would like to continue examining ''rest.''

PROTARCHUS: Fine.

SOCRATES: Before I came upon you here in the Agora, were you sitting alone?

PROTARCHUS: Yes I was.

SOCRATES: Were you resting?

PROTARCHUS: Yes.

SOCRATES: Was it the morning?

PROTARCHUS: Of course it was.

SOCRATES: Were you already tired so early in the day?

PROTARCHUS: No.

SOCRATES: Were you forcing yourself to sit for some other purpose?

PROTARCHUS: No, I was just sitting, Socrates. Have you not done that yourself?

SOCRATES: Certainly, Protarchus—as I get older, I find myself sitting almost all of the time. Now, was this resting of yours a pleasure?

PROTARCHUS: A pleasure? I would not exactly call it a ''pleasure.''

SOCRATES: Were you happy?

PROTARCHUS: I suppose so—I definitely was not sad.

SOCRATES: So, resting was not a pain?

PROTARCHUS: No.

SOCRATES: If it was not exactly a pleasure and it was not a pain, then what kind of activity was your rest?

PROTARCHUS: It was rather neutral; I do not know a word for it.

SOCRATES: Does this mean that actions can lead to some state other than pleasure or pain?

PROTARCHUS: Yes.

SOCRATES: Would you conclude, then, that there are at least three states: pleasure, pain, and neutrality?

PROTARCHUS: That sounds right to me, Socrates.

SOCRATES: And the same act—like "rest"—can give rise to any of these different states, in different circumstances?

PROTARCHUS: Yes yes, Socrates—we had already decided that.

SOCRATES: Good. I was just trying to make certain that we had not been mistaken earlier.

PROTARCHUS: No, Socrates, our reasoning was as sound before as it is now. The content of our reasoning was the same. But the pace, old man—the pace of your reasoning is slowing still further (if that is possible): I am beginning to feel a hint of snow in the air.

SOCRATES: Am I keeping you from some errand, Protarchus?

PHILEBUS: Socrates, ignore Protarchus's comments. We listeners are interested in your argument—please continue.

SOCRATES: Well, Philebus, I do tend to be slow and cautious . . . Now let me see, we have been trying to understand pleasure. Would you agree that happinesses can be brought about by certain acts, Protarchus?

PROTARCHUS: It can.

SOCRATES: And those acts that bring about happiness are acts that we call "pleasures"?

PROTARCHUS: Yes.

SOCRATES: Is pleasure inherent in the act?

PROTARCHUS: It is.

SOCRATES: But, Protarchus, the same act—like eating honey or resting—can bring either pleasure or pain or even some neutral state.

PROTARCHUS: All right, Socrates—then the answer is "no": pleasure is not inherent in the act.

SOCRATES: I see. Then wherein does the pleasure reside?

PROTARCHUS: Obviously, Socrates, pleasure is inherent in the person. We have known this since the beginning of our discussion; there was no reason to go through all this roundabout reasoning.

SOCRATES: Perhaps you are right, Protarchus—but then again, perhaps you are wrong.

PROTARCHUS: *Me* wrong? Hold on a moment, Socrates—I am only following your lead. First you say something, and politely I agree with it. Now suddenly you say that *I* am wrong. Is that any way to behave with a friend?

SOCRATES: Protarchus, let us be clear about this. I have been asking you questions, have I not?

PROTARCHUS: True.

SOCRATES: I did not tell you what to answer—did I? Did you not give answers of your own free will?

PROTARCHUS: Yes I did.

SOCRATES: Now, did you answer honestly? Did your answers represent the best evaluations that you could make?

PROTARCHUS: Yes yes, Socrates.

SOCRATES: Then if we came to a wrong conclusion, was that not your responsibility as much as mine?

PROTARCHUS: I suppose that, in some sense, I share the responsibility—but you have led me astray with your choice of questions. You have been free to wander this way and that, and I have merely tried to oblige by following your meanderings.

SOCRATES: I apologize, Protarchus—I only meant to understand exactly what you are thinking about this thing called "pleasure."

PROTARCHUS: All right, old man, where to next?

SOCRATES: You have said that pleasure is inherent in the person and not in the act. Is pain also inherent in the person and not in the act?

PROTARCHUS: Definitely.

SOCRATES: How about the neutral state—the absence of pleasure or of pain—is that also inherent in the person?

PROTARCHUS: All of these states are the same, in this regard.

SOCRATES: Now let me understand you, Protarchus: When you say "person," do you mean the particular individual who is experiencing the state?

PROTARCHUS: Of course, what else could you imagine?

SOCRATES: Ah, Protarchus, I have a vivid and an unruly imagination. Sometimes I imagine all sorts of wild things—for instance, my imagination has just conjured up Death.

PROTARCHUS: Death? It takes no imagination to create death. Rather, it takes imagination to create life: death can be created by the dullest person and by the most senseless beast and by the most thoughtless and unimaginative acts.

SOCRATES: Of course you are right, Protarchus. Let me speak a little more clearly.

When you said that the states of pleasure, pain, and neutrality are inherent in particular people, my mind immediately pictured the calm and endless condition of death. (I am an old man, and death is not too far off, you know.) Suddenly I felt that there, in the absence of all pleasure and all pain, was a state of neutrality that is independent of any individual person.

PROTARCHUS: Perhaps in that one extreme case we may have a state that is independent of any one person. But, Socrates, please recall what valiant Achilleus said to his mother, the goddess Thetis—

> I, too, shall eventually lie in dust
> When I am dead and just a shade.
> Now let me face a living world
> And do great deeds, bold and unafraid.

Now let us, too, boldly get on with life, Socrates. There are many living pleasures and many living pains, and there must be many living neutral states also. Undoubtedly these living states are all inherent in the particular individuals who experience them.

SOCRATES: So, Protarchus, there are many pleasures, many pains, and many neutral acts?

PROTARCHUS: Of course.

SOCRATES: Then, are pleasures, pains, and neutralities really aggregates or collections or pluralities? Are—

PROTARCHUS: Aggregates, collections, pluralities? Ah Socrates, I have heard you set this verbal trap before.

SOCRATES: What verbal trap, Protarchus?

PROTARCHUS: Well now, just sit quietly a moment. I can save you the exertion—let me play out our inevitable discussion:

> First, you will ask: "Protarchus are you a person?"
> And I reply: "Of course I am."
> "Are you one single person?"
> "Certainly—I am Protarchus," I answer.
> "And is this 'Protarchus' a single entity?"
> "Yes he is."
> "Have you always been the same one entity?"
> "Yes."
> "Have you always been the same height?"
> "No."
> "Or the same weight?"
> "No."
> "Yet you have always been the same Protarchus?"
> "Of course I have."
> "Tell me, Protarchus: Are you happy now?"

"No, I am a bit irritated."

"Were you happier early this morning?"

"I was."

"Have you ever been miserable?"

"Yes."

"But in spite of the changing moods, you have always been the same Protarchus?"

"Of course."

"And is that your arm?"

"Certainly—it is not yours."

"Would you be Protarchus without that arm?"

"Of course."

"And without your leg?"

"Yes."

"Now suppose that you had no parts at all. Would you still be Protarchus?"

"How could I know the answer to such an impossible conjecture, Socrates?"

"Well, let me ask the question this way: What is this thing called 'Protarchus'? Apparently it is not some one size or some one state or some one part or some one mood. Is it the aggregate of all these? Or is it some other thing altogether?"

Now, Socrates, I cannot reply that "Protarchus" is an aggregate; otherwise you will upbraid me for originally claiming that I was one single entity. Therefore, I must agree that "Protarchus" is some other thing altogether.

(Are you following me, Socrates?)

SOCRATES: I am listening attentively, Protarchus.

PROTARCHUS: Very well—we continue:

Now you say to me: "Protarchus, you are not a particular size or a particular shape or a particular body part. In fact, you seem not to be any one particular physical thing. Then what one entity are you?"

"Clearly I am Protarchus—the same one person named by my parents, almost forty years ago."

"And is it only your name that identifies you? Or is there some other special thing that is the essential 'Protarchusness' and that makes you Protarchus and not an urn or a dog or a Socrates?"

"Socrates, there *is* a special single thing: it is my Protarchus soul."

"Ah, your own special soul."

"Yes."

"Now, how about your soul—your own special Protarchus soul—is it a single thing? Or is it an aggregate? Is it a composite collection of things? Is it a plurality?"

Of course if I reply that my soul is a plurality, then I have betrayed my original contention that Protarchus is just one entity. So I must say: "It is one single thing."

But you will respond: "Protarchus, are the Pythagoreans not great philosophers?"

"Yes," I will say.

"What did the Pythagoreans, such as Philolaus, say about the soul? Why, they proposed that the soul is a harmonious mixture of its many diverse parts and essences and natures. (And they have even given this mixture its own unique numerical ratio.)"

"True."

"And as for Empedocles—did he not see the soul as a blended multitude of units?"

"Yes he did."

"Or how about Heraclitus? Did he not consider that the soul is subject to continuous change into other elements (and at death it finally turns into water)?"

"Yes."

"And Leucippus and Democritus—they claimed that the soul comprises a myriad of special animate atoms, atoms that pervade the entire body."

And so on and on, until I am worn down and I give in from exhaustion . . . Well Socrates, what do you have to say to this?

SOCRATES: You have said it all, Protarchus—I have nothing more to add.

PROTARCHUS: Nothing to say? This is a rare occasion, Socrates.

SOCRATES: Apparently, Protarchus, your point is that one can always see many things in any one real object.

PROTARCHUS: Precisely.

SOCRATES: Moreover, you seem to believe that it is common reasoning to try to force an artificial simplicity on things. Have I understood you correctly? Do you contend that we often distort complex real world items to make them seem to be completely pure, single, and homogeneous entities?

PROTARCHUS: Exactly, Socrates.

SOCRATES: Undoubtedly we ought to begin all our arguments by recognizing the truth, Protarchus. Therefore, we had best follow your lead: here we should start with the understanding that most things are actually pluralities, aggregates, or collections.

PROTARCHUS: Fine.

SOCRATES: But wait a moment, Protarchus—I wonder whether I have been honest with you.

PROTARCHUS: Well have you?

SOCRATES: I am not certain. You see, I just said: "*Most* things can be seen as pluralities." But now I wonder: Is this true? Are there are *any* pure and indivisible monads in the real world?

PROTARCHUS: Let me see . . . That is a good question. At the moment, I cannot think of any, Socrates—but I am not sure.

SOCRATES: Let me help: consider the alphabet. Is the letter "a" a single thing?

PROTARCHUS: Yes, it seems to be.

SOCRATES: Is it one sound?

PROTARCHUS: Yes.

SOCRATES: Oh? You must be getting old like me, Protarchus.

PROTARCHUS: Old? Why do you say that?

SOCRATES: You are becoming forgetful; you have forgotten Theuth, the famous Egyptian.

PROTARCHUS: Forgotten Theuth? I have not forgotten him: he was the god who invented the game of knucklebones.

SOCRATES: Yes. In addition, he was also a linguist. He was the first to distinguish vowels and consonants. Also, he classed the letters as noiseless or articulated, and he pointed out that each of the articulated sounds had parts—even a simple letter, like "a," is a sequence of smaller unit sounds. Theuth considered "a" to be an aggregate thing. And then, of course, he pointed out that our use of "a" comprises many variant sounds, as in "apple," "ago," "alms," "arm," "air," "are," and "age."

PROTARCHUS: Well perhaps "a" is an aggregate, Socrates— as I said, I cannot think of any monads in the real world.

PHILEBUS: Just a moment, Protarchus. It is true that everything is divisible—at the same time, things may still be essentially single, individual, and particular entities.

PROTARCHUS: What do you mean, Philebus?

PHILEBUS: I mean that things may be divisible, but they can still be monads. Although they are assemblages, certain things are nonetheless whole and unique unto themselves. These things *behave* like monads, because they have particular, special, universal, and independent definitions.

SOCRATES: That is an interesting idea, Philebus . . . What would you say about people? Is man a monad?

PHILEBUS: I would say that in spite of the diversity among mankind, "person" has a particular, special, universal, and independent definition. Of course the definition is a bit complex: it not only describes the common parts of a human, it also describes his many special abilities. Nonetheless, this definition applies to all people. Thus, man is essentially a monad.

SOCRATES: I see. But I myself am overwhelmed by the diversity. What do you do with the diversity among people?

PHILEBUS: What do I do with it? I simply admit that it exists.

SOCRATES: Would you say that each person is unique?

PHILEBUS: Yes, in many ways.

PROTARCHUS: Obviously people are unique individuals, Socrates—as Hector was reminded in the *Iliad:*

> You cannot hope that every gift
> Be given to you outright:
> Gods grant to one man the swift
> Dance of war and the grace of fight;
> Another gets supple hands, the kind
> For crafting clay and malachite;
> In yet another, bright song we find,
> Or a tongue to speak pure verse aright;
> And deep in someone else's mind,
> Zeus sets fine wit and wise foresight.

SOCRATES: Very well. Now, Protarchus, if each person is unique, then does his perspective of the world differ from every other person?

PROTARCHUS: Yes it does. Actually, his viewpoint differs literally from every other viewpoint.

SOCRATES: Literally?

PROTARCHUS: Yes—literally. Two people cannot occupy exactly the same position in space. Thus, each person's eyes are in a different location from every other person's eyes. At any one time, each person has a slightly different view of the world, and his description of things must differ—no matter how slightly—from that of every other person in the world.

SOCRATES: That is finely said, Protarchus. So, I imagine that you would accept this idea too: each person's description of any item could differ—no matter how slightly—from descriptions given by every other person in the world.

PROTARCHUS: That is a reasonable statement.

SOCRATES: Would you agree that such descriptions define (at least they define for us humans) the things in our world?

PROTARCHUS: Yes.

SOCRATES: Then, because there are manifold people, each thing in the world can have manifold descriptions?

PROTARCHUS: It can.

SOCRATES: Descriptions are the basis of our understandings?

PROTARCHUS: Yes.

SOCRATES: So, as far as our understandings are concerned, nothing is really a simple monad? To us—in terms of human comprehension—each single item must be a plurality? You have told me that humans are varied. Thus, everything in the human world must be equally varied; everything has myriad states and diverse parts and manifold appearances.

PROTARCHUS: Apparently, Socrates.

SOCRATES: Do you agree Philebus?

PHILEBUS: I suppose so.

SOCRATES: Then when reasoning, we must begin with plurality. Monads are only an approximation. An urn, an ox, a particular state of pleasure—in actuality, these are all complex things.

PROTARCHUS: So, the first principle of logic is that everything is complex, Socrates?

SOCRATES: As far as our understandings go, everything in the real world is complex . . . But now, my young friends, there is a strange twist: we love monads.

PHILEBUS: We love monads?

SOCRATES: Yes, we certainly do, Philebus: we are always trying to make our understandings as simple as possible.

PHILEBUS: But if nothing is really a monad, then why should we pretend? Why devise simplicities? Why disguise reality?

PROTARCHUS: Yes, Socrates—why pretend? And what is this business of ''simple understandings'' with which you are suddenly complicating our logic?

SOCRATES: By ''simple understandings,'' I mean this: we

attempt to capture the greatest possible portion of these manifold and complex things in the form of pure, uniform, homogeneous, and indivisible abstractions. We build monads, and these are our simple understandings.

PROTARCHUS: Just a moment, Socrates—earlier you said that simplicities are a distortion of reality.

SOCRATES: Distortion is not the issue, my friend, because at heart, we only comprehend the simple. Our understandings are based on simple, monadic abstractions. Simple abstractions do not embody every single nuance of reality. They cannot embrace all of the indiosyncratic variations of real things. Nonetheless, good simplicities come close to mirroring a great deal of reality.

PROTARCHUS: Well, I still do not understand you, Socrates. Did you not say that the world is everywhere complex and messy?

SOCRATES: Yes—the *real* world.

PROTARCHUS: All right, the *real* world. But why bother to try to create these simple abstractions? Why build simple representative definitions, if they will never be true?

SOCRATES: Protarchus, it has to do with the gods.

PROTARCHUS: The gods? Which gods?

SOCRATES: All gods. You see, my friend, divinity is purity: it is unity and simplicity.

PHILEBUS: Divinity is simplicity?

SOCRATES: Yes, divinity is simplicity. And the mere existence of the gods pushes us to see simplicity, purity, and divinity in all the messiness of reality.

There is a tension between simple and complex, between divine and mortal. This dichotomy was first taught to mankind by Prometheus; it was an insight as bright as fire. Men of old, who were better than ourselves and who lived nearer to the gods, then passed on this understanding to their children in the form of a saying:

> All things consist of many
> But also one pure kind;
> They're both clay and heaven—
> At once dusty and divine.

The true nature of things is a mix of clay and heaven. Still, we ought always to hope for purity, to believe in divinity, and to search for simplicity. "First see the 'ones' in the world"—this was the ancients' credo. Only after discovering divinity and "monadness" should we then face the complexities and search out the "twos" and the "threes" in things. Multiformity is the polish on our raw understanding, which in its naked form is really built of single, simple monads.

PROTARCHUS: So, Socrates, you believe that the gods have committed us to simplicity?

SOCRATES: Yes I do, Protarchus.

PROTARCHUS: And yet the world is essentially complex?

SOCRATES: Yes.

PROTARCHUS: But did not the gods create this world?

SOCRATES: They did, to some extent.

PROTARCHUS: To some extent? I thought that the gods created it all.

SOCRATES: Oh the gods neatened some enclaves, and they constructed some small islands of order. But on the grand scale of matters, they have not had the time or the opportunity to spread their pure and simple divinity throughout. As Hesiod tells us, our mortal world has been condensed from Chaos; it is built on Tartarus, son of Aether and Gaeae and father of Typhoeus and the elder giants.

> The sources and the ends
> Of all the mortal world
> (Which Heaven now transcends)
> Is Tartarus, a gloomy swirl
> Who dank and bleak extends
> Beneath the sea's deep floor

> And who at base descends
> To primal Chaos's door,
> His thick and clotted friend
> Which even gods abhor.

PROTARCHUS: True—our world is founded on the god Chaos.

SOCRATES: Yes, Chaos "which even gods abhor." And it is not only our world, the younger gods themselves emerged from Chaos. Who created the gods, Protarchus? Surely no one with a simple plan, for we have been blessed with a divine rabble.

PROTARCHUS: Socrates, this sounds like blasphemy: you are criticizing the gods. Remember the warning of the ancient goddess Dione, from the *Iliad*—

> Brief are the lives of men
> Who fight the god's design;
> They'll never return again
> From battling the Divine.
>
> Their children will not play
> About their fathers' feet
> Nor watch their sires grow grey
> Through lives long and complete.

SOCRATES: No no, good Protarchus, we do not fight *against* the gods—we join together with the gods in their struggles against complexity.

The gods are divine, and they set for us beautiful standards of purity and simplicity. But gods though they be, they too must struggle against the diverse and variegated complexities that adorn and obscure this tangled fabric. The fabric of our universe is an intricate, warm, and complex cloth.

September 16: PHILEBUS

PHILEBUS: You have strayed from the original issue, Socrates. Did we not began by trying to decide which is best: pleasure or reasoning?

PROTARCHUS: We certainly did.

PHILEBUS: Protarchus and I said that pleasure, luxury, delight, enjoyment, and rapture are the ultimate joys. On the other hand, you claimed that we should aim for other things—truth, reason, knowledge, skillful logic, and clear understandings.

PROTARCHUS: Exactly, Philebus. (You know of course, Socrates, that Philebus and I are supported by that well-known philosopher, Aristippus of Cyrene.)

SOCRATES: I am quite aware of his views, Protarchus.

PHILEBUS: In any case, it is clear that we are not so far apart as it first appeared. Pleasure and reason are not true alternatives; they are not incompatible—reasoning can be a joy.

SOCRATES: Yes, it *can* be a joy.

PHILEBUS: So there is no reason to argue against our position, Socrates. You aspire to clear understandings because they make you happy. You want to be happy, just as we want to be happy— and in your case, thoughtful reasoning makes you happy.

PROTARCHUS: Precisely. Now, Socrates, do not plunge us into interminable semantic convolutions over this issue. Admit that you were wrong, and let us get on with our affairs. You have been trying to wrap us in some dream world of yours. Awake from your complex nightmare; return to the simpler realities of our everyday life.

SOCRATES: My position is a dream, Protarchus? As Achilles said in the *Iliad:* "Dreams are divine, for they come from Zeus."

PROTARCHUS: They may be divine, but sometimes they are frightening and complex distortions of reality.

SOCRATES: Are you referring to nightmares?

PROTARCHUS: Yes I am.

SOCRATES: Can you remember a recent nightmare of yours?

PROTARCHUS: Ah, more of your peculiar questions, Socrates.

SOCRATES: Questioning is my way of understanding you, Protarchus.

PROTARCHUS: All right, all right—continue your inquiry, Socrates.

SOCRATES: We were talking about nightmares. Can you relate a recent nightmare?

PROTARCHUS: Of course I can: I have had many nightmares. Let me see . . . One time I was running through the alleyways of the market, with dark figures behind me. Each figure had a huge club, and they chased me, closing in. My feet were too heavy; I could not make them move quickly—it was as if I were mired in wet sand, in some thick night ocean.

SOCRATES: And when you awoke?

PROTARCHUS: When I awoke, my heart was racing.

SOCRATES: Did your feelings remain vivid, even in the face of the secure reality of your bedroom?

PROTARCHUS: Yes, I remember that clearly. I had to get out of bed and walk about for a moment before the fears subsided. Even then, there was some vague unease left behind, and I had trouble falling asleep again.

SOCRATES: I too am like that, Protarchus. You have awakened me from a nightmare in which I dreamt that reason outweighs pleasures. But although I am newly awakened, a vague unease remains.

PHILEBUS: Socrates, that feeling will fade with time, as do all nightmares.

SOCRATES: Perhaps, Philebus—nonetheless, you could soothe my spirit if you helped to settle a few small points first.

PHILEBUS: Oh? And what small points are those?

SOCRATES: We have been discussing the important goals for one's life, have we not?

PHILEBUS: We have.

SOCRATES: What might those goals be?

PHILEBUS: The goals for life? These are not small points, Socrates: this is the heart of our discussion. Now, Protarchus and I maintain that pleasure is an important goal—

SOCRATES: And I maintain that reasoning is an important goal. But aside from those goals, could there be others?

PHILEBUS: Of course—I would say that good health and comfortable daily living circumstances are also important goals.

SOCRATES: I see. Are there any others?

PHILEBUS: Adequate food and drink.

SOCRATES: Are there any more?

PROTARCHUS: Shelter from excessive heat and from storms, and warmth in the cold weather.

PHILEBUS: Very true, Protarchus—and also some occupation to busy your hands and your mind, and of course friends for fun and for comfort.

SOCRATES: So, you have listed: health, comfortable daily circumstances, food, drink, shelter, warmth, an occupation, and friends. Are there yet more goals in life?

PROTARCHUS: You have forgotten pleasure, Socrates.

PHILEBUS: And (perhaps) reasoning.

SOCRATES: I set those aside for the moment.

PHILEBUS: Then I think that we have listed the most important goals in life.

SOCRATES: What about children?

PHILEBUS: Children can have goals, but I think that youngsters are still rather vague about the important ones. I would say—

SOCRATES: No no, Philebus—I mean: Is having children an important goal in life?

PHILEBUS: I am not sure—I suppose that it is important to some people, but it is not essential to me.

SOCRATES: Is creating epic poetry an important goal?

PHILEBUS: No, I do not think so.

SOCRATES: No?

PHILEBUS: Poetry is a luxury, Socrates.

SOCRATES: Do you remember how, in the *Odyssey,* Odysseus said:

> Honor the epic arena.
> Give poets reverence, esteem, and regard;
> For poets are loved by Athena,
> Who taught them the art of the bard.
>
> As their marble, the wind on the fall roads,
> As their paint, the meadows of spring—
> Poets sculpt the dawn in their night odes,
> Bards sketch our souls when they sing.

PHILEBUS: I recall that passage. Perhaps poetry is an essential part of life to some men, but not to me.

SOCRATES: How are you deciding which things are important goals in life and which things are not, Philebus?

PHILEBUS: I will tell you, Socrates. I ask myself: "Can I live without this thing?" If I cannot live without it, then it is an important goal—in fact, it is an essential goal.

SOCRATES: I see. So, for example, you must have said: "Can Philebus live without food and drink?" And then you answered: "No." Thus, you concluded that food and drink are essential goals in life.

PHILEBUS: Exactly, Socrates.

SOCRATES: And for good health, you must have said: "Can Philebus live without good health?" What was your answer?

PHILEBUS: It was "no."

SOCRATES: Do you agree, Protarchus?

PROTARCHUS: Certainly.

SOCRATES: Protarchus, I saw your father, Callias, in the marketplace last week.

PROTARCHUS: My father? Yes, he gets out occasionally—when his rheumatism is mild. Usually however, he awakens stiff and weak, so he does not come to the Agora until the late morning or the afternoon.

SOCRATES: How long has he been troubled by his joint pains?

PROTARCHUS: It has been years and years, Socrates; I think that he first had problems in his forty-fifth or forty-sixth year, fully two decades ago. Now, his knuckles are quite swollen and his fingers are bent and twisted.

SOCRATES: So Callias has been in ill-health at least twenty years?

PROTARCHS: He has not been ill continuously: there was at least one spell of almost a half year when he seemed quite limber and when he was feeling much better. (I think that this was about ten years ago.) And even today hot baths help considerably.

SOCRATES: Nonetheless, you would say that he has lived two decades in poor health?

PROTARCHUS: I am afraid so.

SOCRATES: Then good health cannot be an essential requisite for life.

PROTARCHUS: "An essential requisite"? Ah, I see what you mean. Listen, Socrates, Philebus and I meant only that *very* bad health is incompatible with life.

PHILEBUS: Exactly.

SOCRATES: How bad is "very bad"?

PHILEBUS: "Very bad" means extremely bad.

PROTARCHUS: Yes—it means mortally ill.

SOCRATES: Mortally ill? Do you mean deathly ill? Are you saying that death is incompatible with life?

PHILEBUS: Well, of course when you define it so precisely, then it sounds a bit trivial. But is it not a fact that we must be alive in order to live?

SOCRATES: Then, in your list of essential goals for life, you would include life itself?

PHILEBUS: Definitely.

PROTARCHUS: Yes, definitely.

SOCRATES: All right. Now we have: food and drink and life itself. Initially you also listed comfortable daily living. Is that essential for life?

PHILEBUS: It is not *essential,* Socrates, but earlier we were talking about the important goals in life, and I still consider comfortable daily living an important goal.

SOCRATES: Oh? By what criteria, Philebus?

PHILEBUS: By what criteria? . . . Well, although these things are not absolutely necessary for life, they are things to which we all aspire.

SOCRATES: Your criterion for an important goal is "universal aspiration"?

PHILEBUS: Yes.

SOCRATES: How do you know that we all aspire to comfortable daily living, Philebus?

PHILEBUS: Why, just ask anyone, Socrates. For instance: Protarchus, do you want to live comfortably?

PROTARCHUS: I certainly do, Philebus. And do *you* want to live comfortably, Philebus?

PHILEBUS: Yes. So you see, Socrates—any normal man would wish the same.

SOCRATES: And me?

PHILEBUS: You, Socrates? I hardly consider you a normal

man. Your meat and drink are of the poorest kind. Summer and winter, your coat is the same patched tunic, and often you go about shoeless and shirtless. As someone has said: "A slave whose master made him live as Socrates does would soon run away."

SOCRATES: You think that this is not normal?

PHILEBUS: Now, Socrates, do *you* think it normal?

SOCRATES: I do not know what "normal" means. It seems to me that he who has the fewest wants is nearest to the gods—but I cannot say whether that is normal.

PROTARCHUS: Believe me, Socrates, you are not normal.

SOCRATES: Then a normal person is one who considers daily comforts to be important goals in life?

PHILEBUS: Yes.

PROTARCHUS: Yes, *that* is normal, Socrates.

SOCRATES: And what of the person who does not consider daily comforts to be important?

PHILEBUS: He is not normal.

PROTARCHUS: He is definitely not normal.

SOCRATES: Philebus, you and Protarchus are remarkable men to know these things so well. Would you consider yourselves to be open-minded?

PHILEBUS: Yes, we entertain all ideas.

SOCRATES: Good—I need some open-minded guidance. Now, gentlemen, we know that there are normal men here in Athens, because you two are clearly normal.

PHILEBUS: Yes, Protarchus and I and most other men are normal.

SOCRATES: All right. We also know that there are men who are not normal—as I have learned from you, Socrates is not normal.

PHILEBUS: True.

PROTARCHUS: True—Socrates is not normal.

SOCRATES: And normal men consider that daily comforts are important?

PHILEBUS: Yes.

SOCRATES: Whereas, men who are not normal consider that daily comforts are unimportant?

PROTARCHUS: Correct.

SOCRATES: Now you are both open-minded—

PHILEBUS: We are.

SOCRATES: So, I assume that you will entertain this possibility: there are some men who are unsure, at present, whether daily comforts are important or are unimportant. Would you agree that there may be some puzzled men?

PROTARCHUS: Certainly, Socrates.

PHILEBUS: Of course, Socrates—I could easily imagine that there might be people who have not thought about this issue.

PROTARCHUS: Or if they *have* thought about it, then they are not certain yet.

PHILEBUS: They still wonder whether daily comforts are important. Perhaps these puzzled men are young, or perhaps they are just befuddled.

PROTARCHUS: Or they have been misled by watching some of the eccentrics such as yourself, Socrates.

SOCRATES: Suppose, Philebus, that we had such a man here before us. (I picture him as an average looking young man, with curly dark hair, pale grey tunic, worn sandals, and a puzzled expression on his face.) Will you grant me an uncertain young man?

PHILEBUS: Very well, Socrates.

SOCRATES: Now, Philebus, I see that this young man wants to ask you a question.

PHILEBUS: All right. What does he want to know?

SOCRATES: It is simple, Philebus.

"Tell me," he begins, "what are the important goals in life?"

PHILEBUS: Does this young man have a name?

SOCRATES: Let us call him Ainigmas.

PHILEBUS: Fine. I would answer like this: "Ainigmas, my young friend, among other things (such as food and drink and the pursuit of pleasure), comfortable daily living is an important goal in life."

SOCRATES: Why, Philebus, he is now turning to me: "Socrates," Ainigmas says, "*you* tell me: What are the important goals in life?" What shall I answer, Philebus?

PHILEBUS: You must speak for yourself, Socrates.

SOCRATES: All right—then I would say: "Anigmas, thoughtful reasoning is an important goal."

PHILEBUS: Socrates, you are causing problems. Now you have left poor Ainigmas unclear about this matter. Therefore, he says to you: "I do not wish to seem impolite, Socrates, but I am afraid that I am puzzled. Do you agree with Philebus and with Protarchus (and apparently with many others) that comfortable daily living is an important goal for one's life?" What do you answer, Socrates?

SOCRATES: I answer: "No. I am afraid, Ainigmas, that I do not agree."

PHILEBUS: And now what does Ainigmas say?

PROTARCHUS: Ainigmas asks: "Who is right?"

SOCRATES: "Who is right"?

PROTARCHUS: Yes—which philosopher has given the right answer: Philebus or Socrates?

SOCRATES: Is there a right answer, Protarchus?

PROTARCHUS: Certainly there is. If Ainigmas is a normal man, then we have already decided that the right answer for him is this: comfortable living is definitely an important goal in his life.

SOCRATES: And if Ainigmas is not normal?

PROTARCHUS: Well if he is like you, then I suppose that comfortable living might not the be right answer.

SOCRATES: Now let me understand you, Protarchus: Are you saying that the right answer for normal men is different from the right answer for men who are not normal?

PROTARCHUS: Yes.

SOCRATES: So, for me the right answer is that comfortable living is not an important goal?

PROTARCHUS: Apparently.

SOCRATES: Do you contend that there is no universal right answer? Does the rightness of the answer depend on the nature of the particular man in question?

PROTARCHUS: Yes—that is definitely the case.

SOCRATES: Philebus, do you agree with Protarchus?

PHILEBUS: I do.

SOCRATES: Then what do we tell Ainigmas, when he asks for the right answer?

PHILEBUS: We tell him: "Ainigmas, comfortable living is an important goal in life."

PROTARCHUS: Exactly.

SOCRATES: But comfortable living is not an important goal for everyone: it is only important for those men who are normal.

PHILEBUS: Undoubtedly Ainigmas is a normal man.

SOCRATES: How do we know that he is normal?

PROTARCHUS: Now, Socrates, you cannot be so self-centered as to assume that most people agree with your views. Most people, I am afraid, are normal.

SOCRATES: Well you are probably right, Protarchus, but let us test Ainigmas to be certain. Did we not have a definition of normal, earlier in this discussion?

PROTARCHUS: Yes.

SOCRATES: Do you recall it?

PHILEBUS: I do, Socrates—it was: "A normal person is one who considers daily comforts to be important goals in life."

SOCRATES: That is what I remember also. Do you agree, Protarchus?

PROTARCHUS: Yes.

SOCRATES: Very good—now we can test Ainigmas. Is he a typical, normal man? We need only find out whether he considers daily comforts to be important goals in life.

PROTARCHUS: Exactly, Socrates.

PHILEBUS: Exactly.

SOCRATES: So let us ask him.

PHILEBUS: Very well.

PROTARCHUS: Yes, ask him by all means.

SOCRATES: "Ainigmas, my young friend, do you consider daily comforts to be important goals in life?" . . .

   Well? I am listening closely for his reply, Philebus, but he seems strangely silent. Ah, wait, I think that he is speaking now. Can you hear what he is saying?

PHILEBUS: I am not certain . . . Protarchus, can you hear him?

PROTARCHUS: Of course I can hear him—he says: "Philebus, I consider daily comforts to be important."

SOCRATES: Protarchus, that is not Ainigmas speaking—perhaps it is his companion.

PROTARCHUS: No, he is alone, Socrates. Why do you say that it is not Ainigmas talking?

SOCRATES: Think back, Protarchus. Remember, we chose Ainigmas because of an important trait: we specifically wanted to examine a young man who was undecided about the importance of daily comforts. Being open-minded men, you and Philebus agreed that there must be people who do not know whether daily comforts are truly important goals in life. Did you not accept this condition, Philebus?

PHILEBUS: Yes.

SOCRATES: And you, Protarchus?

PROTARCHUS: I suppose so.

SOCRATES: Then it does not seem possible for our Ainigmas to answer your question, Philebus. By definition, Ainigmas is a man who does not know whether daily comforts are important goals in life.

PHILEBUS: So, is he normal or is he not, Socrates?

SOCRATES: I do not know, Philebus.

PHILEBUS: Socrates, you have backed us into a corner. We cannot answer Ainigmas's original question.

Here is the situation. If Ainigmas is normal, then Protarchus and I can tell him confidently that comfortable living is an important goal for his life. On the other hand if Ainigmas is not normal, then Socrates can tell him to disregard comfortable living. To know what to say, we must know whether Ainigmas should listen to me or to Socrates. But to decide this, we must first know: Is Ainigmas normal or is he not?

PROTARCHUS: Hold on a moment, Philebus; you surrender too easily to Socrates's verbal sleight-of-hand. Listen, gentlemen, we should be talking about universals here. Forget comfortable living. Instead, consider food and drink. Are these not things that all men require?

PHILEBUS: Certainly.

PROTARCHUS: Good. Then there is no question that food and drink are important, and they are essential goals in life. Also, consider good health (or as Socrates would say "life itself"). Is that not essential?

PHILEBUS: Yes, it definitely is.

PROTARCHUS: Then let us stick to these absolutes and universals. The other goals are too subjective; they are like thick jungles filled with all manner of vines and tendrils that Socrates can use to wrap about your feet and to ensare your arms.

Do not deny it, Socrates: you enjoy playing in the underbrush.

SOCRATES: I guess that you are right, Protarchus—the world is a complex place, and I enjoy the complexities.

PHILEBUS: You say this often, Socrates. You say that you revel in "complexities." Now tell us: What exactly do you mean by "complexity"?

SOCRATES: Basically, Philebus, complex things are manifold: they are made of many and diverse parts, all interlaced in many and diverse ways.

PHILEBUS: So, Protarchus's jungle metaphor is accurate?

SOCRATES: It is very accurate. Complexity is a jungle, woven with underbrush and tangled with vines. When we become enmeshed in the complexities of the world, we need both hands and both feet to make our way.

PROTARCHUS: In addition, we need a sharp axe.

SOCRATES: An axe, Protarchus?

PROTARCHUS: Yes. We need an axe to clear a path.

SOCRATES: You have unravelled knots of yarn—have you not, Protarchus?

PROTARCHUS: Of course I have.

SOCRATES: Did you use a knife?

PROTARCHUS: At times, when I was in a hurry. (But then I ruined the yarn.)

SOCRATES: It is the same with any true complexities, Protarchus. Complex things are interlaced with a confused scramble of interconnections, and it can take hours or days to unravel the tangles. When we are in a hurry, we are always tempted to use a knife: we would love to hack through the complexities of the world. But as with a tangled ball of yarn, it can be worthwhile to take the time for patient handwork—

PROTARCHS: Handwork? Socrates, we are talking about the art of reasoning.

SOCRATES: That we are, and complex philosophical problems require patient logical handwork. When we have enough time to dissect complexities leisurely, then we end up with an archive that is full and rich. With patience, we build a collection of parts and arms and bits and connectors, full colorful, variegated, and diversified.

This, Philebus, is complexity—motley, mosaic, and multifarious, sundry, assorted, and polypsychical.

PHILEBUS: So, "complex" means "intricate"?

SOCRATES: Complex means intricate, involved, and irregular. Complex things take careful patience to unravel—and our world is thoroughly complex. Moreover, it has pockets of incondensable complexity, places where—

PHILEBUS: "Incondensable"? What is this "incondensability," Socrates?

SOCRATES: "Incondensability" means that for a full understanding of something we need the whole thing—there is no smaller form; the thing cannot be condensed.

PROTARCHUS: Socrates, you are wildly introducing all manner of tangents. Why worry about condensed forms?

SOCRATES: This is no tangent: this is the heart of the matter because it is about truth. We would always like the truth in a condensed form, Protarchus, so that we may cart it off easily in our own two hands. Incondensability describes those places whose intricacy can never be fully captured. For these regions, we must return again and again. We must reimmerse ourselves if we are to experience their complete richness, because incondensable thickets are warrens of idiosyncratic diversity.

PROTARCHUS: Socrates, your reasoning is complex and your speeches are ornate and incondensable. Do you think that you might shorten matters a bit? How about giving us a simple, real example?

SOCRATES: Gladly. Consider a person, Protarchus: we learn a bit about him from his toe or his finger or his laugh or his name. But the person is the whole person, and he is incondensable.

PROTARCHUS: All right, Socrates. A person may not be fully condensable. Nonetheless, I suspect that there are a great many things—things that *seem* big and complex—that really are quite condensable.

PHILEBUS: Oh? What is an example, Protarchus?

PROTARCHUS: Well . . . I am not certain that I have one on the tip of my tongue—

SOCRATES: Perhaps I can help out here, my friends.

PROTARCHUS: You, Socrates? You are supposed to be arguing on the other side.

SOCRATES: There are no sides here, Protarchus—there is only good reasoning—and if you are making a good point, then I would like to help.

PHILEBUS: What would you like to add, Socrates?

SOCRATES: Look at that long stone wall over there, Philebus.

PHILEBUS: The one just beyond Eudicus?

SOCRATES: Yes.

PROTARCHUS: What of it?

SOCRATES: That wall is made of hundreds of even, smooth, and almost identical stones. Can that wall be condensed?

PROTARCHUS: Perhaps it can be condensed by a god—some Titan, an Atlas—but not by a mortal.

SOCRATES: No mortal can squeeze that wall into any smaller form, but I would say that the wall *can* be condensed. It is big—

PROTARCHUS: It is big—and it is long.

SOCRATES: Nonetheless, the entire wall is simply the same roundstone pattern repeated hundreds of times, over and over again.

PHILEBUS: (Thousands of times, I would wager, Socrates.)

SOCRATES: That roundstone pattern is quite simple, Philebus. But is that little, simple pattern not a very condensed version of a quite extensive wall?

PHILEBUS: Well yes, I guess that it is, Socrates. I suppose that each miniature pattern is a condensed version of the entire wall; so, in a sense, the wall can be condensed . . . And now that you have given us an example of condensability, another example comes to mind—

SOCRATES: Oh? What is that?

PHILEBUS: The triangular numbers of Pythagoras 1, 3, 6, 10, 15 . . .

SOCRATES: Ah yes—the sums of numbers, built as the rows of a triangle:

triangle	row	sum
1	1	1
1 1	2	3
1 1 1	3	6
1 1 1 1	4	10
1 1 1 1 1	5	15

PHILEBUS: Precisely, Socrates. With the simple triangle rule, one can find the sum of a triangle of any size. You know, Protarchus, this rule could be written on a small piece of parchment, and it condenses triangles of immense magnitude as well as small triangles.

SOCRATES: This is a fine example, Philebus.

PHILEBUS: Thank you, Socrates.

SOCRATES: I would go so far as to say that it is a wonderful example. Like the wall that we were discussing, the triangular numbers are condensable—

PHILEBUS: Yes—they are pocketable.

SOCRATES: Exactly. And such condensable things are simple things. Even when something appears outwardly to be intricate or ornate or just very large and "unsqueezable," it still may be simple—which is the opposite of complex.

Now, both simplicity and complexity are about beginnings, because—

PROTARCHUS: Just a moment, Socrates. Once again you have strayed far from the subject at hand: we were talking of pleasure versus reason, not walls versus triangles.

SOCRATES: It is not "walls *versus* triangles," Protarchus, it is ''walls *and* triangles.'' In our examples, both the walls *and* the triangles are comparable—they are both simple things.

PROTARCHUS: ''Versus'' or ''and''—never mind, Socrates. I think that you are avoiding the issue, because you know that your position is wrong. You certainly have ignored my last point.

SOCRATES: Remind me again, Protarchus: What were you saying?

PROTARCHUS: Very well, Socrates. I pointed out that we slipped into your complexities only when we strayed into the messy realm of conditional things—conditional things like comfortable living. But when we dealt in universals, like food and drink, then we remained on solid ground.

SOCRATES: I quite agree, Protarchus.

PROTARCHUS: You agree with me, Socrates?

SOCRATES: Absolutely, Protarchus.

PROTARCHUS: Then what were we arguing about?

SOCRATES: We have not been arguing. I have been trying to understand your ideas; I have been trying to learn by questioning you. And now you have told me something that I can see quite clearly. You have told me something with which I agree. You say that universals are simple; they are like divine truths—they are absolute and pure.

PROTARCHUS: Yes, Socrates—that is correct.

SOCRATES: In contrast, conditional things are complex; they are like the mortal truths: they are transient and intricate. And as I was saying to Philebus, this difference—the difference between the divine and the mortal, between simple and complex—has to do with beginnings.

PHILEBUS: With beginnings, Socrates?

PROTARCHUS: Beginnings?

SOCRATES: Yes, my friends, with *beginnings*. Simple things have small and manageable beginnings. In contrast, complex things have extensive beginnings.

Consider your wall over there. How would you instruct a mason to build it?

PHILEBUS: Are you asking *me*, Socrates?

SOCRATES: Yes.

PHILEBUS: First, I would tell the mason to collect a large pile of stones. Each rock should be round, it should be as similar to the others as possible, and it should be about one palm in width. Then the mason should neatly mortar the stones into an even, hexagonal pattern.

SOCRATES: If the wall were only to be a few feet long, then how would the instructions differ?

PHILEBUS: They would not differ at all, except that the initial pile of stones would be quite modest.

SOCRATES: What if the wall were to extend from here to Peiraeus—

PHILEBUS: Do you mean: What if it were one of the Long Walls?

SOCRATES: Yes—suppose that it were the North Wall (the one that Pericles finished some sixty years ago); that wall is at least forty stadia long. How would your building instructions differ, if the mason were supposed to construct the North Wall?

PHILEBUS: Again, Socrates, the basic instructions could remain the same. However, the mason would now need a massive pile of stones at the start.

SOCRATES: Ah, this is it, Philebus.

PHILEBUS: This is *what*, Socrates?

SOCRATES: This is exactly why the wall is simple: even a long wall, such as the North Wall to the Great Harbor in Peiraeus, could be built with almost the same modest beginnings as a very short wall.

PROTARCHUS: Those beginnings are not modest, Socrates. The mason would need fully forty stadia of stones in order to build a wall that is forty stadia in length, and those stones would not appear magically from thin air.

SOCRATES: True, Protarchus, but we are talking about the *instructions* for the mason. Now, the minimum instructions for building the wall—that is, the essential specific information that you must provide—include two things: a description of the size of the individual stones, and an order for a certain number of stones. For the North Wall, you could write the full instructions and the order on a scrap of papyrus, a scrap that you then could hide in the palm of one hand.

PROTARCHUS: Yes, I suppose that I could.

SOCRATES: The wall comes from simple instructions, from small beginnings.

PHILEBUS: Simple and small.

SOCRATES: "Simple and small," Philebus—in contrast, "complex and large."

PHILEBUS: Complex and large?

SOCRATES: Complex and large—truly complex phenomena have large, involved, and intricate beginnings. Specifically, complex things are the progeny of parents that are as large as the things themselves. Complex things have many diverse parts and many diverse inteconnections, and the natural predecessors of complex things also have many diverse parts and many diverse interconnections. To build complex things, you need complex instructions.

PROTARCHUS: This is easy for you to say, Socrates, but I am not sure that you are right.

PHILEBUS: Yes—why could I not write down the instructions for a complex thing just as easily as for a simple thing?

SOCRATES: Think of a specific example, Philebus. Picture a very complex thing—something that is incondensably complex.

PHILEBUS: Like what, Socrates?

SOCRATES: How about the great frieze of the Parthenon?

PHILEBUS: All right.

SOCRATES: The frieze is the Panathenaic procession. It is filled with diverse characters, and it is truly complex. On the western face alone (where the preparations for the parade begin) there are three old bearded men, twenty-five youths, and two boys—some men are sandled, some booted, some barefoot, and one is just tying on his shoes; one man has a helmet with an eagle and a serpent, and others wear Thracian fur hats or broad-rimmed sun hats. Fourteen of the riders are already mounted, and the twenty-three horses have twenty-three different manes—including one mane that has been left long and totally uncropped. Of course I could go on and on, describing the infinite detail and the endless variety that is carved around the rim of the inner colonnade.

PHILEBUS: True, Socrates. Each time I go to the Temple, I see something different in that frieze.

SOCRATES: *That,* Philebus, is complexity. In fact, it is incondensable complexity.

PHILEBUS: Ah, incondensable complexity.

SOCRATES: And no scrap of parchment, no modest wax tablet, could have inscribed upon it a full description of the great frieze of the Parthenon. The instructions for recreating the Parthenon will always be extensive. In a sense, the instructions must be as large as the original—for, no abbreviations or summaries could be employed. The great frieze cannot be condensed.

PHILEBUS: Yes, this is incondensable complexity.

SOCRATES: Now, discovering the natural predecessors of a very complex thing will teach us about its origins—

PHILEBUS: Its beginnings, the necessary instructions—

SOCRATES: Yes—the origins of the complex thing. But discovering the beginnings will never give us smaller things to carry around. Complex things require extensive rolls of papyri.

PROTARCHUS: If you are correct (and I am not certain that you are, Socrates), then you nonetheless support my position. Stick to universals, I say. Do not mess with the confusing "ifs," with the bewildering "sometimeses," and with the befogging "maybes" of this world.

SOCRATES: Look only at the perfect?

PROTARCHUS: Yes.

SOCRATES: Attend only to the pure?

PROTARCHUS: Correct.

SOCRATES: Study only the absolute?

PROTARCHUS: Exactly.

SOCRATES: Consider only the simple?

PROTARCHUS: Precisely.

SOCRATES: Think only of the divine?

PROTARCHUS: Absolutely.

SOCRATES: Ah, Protarchus, I would gladly see only the simple divinities.

PROTARCHUS: You would?

SOCRATES: Yes I would, but I cannot sit still.

PROTARCHUS: Oh? And how does that relate to the universal absolutes?

SOCRATES: When I walk, the dust and the underbrush of our earth get caught in my toes. When I lie down, all manner of twigs entwine my fingers. The mortal complexities are unavoidable.

Besides, Protarchus, for the universal truths, we can always turn to the gods. But for the complex and mortal truths, we must turn to ourselves. Originally, you had asked about the important goals in life. If we did not need to wrestle and to create mortal understandings on our own, then why should we bother with this mortal life at all? For, after death, as the Ancient Proteus foretold to Odysseus:

> You'll travel to the Elysian plain
> And live with fair-haired gods again
> Until our mortal cities wane.
>
> There, your days are dreams of ease,
> At the world's edge, where Hesperides
> Shepherd golden apple trees.

           September 16: PHILEBUS

Snows and frost are never known,
Warm breezes play, flowers lightly blown;
No torrents of rain will drench your home.

Only the gentlest touch upon your door
Of western winds, from far offshore,
To hint of your mortal life outwore.

September 16: PROTARCHUS
(Part II)

PROTARCHUS: Simple versus complex? By reiterating this dichotomy, Socrates, you are once again glorifying your favorite god. But the real issue is pleasure versus reason.

If we were not here to keep you on the correct path, you would meander forever. You never would get anywhere, you never would find a firm resting place.

SOCRATES: I do tend to follow side paths wherever they lead—

PROTARCHUS: Yes you do.

SOCRATES: And I am always amazed that these tributaries lead to the innately complex nature of our world.

PROTARCHUS: Well, your digressions certainly generate complex discussions: many of your ornate arguments seem unnecessarily complex, Socrates.

SOCRATES: Why, this is just as it is in the real world, Protarchus! Many of Nature's ornaments are also unnecessarily complex.

PROTARCHUS: Socrates, that is your old heresy speaking. How can you say that anything in the world is "unnecessary"? Would you claim that the gods work without divine purpose? Take care, Socrates—as Apollo warned Diomedes, the brave prince of Argos:

> It is not your fate
> To understand the gods;
> Do not speculate
> On divine designs—
> Immortals live at odds
> From you, whose life declines.

But, Socrates, that is another issue; we are not here to judge your religious views. We are simply trying to decide whether pleasure or reason is the better goal in life.

SOCRATES: Very well—then let us decide.

PROTARCHUS: Fine. Now, Socrates, do you enjoy good reasoning?

SOCRATES: I do.

PROTARCHUS: Does good reasoning give you pleasure?

SOCRATES: Yes.

PROTARCHUS: Then I rest my case. Pleasure is the ultimate goal of reasoning—and pleasure is certainly the ultimate goal of pleasure. Therefore, pleasure is the ultimate goal of man.

SOCRATES: Do you agree, Philebus?

PHILEBUS: Yes. Protarchus has set out the argument in plain logic.

SOCRATES: What plain logic is that?

PHILEBUS: It is the standard form of argument, Socrates—it is in the form of:

> All men are mortal.
> Socrates is a man.
> Therefore, Socrates is mortal.

SOCRATES: Did Protarchus's argument fit that form?

PHILEBUS: Of course. Protarchus, you said it better than I. Would you repeat it for Socrates?

PROTARCHUS: Gladly. Now let me see—to fit the form that you set out, Philebus, I suppose that the argument would be:

> All pleasures give enjoyment.
> Reasoning gives enjoyment.
> Therefore, reasoning is a pleasure.

SOCRATES: I see. This outline is so clean that it shows your reasoning quite clearly.

PROTARCHUS: Good.

SOCRATES: But at my age, Protarchus, even clear statements are slow to sink in. Let me be certain that I understand exactly what you are saying.

PROTARCHUS: Fine.

SOCRATES: You began with: "All pleasures give enjoyment." Does this mean that every single pleasure gives the feeling of enjoyment?

PROTARCHUS: Yes.

SOCRATES: Are there other things that give enjoyment?

PROTARCHUS: Other than pleasures? No. Pleasure is synonymous with enjoyment, and enjoyment is identical to pleasure.

SOCRATES: Then why distinguish the two ideas, pleasure and enjoyment?

PROTARCHUS: I did not invent language, old man. We have inherited these two words; it happens that they mean one and the same thing.

SOCRATES: Then there is no practical reason to use two terms.

PROTARCHUS: I suppose not.

PHILEBUS: Just a moment, Protarchus. There are many differences between pleasure and enjoyment.

PROTARCHUS: What differences?

PHILEBUS: "Pleasure" describes a thing; whereas "enjoyment" describes a feeling. For instance, a hot bath is a pleasure; whereas warm contentment is an enjoyment.

PROTARCHUS: Ah yes, very good, Philebus. I spoke too quickly, Socrates: pleasures do differ from enjoyments.

SOCRATES: So, how would you amend your statement that pleasure is synonymous with enjoyment?

PROTARCHUS: A more accurate statement would be: pleasures are inseparably tied to enjoyment, and enjoyments are inseparably linked to pleasure.

SOCRATES: Is this what you meant by: "All pleasures give enjoyment"?

PROTARCHUS: Exactly.

SOCRATES: If you have a pleasure, then you always have an enjoyment?

PROTARCHUS: Yes yes, Socrates—I think that our audience may be falling asleep. Can we get on with this discussion?

SOCRATES: I cannot leave this point yet, Protarchus, because I am a bit confused.

PROTARCHUS: Socrates, either old age is muddling your thinking or you are getting sleepy yourself.

SOCRATES: If I am getting sleepy, Protarchus, then undoubtedly it is because I keep thinking of warm baths.

PROTARCHUS: Warm baths?

SOCRATES: Yes—it is Philebus's example of warm baths. Do you agree that a warm bath is a pleasure?

PROTARCHUS: Certainly.

SOCRATES: And you have told me that pleasures cannot be separated from enjoyments?

PROTARCHUS: Yes.

SOCRATES: Protarchus, let me tell you about last week.

PROTARCHUS: Last week? Socrates, I have enough trouble keeping you on today's discussion; by adding last week's discussions, we will be hopelessly asea.

SOCRATES: It is good that you mention water, Protarchus, because it is not last week's discussions that I wish to review, it is last week's bath.

PROTARCHUS: Socrates, just make your point.

SOCRATES: Very well, Protarchus.

Last week my wife, Xanthippe, had the servants heat a tub of water, and then they poured me a warm bath. Actually I should be more accurate—you may have met Xanthippe, and so you will understand that the bath was not intended for me initially: it was for her, but she had gotten distracted. You see, Xanthippe became a little irritated, breakfast was prolonged, some dishes were broken, and a few cross words were said.

Anyways, one thing led to another, and the bath was forgotten. One of the servants thought it a shame to waste the bath; quietly she told me that I could probably slip in and enjoy the water unnoticed. Unfortunately by the time that I climbed into the bath, the water was cold. Ah well, at least it woke me up.

PROTARCHUS: Interesting, Socrates.

SOCRATES: I think so, Protarchus, because it puts me in mind of a question. Early in the morning there was a pleasure, a warm bath. Was there not?

PROTARCHUS: Yes.

SOCRATES: But somehow the Fates did not let it lead to an enjoyment. By the time that I sat in the water, the bath was cold. Now how can this be? Here was a pleasure that was clearly separated from any enjoyment.

PROTARCHUS: Well it should have led to an enjoyment.

SOCRATES: But it did not.

PROTARCHUS: Socrates, although it was an unrealized potential, the bath still *could* have led to an enjoyment.

SOCRATES: "Potential"? Hmm, this is a new addition. Did you not tell me that pleasures are inseparably linked to enjoyments? Yet you now say that pleasures only have the *potential* to be linked to enjoyments.

PROTARCHUS: Well, if you wish to be very precise, Socrates, then I suppose that is right.

SOCRATES: Yes let us be precise, Protrachus. In this precise light, how would you revise your original statement: "All pleasures give enjoyment"?

PROTARCHUS: We have already made that improvement,

Socrates. We now agree that the statement should be: "All pleasures have the potential to give enjoyment."

SOCRATES: I see. But I am still not satisfied, Protarchus.

PROTARCHUS: That does not surprise me, Socrates: you walk around in a vague mist of dissatisfaction.

SOCRATES: This is no vaguery—I am dissatisfied by a very specific word.

PROTARCHUS: What word is that?

SOCRATES: It is the word "potential." It leaves me uncomfortable because it is so irresolute.

PROTARCHUS: I am sorry, Socrates, but we need words that express irresolution as well as words that express resolution.

SOCRATES: Perhaps we need them for colorful speech, Protarchus, but they are a problem in precise logic. "Potential" is "maybe," it is "perhaps" and "if the mood suits," and these concepts are capricious. At this point I would like to remove "potential" and its capricious implications from your statement. Specifically, I would like to know firmly that all pleasures do (or do not) lead to enjoyment.

PROTARCHUS: But, Socrates, it was you who insisted that we must introduce "potential": sometimes pleasures lead to enjoyment, and sometimes they do not.

SOCRATES: True. "Potential" encodes "sometimes," and by using "potential" we made the statement more accurate. Now I would like to make the statement not only accurate, I would like it also to be precise. I want to take a farther step and say firmly *when* that "sometimes" occurs. Can we not improve on: "All pleasures sometimes lead to enjoyment"? I would like a declaration that says: "All pleasures lead to enjoyment when . . ." Can you give me such a statement?

PROTARCHUS: Well, all pleasures lead to enjoyment when they are fulfilled.

SOCRATES: Fulfilled?

PROTARCHUS: Fulfilled—when they are played out through a person.

SOCRATES: Ah, this is progress. "All pleasures lead to enjoyment when they are played out through a person." Would you agree, Philebus?

PHILEBUS: Definitely—and now the logic is:

> All pleasures lead to enjoyment when played out through people.
> Reasoning gives enjoyment.
> Therefore, reasoning is a pleasure.

SOCRATES: Very well, Philebus. But I am still not satisfied.

PROTARCHUS: Of course, Socrates, that would be too much to expect.

PHILEBUS: What is the difficulty, Socrates?

PROTARCHUS: We have already polished the first statement, Philebus, so he must be unhappy with the second statement: "Reasoning gives pleasure."

SOCRATES: Yes, that statement bothers me.

PROTARCHUS: Then you have no one to blame but yourself. Initially, we got that statement from you.

Let me remind you of our earlier conversation, Socrates: I asked whether you enjoy good reasoning, and you said that good reasoning gives you pleasure. Do you remember?

SOCRATES: Yes. Undoubtedly, I have no right to complain—but I cannot help being reminded of last week.

PROTARCHUS: Last week, again? It seems to have been an historic week for you, Socrates.

SOCRATES: No more historic than all other weeks.

PROTARCHUS: What are you reminded of this time?

SOCRATES: It was a discussion that I had with Eryximachus. He—

PHILEBUS: Eryximachus the physician?

SOCRATES: Yes, Philebus. Eryximachus was working on a

difficult case, and he was talking aloud to me. (Sometimes he uses me as a test of his medical inferences.)

"Socrates," he began, "I saw a small boy who worries me very much. His mother first brought him to me last year, because he was too thin. I found him pale; his skin sagged and he looked shrunken. I began to suspect the worst. At that time, I recommended a diet of goat's milk, and I told his mother to set him quietly in the sun whenever possible."

"Unfortunately," continued Eryximachus, "the child remained weak; so his mother returned after a few months. This time, I was forced to ask three disturbing questions:

> Is the boy always thirsty?
> Is he always hungry?
> Does he urinate uncommonly large amounts of water?

Her answer to each question was 'yes.' 'And he has no pain?' 'Correct,' she answered, 'there is no problem with pain—nothing special is hurting him.'"

Eryximachus hesitated a moment; then he went on: "At that point, the young mother seemed relieved. I had inferred the exact symptoms: she assumed that I must know what is wrong and thus that I could offer a cure.

"Well, Socrates, I knew what was wrong—but there is no cure. To be certain of my inferences, I tasted his urine. It was sweet, and there was no question that my reasoning was correct. This boy has the progressive wasting disease that passes more and more water, and he will die slowly."

"Is there nothing to do for him?" I asked.

"Some physicians recommend bleeding the patient; others claim that it is helpful to eat absolutely no sweet foods. But I myself do not think that any of these things make much difference," said Eryximachus. "It is very sad. Soon he will tire more often, his skin will become itchy, he will get sores, and then the end is slow but inevitable."

PHILEBUS: That is a sad case.

SOCRATES: Clearly it pained Eryximachus. Nonetheless, his reasoning was methodical and clean and accurate.

PHILEBUS: And this is why you relate the story?

SOCRATES: Well, would you agree that Eryximachus argued thoughtfully and carefully? Was his reasoning precise and methodical?

PHILEBUS: It was.

SOCRATES: As usual, Eryximachus played out a cogent logical argument. But here, reasoning led to no enjoyment; it led only to distress—distress to the mother and distress to Eryximachus. Unfortunately, reasoning—even good reasoning—does not always give enjoyment.

PROTARCHUS: All right, Socrates—I suppose that reasoning does not *always* lead to enjoyment. But it does sometimes.

SOCRATES: Oh? Then would your standard logic statements now be:

> All pleasures lead to enjoyment when played out through people.
> Some reasoning gives enjoyment.
> Therefore, reasoning is a pleasure.

PROTARCHUS: Yes, so it seems.

SOCRATES: But now, my young friend, the logic is not accurate.

PROTARCHUS: Where is the problem?

SOCRATES: We must amend the conclusion—the accurate logic is:

> All pleasures lead to enjoyment when played out through people.
> Some reasoning gives enjoyment.
> Therefore, *some* reasoning is a pleasure.

PROTARCHUS: All right—but it is a small difference.

SOCRATES: It is a large difference to me, Protarchus.

PROTARCHUS: Why?

SOCRATES: Let me review: You claimed that pleasure is the ultimate goal, did you not?

PROTARCHUS: Correct.

SOCRATES: I contended that thoughtful reasoning is the most worthwhile goal?

PROTARCHUS: Yes, you did.

SOCRATES: Next, you pointed out that reasoning is a pleasure for me, and so pleasure must also be *my* ultimate goal. Was this not your argument?

PROTARCHUS: Yes.

SOCRATES: Should one always strive to fulfill man's ultimate goal?

PROTARCHUS: He certainly should.

SOCRATES: Regardless of the outcome?

PROTARCHUS: Yes yes, Socrates—regardless of the outcome. Now get to the point.

SOCRATES: Very well, Protarchus. I am like you: I too believe that one should do one's best boldly to achieve the ultimate goal in life.

PROTARCHUS: Is that your point?

SOCRATES: Yes, it is.

PROTARCHUS: How does this relate to your unnatural distinction between pleasure and reason?

SOCRATES: Unnatural? I think that the distinction is natural and also that it is very important.

PROTARCHUS: Socrates, you are talking all around the issue—just say directly what is on your mind.

SOCRATES: We have just confirmed that reasoning does not always lead to enjoyment. Now, would you agree that we should *always* do the heroic? Should we always walk resolutely and unwaveringly toward our ideals?

PROTARCHUS: Yes.

SOCRATES: For me to do this, I must always question, and I must follow the questioning wherever it leads.

PROTARCHUS: So you have said many times.

SOCRATES: I find that this questioning can be a pleasure, but sometimes it is painful. Questioning is my form of reasoning. My reasoning does not always lead to pleasure; nonetheless reason I must, in all weathers. No matter how heroic my effort, enjoyment cannot be guaranteed—but, Protarchus, good reasoning is always possible.

This is why the distinction between reasoning and pleasure is important. To stop short and to accept pleasure as the ultimate end can be a diversion, and it is definitely a weakness. The weak man avoids painful reasoning, and the weak man dies with only a shallow happiness.

PROTARCHUS: Socrates, you have slid from Reasoning to Death, and you have equated weak men with those who honestly seek pleasure. Colorful rhetoric is once again obscuring your logic, old friend. Let me help you retrace your steps.

SOCRATES: All right.

PROTARCHUS: We begin with pleasure and with reasoning. Now, do you wish to distinguish them?

SOCRATES: Yes.

PHILEBUS: Protarchus, we do not have to go over this again. We can accept Socrates's points: reasoning is not always a pleasure, and it is useful to separate the two things, reasoning and pleasure.

PROTARCHUS: Very well, Philebus. Now, Socrates, one of these two things is the ultimate goal of man. Are we together so far?

SOCRATES: I do not know, Protarchus?

PROTARCHUS: What?! I am just laying the foundations. Surely you agree that either a thing is in one state or the thing is not in that state. Is this not the most elemental principle of logic?

SOCRATES: I am not certain that it is the most elemental

principle. However, I would agree that a pure single thing is either in one state or it is not in that state.

PROTARCHUS: Then we agree that the ultimate goal of man is either pleasure or reasoning?

SOCRATES: I do not know.

PROTARCHUS: Now what is the problem, Socrates?

SOCRATES: It is this, Protarchus: man is not a pure single thing. When you say "man" you really mean "men," and men are a diverse and varied lot. In fact, men are as manifold as anything in nature. Humankind is incondensably complex. Remember how the old poet said that men

> Are each unique—through people rife
> Diversity is brought to life.

PROTARCHUS: So, Socrates?

SOCRATES: So, Protarchus, I suspect there may be many ultimate goals for men. Perhaps there is a different goal for each different man.

PROTARCHUS: But, Socrates, originally you said that reasoning was the ultimate goal. Were you telling us a lie?

SOCRATES: Yes, Protarchus, I am afraid that I am guilty—I did overstate my position. Reasoning is the ultimate goal for Socrates. Reasoning could be the ultimate goal for many other men. However, reasoning is not the only candidate from which men can choose when they decide how best to live their lives.

PROTARCHUS: Oh? Then would you allow that pleasure is also a legitimate ultimate goal?

SOCRATES: Not for me, Protarchus—but I do concede that it may be the appropriate goal for some men.

PROTARCHUS: Well, well, Socrates, this is a reversal. Finally you admit that pleasure can be the ultimate goal in life.

SOCRATES: I think that is possible, for some men.

PHILEBUS: Socrates, this discussion has taken a surprising

turn. Do you propose that there may be no one universal goal for men?

SOCRATES: That is not exactly my position, Philebus. Actually, I am not certain whether there are one or many ultimate goals for men.

PHILEBUS: You are not certain?

SOCRATES: No.

PHILEBUS: Well how are you going to decide?

SOCRATES: I do not think that it is for me to decide.

PHILEBUS: Socrates! Have I heard you correctly? We are philosophers: a philosopher cannot have walls. He cannot admit boundaries; he cannot allow impediments to his access to knowledge. Many times you have said: "Be bold. Follow your reasoning wherever it leads!" How can you now acquiesce so timidly and so quietly? Do you really believe that we should not inquire into whether there is only one ultimate goal for man?

PROTARCHUS: Socrates, suddenly you are wearing out in your old age. After a lifetime of fighting with us, you have lost your spirit of battle.

SOCRATES: Let me show you something, Protarchus.

Acumenus, I see that you have a waxed table. Would you etch a few words on it, in your tiniest writing?

ACUMENUS: Certainly, Socrates . . . There—I have written a miniature sentence.

SOCRATES: Good. Would you pass it to Protarchus . . . Now, Protarchus, can you read that sentence?

PROTARCHUS: Yes (although it is barely visible), it says—

SOCRATES: Wait just a moment, Protarchus. First, pass the tablet to me . . . Thank you. Hmm, even when I hold it at arm's length, I cannot make out the words.

PHILEBUS: Not at all?

SOCRATES: Well the first word begins with an "S." Perhaps it is "Socrates." But I cannot decipher the remainder.

PROTARCHUS: It says: "Socrates is a man; therefore, Socrates is mortal."

SOCRATES: Is that correct, Acumenus?

ACUMENUS: Yes.

SOCRATES: Now, Protarchus, look at that temple over there.

PROTARCHUS: The Temple of Dionysos?

SOCRATES: Yes. Can you read the inscription along the top?

PROTARCHUS: Not from this distance—however, I think that I can make out the name "Dionysos."

SOCRATES: I too, Protarchus—even from here, I can read the word "Dionysos." In my old age, I can still see things well when I look far and into the distance, but I can no longer discern all the fine details of things that are close by.

This is what happens in old age: we can attend to fewer things in the world. In particular, it is the immediate, petty, and close intricacies that lose their definition, that become fuzzy along the edges. In contrast, the broad, far, and wide-ranging vistas remain clear. Eventually, Protarchus, these large horizons come to dominate our aging vision, because we are no longer distracted by the petty multitudes that crowd up close against us.

You ask whether I have lost my fighting spirit. I never had a fighting spirit, I have only had a strong resolve to make sense of my world. The strength of this resolve has not diminished—it is stronger and purer. But I have become far-sighted in my old age. Now my drive to understand is increasingly concentrated on things that I see at a distance.

PROTARCHUS: So, Socrates, your presbyopic far-sightedness makes you unwilling to decide whether there is a unique ultimate goal for man?

SOCRATES: Not "unwilling," Protarchus—"unable." The uniqueness of the ultimate life goals is a rather small point, and I cannot see it very distinctly; other aspects of the problem have much clearer outlines. This is a natural consequence of old age.

PROTARCHUS: Oh? And what aspects of these problems *can* an old man see clearly?

SOCRATES: An old man can see old man aspects.

PROTARCHUS: "Old man aspects"?

PHILEBUS: "Old man aspects," Socrates?

SOCRATES: Yes. I no longer have much of a future, so I do not look at future goals. My future is so short, so small, and so close to me that I cannot see it well. But the past, gentlemen—now *that* extends out far behind me, and with my long-range vision I can see it quite well. The future is "young man aspects"; whereas the past is "old man aspects."

PROTARCHUS: Of course, Socrates—clearly each of us is concerned with different things at different stages in his life. But how does this relate to the problem of pleasure versus reasoning? What does it mean for the problem of choosing ultimate goals?

SOCRATES: Protarchus, what does this really mean: "ultimate goals"?

PROTARCHUS: Ultimate goals are what we wish to achieve.

SOCRATES: Why do we wish to achieve them?

PROTARCHUS: Why? I suppose it is so that when we achieve them we have become satisfied.

SOCRATES: And we are not satisfied until we have actually achieved our goal?

PROTARCHUS: Correct.

SOCRATES: Can you know in advance what will satisfy you in the future?

PROTARCHUS: Often you can. For instance, I think that a good meal will satisfy me this evening.

SOCRATES: You say: "I think." Does this mean that you are not absolutely certain?

PROTARCHUS: I am not *absolutely* certain. But really, I have little doubt, Socrates.

SOCRATES: What if you wanted to be absolutely certain?

PROTARCHUS: Then I would have to wait until this evening—

the closer that I came to the evening, the more certain I would become that a good meal would satisfy me.

SOCRATES: What if you found that a good meal did not satisfy you?

PROTARCHUS: Obviously I would not have picked the best possible goal: a good meal would not have been what I really needed.

SOCRATES: So, a goal must always be satisfying at the time that it is achieved?

PROTARCHUS: That would seem to be the elemental requirement.

SOCRATES: Would you say that the best time to judge a goal is near to its achievement, perhaps even after it has been achieved?

PROTARCHUS: Of course.

SOCRATES: Now, Protarchus, you and I have been speaking of *ultimate* goals.

PROTARCHUS: True.

SOCRATES: When will such goals have been achieved?

PROTARCHUS: Well we continually attempt to achieve them, but certainly they should be achieved by the end of one's life.

SOCRATES: Do you mean that the ultimate life goals will have been achieved in old age?

PROTARCHUS: I would say that they may have been achieved earlier—but then again they may not.

SOCRATES: So, when is the best time to judge ultimate goals?

PROTARCHUS: With our rule that goals should be judged near to their achievement, we had best judge the ultimate life goals in old age.

SOCRATES: Would you say that evaluating ultimate goals has now become an old man's problem, to be seen with old man's eyes and to be judged with an old man's mind?

PROTARCHUS: Apparently so, Socrates.

SOCRATES: Fortunately, we have here an old man with whom to discuss this problem.

PROTARCHUS: Yes we do. So, what do you say, old man?

PHILEBUS: With your old man's voice.

SOCRATES: With my old man's voice, I say this: ''Backwards.''

PROTARCHUS: Backwards?

SOCRATES: Yes—backwards. With my old man's eyes, I look backwards.

Now, some of the things that I see in retrospect have been satisfying. Other things have not been satisfying. I find that reasoning has always been satisfying—it has not always been a pleasure, but it has always satisfied.

PROTARCHUS: Just reasoning, Socrates?

SOCRATES: Well, it is reasoning within my world picture, Protarchus. You see, by continual questioning, I have created an orderly picture of the world. Now do not mistake me here: although it is orderly, my world picture is complex and it is tangled. In places, this vision is overwhelmingly intricate, detailed, and ornate. But with methodical reasoning I can usually find my way around within the picture, and this is quite satisfying. Other supposed pleasures remain with me only as vague, dim, and weak memories. But my reasoning? It is always with me and it is always a firm comfort. So when I say: ''Reasoning is my ultimate goal.'' It is simply because I look backwards with my old man's eyes. And looking behind me I see that good reasoning has always made me content.

September 21: PLATO

SOCRATES: Plato, I am tired of listening to these men argue; let us walk a little and stretch our legs.

PLATO: Very well, Socrates—but I thought that you enjoyed listening to philosophical combat.

SOCRATES: This was not artful combat—it was crude bludgeoning. But, Plato, I fear that Socrates the philosopher does not enjoy listening to philosophy.

PLATO: Socrates does not enjoy philosophy? Then he has fooled a great many Athenians.

SOCRATES: Socrates the philosopher enjoys philosophizing— it is listening to other philosophers that he does not like.

PLATO: Oh? Then Socrates must be like Timros.

SOCRATES: Who is Timros?

PLATO: You know him, Socrates: he is the old man who always sits on the stone bench by the Temple of Pan.

SOCRATES: Do you mean the toothless old man who is always smiling?

PLATO: Yes, that is Timros.

SOCRATES: And how is he like Socrates?

PLATO: Timros is always smiling. But ask him how he feels, and he replies: "Terrible." If you wish him a good day, then he says simply: "Bah." On the outside he looks as if he were completely content and as if he were enjoying life. However, on the inside he must be discontent and unhappy.

SOCRATES: Do you think that this is like Socrates?

PLATO: Well, you have been known to smile and to nod and

even to be drawn irresistibly into speech at public arguments, arguments where you were in the audience. Yet you now claim to dislike these philosophical discussions. Are you destined to be a Timros, when you grow old?

SOCRATES: Plato, my friend, I am old already.

PLATO: Then are you a Timros?

SOCRATES: I would imagine that I am like both Timroses.

PLATO: *Both* Timroses?

SOCRATES: Plato, you do not imagine that it is one and the same person who is both smiling and grumpy all at once, do you?

PLATO: He looks to be one and the same man to me.

SOCRATES: He does?

PLATO: Yes, he certainly does.

SOCRATES: Then let me ask you a question, Plato: Do you remember our walk to Peiraeus last summer?

PLATO: Of course, Socrates—we walked the Long Walls. It was a golden morning.

SOCRATES: The late morning sun baked the road.

PLATO: Then the afternoon heat shimmered, like an ocean—

SOCRATES: With wave upon wave of dry heat.

PLATO: It is those waves, those tides of heat, that I remember most clearly.

SOCRATES: When you looked off down the road—squinting at the horizon—it was as if you were about to slip into an endless shining pool of water.

PLATO: Exactly.

SOCRATES: But it was not water—it was the glow of the sun, through which we waded.

PLATO: True.

SOCRATES: The shimmering pools were water to the eye, and they were sunshine to the touch?

PLATO: Yes, that they were.

SOCRATES: So, one and the same thing was at once two and different things?

PLATO: You mean like Timros?

SOCRATES: Yes, like the two Timroses.

PLATO: All right, like the two Timroses—and you say that you are like them? You are two Socrateses, one who smiles at philosophy and one who frowns at philosophy? Why is that?

SOCRATES: Tell me, Plato: For whom does the painter paint?

PLATO: Painters? I thought that we were talking about philosophers.

SOCRATES: Think of them as philosophical painters. Now what do you say, young man? For whom does the painter paint?

PLATO: He paints for all men.

SOCRATES: For *all* men?

PLATO: Yes, for all men.

SOCRATES: For me, for instance?

PLATO: Yes.

SOCRATES: For you also?

PLATO: Yes.

SOCRATES: For Paeroles?

PLATO: The blind singer?

SOCRATES: Yes.

PLATO: Painting can only be appreciated by the sighted.

SOCRATES: Then how about Lasicus?

PLATO: The old man who goes about the marketplace nibbling bits of pottery? No, painters do not paint for Lasicus: he can hardly attend to anything at all.

SOCRATES: How about Antisthenes' son?

PLATO: Antisthenes' boy is less than two years old, Socrates.

SOCRATES: Would you say that a painter like Zeuxis or Polygnotus paints for Antisthenes' son?

PLATO: Certainly not.

SOCRATES: So, painters do not paint for all men?

PLATO: Antisthenes' son is hardly a man.

SOCRATES: True—but the question remains: Do painters paint for all men?

PLATO: No, not for *all* men.

SOCRATES: Then how would you define those men for whom painters paint?

PLATO: I would say that painters paint for all mature men who can appreciate the visual arts.

SOCRATES: Would you say that painters paint for men who have the ability to see and who have the ability to enjoy what they see?

PLATO: Exactly.

SOCRATES: Now, Plato, suppose that we meet an eccentric man. This strange character closes his eyes every time that he is in the presence of a painting. Is he included in the class of men for whom painters paint? Does this class of men also include men who can see and who have the ability to enjoy what they see but who, for some inexplicable reason, do not want to see these things?

PLATO: No. One must also want to see paintings in order to be a painting appreciator.

SOCRATES: All right. Now does this class of men—the painting appreciators—include poets?

PLATO: Certainly. (Of course I mean *sighted* poets.)

SOCRATES: Does your class of men for whom painters paint include philosophers?

PLATO: It certainly does: you will recall that we began with a philosophical painter.

SOCRATES: And does it include painters themselves?

PLATO: Most definitely.

SOCRATES: In their capacity as men who appreciate the visual arts?

PLATO: Of course.

SOCRATES: How about painters in their capacity as painters?

PLATO: Absolutely—here more than in any other way, because painters are men for whom other painters paint.

SOCRATES: Let us be very clear about this, Plato: Exactly what is a painter?

PLATO: Do you want a definition, Socrates?

SOCRATES: Yes please.

PLATO: A painter is a man who creates visual images on flat surfaces, using pigments and a brush.

SOCRATES: I see. Would you distinguish between painters and copyists?

PLATO: What do you mean by a "copyist"?

SOCRATES: I mean a person whose goal is to make an exact reproduction of something.

PLATO: Then, no—I do not think that I see a fundamental difference between a painter and a copyist.

SOCRATES: I would have guessed that they differ.

PLATO: I assume that you are thinking this way, old man. A painter is someone who invents something completely original. On the other hand, a copyist only recreates something that another man (or perhaps even a god) has made originally. Am I correct?

SOCRATES: Yes, that was my idea.

PLATO: Socrates, it seems to me that any fabricator—be he painter, sculptor, poet, or copyist—recreates a thing that is at once original and also a copy.

SOCRATES: Artworks are always originals *and* copies at the same time?

PLATO: Yes. Nothing is created completely ex nihilo; all things are compiled from materials at hand, and all creations are at least partial copies of extant entities. Thus, in a sense, all our mortal creations can be considered to be variants, collages, pasticcios, and potpourris of the pure ideal forms of which we dream and to which we aspire.

SOCRATES: Then you would say that all artists are dependent on various aspects of the outside world, so all artists are in part copyists.

PLATO: Precisely—as copyists, artists require a world beyond their inner imaginations.

SOCRATES: All right, I see why you could claim that all artworks are copies. Now, tell me why you maintain that all artworks (even those of copyists) are also originals.

PLATO: Artworks are creations of men. Let me ask you, Socrates: Can the artwork be separated from the man?

SOCRATES: Certainly—the wonderful statue of Athena by Phidias still sits alone in our Temple, does it not?

PLATO: It does.

SOCRATES: Phidias is now dead; his mortal remains are buried in Delphi, and his shade is in Elysium.

PLATO: True.

SOCRATES: Then the artwork is separated from the artist.

PLATO: It is separated *physically*. But, Socrates, there is a more important sense in which the artwork is still integrally tied to the artist: Can we pretend that the statue was made by Polyclitus of Argos?

SOCRATES: No.

PLATO: Would the same statue of Athena have been made if Phidias had never lived?

SOCRATES: No.

PLATO: Would you agree that this statue of Athena has special features and certain touches that are characteristic of all of Phidias's work? In fact, are these special characteristics unique to the sculptures of Phidias?

SOCRATES: Yes.

PLATO: Then that is what I mean when I say that the artwork cannot be separated from the man.

SOCRATES: I see.

PLATO: Moreover, Socrates, what does the word "original" actually mean?

SOCRATES: "Original"? In the context of artwork, it means "specially created" and "peculiar to the artist."

PLATO: Exactly. Therefore, would you agree that an original artwork is one that cannot be separated from the artist?

SOCRATES: Yes, Plato, I like that definition. So, the *original* aspects of an artwork stem from the inner, unique imagination of the artist; whereas the *copied* aspects stem from other parts of the world.

PLATO: Correct. That is why I say that artworks are original at the same time as they are also copies.

SOCRATES: All right. Now, Plato, before we took this digression, I had been asking you the question: For whom do painters paint? And you told me that painters paint for all men who appreciate painting.

PLATO: True.

SOCRATES: Then I asked whether the painting appreciators include painters themselves, and you answered: "Yes."

PLATO: I did.

SOCRATES: Now, we have decided that painters (like all artists) make works that are at once originals and also copies.

PLATO: Yes.

SOCRATES: For the copied aspects of the artwork, the artist depends on the world about him. On the other hand for the original aspects, the artist looks to his inner imagination.

PLATO: Yes. For the copied aspects, the artist has opened wide his eyes; for the original aspects, he has closed them tightly.

SOCRATES: Could we say that an artist is two men in one? Is the artist both a sighted man and a blind man?

PLATO: We could use that metaphor.

SOCRATES: Do painters paint for both men?

PLATO: What do you mean?

SOCRATES: I mean this. Earlier, we agreed that painters paint for sighted men and not for blind men. Does this dichotomy also extend to our metaphor? Do painters paint for the sighted man within the artist and not for the blind man within the artist?

PLATO: I am not certain that I follow you, Socrates.

SOCRATES: The sighted aspect of the artist is the copyist: he is a man who looks to the world in order to learn what to paint or to sculpt or to write. On the other hand, the blind aspect of the artist is the originator: he closes his eyes to the world, and he looks into his innermost, personal, and unique imagination in order to learn what to create.

As copyist, the artist is a willing student of other painters. However, what of the other man within the artist? The blind man is not a student of anyone but himself: for the originator within the artist, an outside painter is of no help.

PLATO: I see what you mean.

SOCRATES: I would go even farther, Plato: picture a trireme, imagine a galley ship rowing smoothly through the seas.

PLATO: All right.

SOCRATES: You are sitting on one of the benches, rowing in an even rhythm. Suddenly, the man in front of you begins to stroke in a different rhythm. He distracts you, and you also begin to row at a new tempo. Now the ship slows down; it wobbles and it bucks in the waves.

PLATO: Yes, it would.

SOCRATES: At first, you were both copyists: your rowing rhythms were coordinated, and they were templeted by the outside world. Suddenly, though, each rowing rhythm became original to the individual man. Your rhythm is your own invention, and your companion's rhythm is also idiosyncratic. And because they interact—because the rhythms are forced to encounter and to attend to each other—each begins to interfere with the other.

PLATO: True.

SOCRATES: Plato, it is the same with all artworks, it is the same with all creations of any type. The original aspects of our creations stem from personal, private, "blind" visions.

PLATO: Yes, the originator is blind.

SOCRATES: Furthermore, the originator *must* be blind. Any outside visions can only dilute and diffuse and confuse; the outside world interferes with the uniquely original aspects of our art.

PLATO: The sighted man within an artist learns from the world, but the blind man within the artist must actively ignore the world?

SOCRATES: Exactly.

PLATO: So, painters only paint for one half of a man—the sighted half?

SOCRATES: I think that is the case.

PLATO: Socrates, I have forgotten why we began this discussion of sighted and blind artists.

SOCRATES: We decided that I am like old Timros, two men in one.

PLATO: Oh yes—you are two philosophers: one Socrates who likes listening to philosophy and one who does not.

SOCRATES: I learn from the world, but at the same time the outside noise distracts my personal rhythm.

PLATO: And these two Socrateses are within the same body— it must be confusing.

SOCRATES: When the gods created man, Plato, they made a complex being; many different people are all jumbled together in one body. So, we do our best. We try to make peace between the warring parties, we try to integrate the many artists tumbling and scrambling about within our souls.

PLATO: Is this why you had to leave today's discussion?

SOCRATES: In part—but then the harangue itself was so pompous that even the sighted philosopher within me was forced to close his eyes. Leotychides is such a difficult man with whom to talk. He blathers on and on, and he refuses to listen at all.

PLATO: Leotychides makes it clear that he is royalty. But you know the rumors, Socrates: instead of being the great grandson of Leotychides—

SOCRATES: The Leotychides who was king of Sparta for twenty years—

PLATO: The Leotychides who captured Aegina and Delos—

SOCRATES: The Leotychides who crushed the Persian army at Mycale and then at Samos.

PLATO: Instead of being a descendant of this royal Leotychides—this Spartan aristocrat—it is rumored that our Leotychides is actually the illegitimate son of Alcibiades.

SOCRATES: Leotychides is the son of Alcibiades? Poor Alcibiades, to be saddled with such a son.

PLATO: Poor Alcibiades? He deserves Leotychides: Alcibiades was a traitor, Socrates.

SOCRATES: You know, Plato, Alcibiades was a beautiful man with a reckless, wild soul. I am certain that his treachery against Athens, his collusion with Sparta—

PLATO: The collusion that caused all our recent Athenian defeats.

SOCRATES: I am certain that this collusion was not some well thought out traitorousness. Alcibiades lived life so fully and with such passionate abandon that he flew headlong into whatever course of action was most dangerous.

PLATO: Alcibiades spent many years walking and talking here in the Agora. But Alcibiades never learned the lessons of his masters, Protagoras or Prodicus, and he never began to comprehend *your* ascetic life. If Leotychides is Alcibiades's son, then he is of ignoble birth indeed.

SOCRATES: I am not certain which paternity is the most

ignoble. Remember, Plato, the original Leotychides—the Spartan king—eventually accepted a bribe from the Persian generals to withdraw from his seige of Samos.

PLATO: True.

SOCRATES: For this misdeed, old Leotychides was brought to trial at Sparta.

PLATO: Then to save his life, he fled to the temple of Athena at Tegea.

SOCRATES: And in his absence, he was sentenced to exile, his house was torn down, his possessions were seized, and his name was condemned.

PLATO: Nonetheless, the family maintained its royal lineage, and eventually his grandson, Archidamus II, ascended the Spartan throne.

SOCRATES: True, my young friend—quite true. What complexities are these political careers of men . . . It is not the same with sticks and stones. Look down here, Plato; I envy the simple brown rocks along our road. It is just as that fine old poet wrote:

> How happy is the little stone
> That rambles in the road alone,
> And doesn't care about careers,
> And exigencies never fears;
> Whose coat of elemental brown
> A passing universe put on;
> And independent as the sun,
> Associates or glows alone,
> Fulfilling absolute decree
> In casual simplicity.

PLATO: A beautiful poem, Socrates. Stones never face political complexity; nonetheless, I have always felt sorry for these little pebbles: to me they seem lonely.

SOCRATES: Why is that?

PLATO: They are cold and smooth. They can never intertwine. They can never share a warm touch, never rub shoulders, never hug. Stones have no sheltering parents, and their children never run to them.

These stones may be simple. But the simple, the absolute, the pure, and, I fear, the divine are too clean and too cold. On the other hand, complexity—thick, messy complexity—complexity is humanness, and *humanness* is warmth.

SOCRATES: Ah Plato, that it is—give me your hand, my young friend, my friend.

September 24: THEAGES

HERMOGENES: The beginning of the *Iliad?* Of course I remember it: "Sing my Muse—make me the biographer of heroes—fill the rhapsode with Achilles's black anger . . ."

THEAGES: Well not exactly, Hermogenes. Actually, it goes:

> O Muse, give me wing as heroes' biographer,
> Help me to sing of Achilles' anger—
> That blackest wrath which set Death's toes
> Onto their path and rained grim woes
> And anguish untold on Agamemnon long ago
> And on Achaeans bold, hurling heros
> From the throng to Hades' doors,
> Sending the strong Achaean warriors
> Fair-haired and tall, grey-eyed and brave,
> To the Final Hall, from Troy's bloody grave.

HERMOGENES: Yes, yes of course, Theages: "Brave Achilles, Pelles's son . . ."—and all that. It is beautiful verse, simply beautiful; you have a fine memory.

THEAGES: Hermogenes, Achilles was *Peleus's* son—and he was Aeacus's grandson.

HERMOGENES: Aeacus? Aeacus of Aegina?

THEAGES: So we are told.

HERMOGENES: Aegina is one of my favorite islands. It is a wonderful place, is it not, Socrates?

SOCRATES: It certainly is, Hermogenes. Do you agree, Theages?

THEAGES: You know, Socrates, as near as Aegina is, I have never been there. My weak constitution allows very little travel.

I just pass my days sitting in the sun and resting. I listen to verse, and I talk with you philosophers, when I am feeling strong.

SOCRATES: Aegina is only a half day's sail from Peiraeus—

THEAGES: Less than 200 stadia?

SOCRATES: Yes.

THEAGES: I am afraid that even a short sail is too tiring for me, Socrates. I have always been frail. When I was little, I could play only for short spells—then I had to sit down or squat, until I could catch my breath. Now I seem to need even more rest. Sometimes my lips and fingernails get dark and bluish. I am a strange character, I fear.

SOCRATES: I have noticed your blue nails, Theages. Nonetheless, this has not kept you from reciting poetry or from wrestling with philosophy; you have a keen mind and a wonderful memory.

THEAGES: Poetry and philosophy are my passion . . . But gentlemen, you were telling me about Aegina.

SOCRATES: Oh yes—I am certain that if you could get there, then you would enjoy it. In spite of its recent political problems, Aegina remains a healthy-climated island with plenty of cotton, grapes, almonds, and figs.

HERMOGENES: Do not forget sponges, Socrates—Aegina is well known for its sponge fishing.

SOCRATES: Yes, Hermogenes, one must not forget the sponges. It is too bad that the fine residents of Aegina were scattered—

HERMOGENES: (In their defeat by Athens, some thirty years ago.)

SOCRATES: Now you have to go to Thyreatis (on the border between Laconia and Argolis) to find most of them. Aeginaians are skilled, and they are efficient. Did you know that Aegina was the first state to coin its own money? Long ago, the Aeginetan scales of coins, weights, and measures became the standards throughout the Greek world.

HERMOGENES: Aeginaians have always been renowned businessmen.

SOCRATES: And they are peace-loving. Their large navies were entirely for commerce: Aegina never founded a single colony.

THEAGES: The Aeginaians are peace-loving? But I thought that the warrior Achilles was their famed model son.

SOCRATES: Achilles was a famed *ex-patriot* son. The true Aeginaian spirit comes down through Achilles's grandfather Aeacus. Aeacus—

THEAGES: Who married Endeis.

SOCRATES: Yes (you remember well, Theages)—Aeacus and Endeis were the parents of Telamon and Peleus—

HERMOGENES: Achilles's father.

SOCRATES: Now, Aeacus himself was the son of Zeus and Aegina—

THEAGES: (The daughter of the river-god Asopus.)

SOCRATES: Exactly, Theages. In fact, that is where the name of the island originated. You see, Aegina had been carried off by Zeus to the island of Oenone.

HERMOGENES: Oenone? I have never heard of that island.

SOCRATES: Oenone is now Aegina. The old name no longer exists: Zeus changed the name of the island to Aegina, in honor of the nymph.

Aeacus roamed the island as a young godling, and when he grew up, he became king of Aegina. As king, good Aeacus repeatedly interceded with his father Zeus to repair all manner of evils that befell his land. For instance, once through prayer he ended a terrible drought—the famed temple of Aeacus at Aegina commemorates Aeacus's month-long fast which convinced Zeus to bring the rains.

HERMOGENES: And how about the the ant story, Socrates?

THEAGES: I know that legend, Hermogenes. A pestilence entirely depopulated the island. In order to re-fill the towns and the farms, Aeacus persuaded Zeus to change all the ants on the island into human beings.

HERMOGENES: This is why the Aeginaians are sometimes called Myrmidones, and it is why the Aeginaians are so industrious. And Aeacus gave rise to all sorts of other colorful legends. It is said that he helped Poseidon to build the great walls of Troy.

THEAGES: I thought that it was Apollo who helped Poseidon.

HERMOGENES: Well he helped too, of course.

THEAGES: But where did the peace-loving tradition come in, Socrates?

SOCRATES: During the half century when Aeacus reigned in Aegina, no war was ever fought. Moreover, Aeacus ruled over the island with such justice and such impartiality and with such an even hand, that after his death he was made a Judge and an arbitor of the lower world.

THEAGES: An arbitor in the Land of the Dead?

SOCRATES: With Minos and his brother Rhadamanthus, Aeacus was given the task of deciding to which House of the Dead each shade would be assigned.

THEAGES: Oh? And how did Aeacus get this job?

SOCRATES: Well to explain this, I had best go back to the beginning. As you recall: Zeus, Poseidon, and Pluto divided their earthly kingdom among themselves, after inheriting it from their father.

HERMOGENES: Kronos.

SOCRATES: Yes—from their father Kronos. Now, in those days if a mortal had led an upstanding, godly, and righteous life, then his shade lived forever on the Isles of the Blessed, in the gentle Elysian Plains. But if he had been wicked, godless, and evil, then he departed to a prison of vengeance and punishment in the underworld of cruel Tartarus.

HERMOGENES: Yes, he did.

SOCRATES: At first, Zeus followed the tradition that had been established by his father, Kronos: living men rendered this eternal judgment on other living men. There was a vital court; god-appointed mortal jurors pronounced sentence at once, on the very day when a man was due to die.

THEAGES: How did the jurors know when someone was destined to die?

SOCRATES: All foreknowledge of a man's destiny was given by Prometheus.

HERMOGENES: It was foretold by Prometheus.

SOCRATES: You will recall, Theages, that Prometheus was given the gift of prescience, and he shared the future with his chosen flock—the great mortals of the time.

THEAGES: I am amazed that Prometheus could then accomplish anything else in his life. People die continually—the daily death roll is long, and its chronicle must have occupied a great deal of time. Prometheus must have spent all day warning the families and the friends of the about-to-be-departed.

SOCRATES: Undoubtedly Prometheus delegated some of the heraldic chores, my friend.

THEAGES: Undoubtedly, Socrates. Nonetheless, just compiling the list of those who will be doomed each day and then distributing the roster—this task must have been quite time-consuming.

SOCRATES: Theages, do you think that I am inventing this story?

THEAGES: I do not know.

SOCRATES: My good Theages, one would think that you doubt the gods.

THEAGES: Ah, Socrates, I should not want to be accused of impiety—please continue your tale.

SOCRATES: Very well.

In this setting, some decisions were rather hasty and often there were disputes. For instance, one man—a certain Kenan—was mistaken for another man named Kenon. Kenan was a priest, and Kenon was a murderer; but poor Kenan was mistakenly cast into Tartarus, while the evil Kenon was given a palace in Elysium.

HERMOGENES: A sad state of affairs indeed.

SOCRATES: Understandably a clamor arose, and Pluto and the stewards from the Elysian Isles of the Blessed and the gaolers from chaotic Tartarus all came together, and they told Zeus that the wrong people were going to each of the final resting places.

Zeus listened thoughtfully. "Well, gentlemen," he said, "I will put a stop to this."

"What we need," said Zeus, "are Judges—and not mortal judges but great and immortal Judges. We need divine Judges."

All the petitioners agreed. However, the young god Pan spoke up. He said—

THEAGES: Pan, Socrates? What was he doing as part of this delegation?

SOCRATES: He was not one of the petitioners: Pan was there in the Olympian court visiting with his father Hermes. Anyways, Pan said—

THEAGES: Just a moment, Socrates. I do not think that I have ever heard of an interchange between Pan and Zeus, and I have never heard any tales of Pan on Mount Olympos.

SOCRATES: Do not be so impatient to grow up, Theages: you are just a young man, and you have not had time to hear all the unusual divine events that have occurred. Pan was not on Olympos often—this was a rare occasion. Perhaps I should remind you of another time that he visited with Zeus?

HERMOGENES: Yes, please do, Socrates.

SOCRATES: Now, as you both remember, Pan was the music teacher of Daphnis, his half-brother.

HERMOGENES: Ah yes.

SOCRATES: Daphnis was a thin, weak young man—not unlike yourself, Theages. He had pale blond hair and thin spidery fingers and pure white skin. He passed most of his days quietly, inventing shepherd's songs in shady glades and sitting amidst cool hummocks, in the backlands of his native Sicily.

HERMOGENES: Sicily.

SOCRATES: One day, a young nymph, Nana—

THEAGES: The daughter of the Sicilian river Sangarios.

SOCRATES: Exactly, Theages. Nana the daughter of Sangarios found Daphnis alone in a woods. Instantly, she fell in love with Daphnis, but he was too shy to speak to her. Now, I am afraid that Nana was rather hot-tempered, and in her anger, she blinded poor Daphnis.

HERMOGENES: She blinded him, Theages.

SOCRATES: Daphnis, sad and deep-hearted, forgave her; he groped about, and he handed her a small white flower, which she put in her hair. Then not long afterwards, young Nana had a son, whom she named Attes.

Daphnis wandered off, and in his blindness, he fell from a precipice. Hermes was Daphnis' father; sad Hermes took Daphnis' thin body, and he set it in the Heavens. There, a great and mighty river springs from the side of a cliff, and it runs down the boulders of the highest mountains and it feeds the deep Ocean's thundering streams.

HERMOGENES: The deep Ocean's thundering streams, Theages.

THEAGES: I see. And how was this connected with Pan's visit to Zeus?

SOCRATES: Pan? Oh yes—well, Nana heard of Daphnis' death, and she knew that it had been her doing. She sat beneath an olive tree, and she cried for two days. Then she killed herself and her child, Attes. It was Pan who found the bodies, in a clover field far inland in Sicily. Pan took the tiny Attes to Zeus, and he begged the great god to revive the infant. Zeus agreed, and he returned the child alive to earth, where Attes was raised by Agdistis

THEAGES: Socrates, is that the same Attis who became the patron god of Phrygia?

SOCRATES: Yes. Attes or Attis or Atys—he was one and the same god.

THEAGES: I think that your version of the story is not exactly as I had originally heard it.

SOCRATES: Nor is it as I had originally heard it, Theages.

THEAGES: Socrates, have you changed the true old legend?

SOCRATES: "True," my young friend? What is the *true* old legend? Legends are things that we discover within ourselves. There are Theages legends, there are Hermogenes legends, and there are Socrates legends. This is a Socrates legend—and now that I am an old man, I see these Socrates legends more clearly than ever.

THEAGES: I am not certain that I understand you, Socrates. But we are on a digression of a digression—originally, you were telling me about Pan and the petitioners of Zeus.

SOCRATES: Let me see . . . Oh yes, Pan spoke up. He said: "Zeus, if I may add a word here—wisely, you have pointed out that mortal judges make for mortal judgements."

"Precisely," replied Zeus, "it is only the immortals who have both suficient time and the endless perspective necessary to decide an endless fate."

"I understand," said Pan, "but I would like to suggest yet another qualification for the arbitors of a mortal's fate."

"Oh—and what is that, my small godling?" asked Zeus.

"I think that the judges of men must have lived as men."

"As men? Why?"

"Good Zeus, I roam the fields and the villages of mortal earth," said Pan. "I see the farmers and the dust and the housewives and the sticks and the children and the dried grasses of all the lands below. There are many hard and cold nights; there are many hot and dry days. No god who lives in Olympian splendor can truly understand a man."

"What!" said Zeus, "Do you think that I, the all-knowing and the all-wise, or that Athena, who actually created man—do you imagine that *we* do not know more than any poor mortal on the earth?"

"You certainly know more, great Zeus,"said Pan, "but I think that you do not feel the same things as men do. For this reason, I suggest that men themselves should be the final judges of the fates of men."

"And how—young god—do you propose to have mortal men make immortal judgements?"

"I would say, great Zeus, that you should choose three of the wisest and the fairest of men. Then give to these men an immortality. Assign them to be the gate-keepers and the arbitors of the final resting places of all mortals," said Pan.

And Zeus answered: "Well, I do not—"

But then Prometheus bravely interrupted: "He is right, great Zeus."

Zeus was silent for a moment, and then he said: "Well, Prometheus, because it is you who are giving the foreknowledge of their destinies to men, you must take a vow: forever remain silent on *all* prescience and on *all* prognostication."

"*All* of my future knowledge must remain hidden from mankind, Zeus?" asked Prometheus.

"Yes," replied Zeus. "I so decree."

"And now I will follow Pan's advice. Moreover," added Zeus, "I will take further steps. Cases are now judged badly for many reasons, besides the haste of the decisions and the short-sightedness of the judges. Men are tried in their clothes and their finery, and these fripperies cover the true man, and they hide his true soul. So from now on, all men will be judged naked—and they will be judged after their deaths.

"And I will appoint mortal sons of mine as the final arbitors. They shall be the gatekeepers to the other world, and they will be the final Judges. In accord with the populations of the world, two Judges—Minos and his brother Rhadamanthus—will come from Asia, and one Judge—Aeacus—will come from Europe. When these three just men, these absolutely incorruptible and fair-minded men (now alive) are finally dead, then they shall become immortal Judges in the other world.

"The three will hold court in the Great Meadow, at the crossroads from which the two paths lead—one road goes to the

Elysian Isles of the Blessed, the other road goes to Tartarus. Rhadamanthus will judge those who come from Asia, and Aeacus will judge those from Europe. To Minos, I will grant the privileges of court of appeal: if the other two Judges are in any doubt, then Minos will cast the deciding vote.

"And how will it all proceed? It shall be like this: as each shade passes the great stone bench at the crossroads, a Judge shall seize hold of him and stare deep and long into the shade's soul from the black sockets of the Judge's long-dead piercing eyes. The final stare will last one year and one day, the truth shall be laid bare, and a final judgment will be passed, forever."

And this, Theages, is the evidence that the fine men of Aegina come honestly by their fair, equitable, and truth-loving spirit. They inherited the spirit of Aeacus, who is the arbitor of shades from times immemorial.

THEAGES: Aeacus, Minos, and Rhadmanthus—and each passes final judgement by staring into the dead man's soul?

SOCRATES: Yes.

THEAGES: Tell me honestly, Socrates: Do you believe this tale?

SOCRATES: Do you, Theages?

THEAGES: I would say that it is a fine legend, but . . .

SOCRATES: But?

THEAGES: But it stretches my credulity to believe that any mortal can see into a soul.

SOCRATES: Theages, you do it every night.

THEAGES: I do? Do you mean when I dream?

SOCRATES: When you dream—and even before you fall asleep.

THEAGES: How is that?

SOCRATES: Well let me ask you this, Theages: Do things look the same to you at night as they do during the day?

THEAGES: I think that objects take on a different cast in the deep night.

SOCRATES: Let us be certain: Is there a recent night that you can picture vividly—one in which you remember how things looked to you?

THEAGES: Well last night I did not fall asleep until late, and I remember staring at the walls and at the shelves in the dark.

SOCRATES: Is there a particular object from the shelves that you can describe to me?

THEAGES: Yes, I have a small red vase; actually, it is a child's water jug. And I remember looking at it.

SOCRATES: I cannot picture it yet, Theages.

THEAGES: Let me describe it to you. This vase is about the size of your fist. It has a standard shape: it is fat and round at the bottom, with a squat tapered neck and a slightly flared lip.

SOCRATES: What about its color?

THEAGES: It is a dull red—evenly red all about—and it has two fine white lines running around its middle, like thin parallel strings. How is that?

SOCRATES: Yes, I see it quite clearly now. Did it look the same at night?

THEAGES: I have to think a moment . . . It was rather dark last night—but yes, I would say that it looked the same to me then.

SOCRATES: Now, Theages, I need your help, because only you can satisfy me on this point. Be very critical of your vision. Are you absolutely certain that it looked the same last night?

THEAGES: I must confess, Socrates, I have seen that vase so many times that I am not certain whether I remember exactly how it looked from last night. The night was black, and I was tired. I can see the vase in my mind, but I do not know whether I remember it from last night or from some other night or even from some day months ago.

SOCRATES: Concentrate, Theages: tell me exactly what you remember from last night.

THEAGES: All right. There was a black shape on the shelf, and of course, the shape was my vase. But it is strange—the harder that I think, the less certain I am that I remember one vision of it.

SOCRATES: What do you mean?

THEAGES: I cannot escape the feeling that I am remembering a whole collection of visions, all mixed together. I knew what the vase should look like, and that is what I saw. Did I actually see all the details of my vase last night? I am not sure.

SOCRATES: You are not sure?

THEAGES: For instance, at the moment I am not certain that (in the dark) I could have discerned the white lines around the middle.

SOCRATES: Do you think that you actually saw the vase at all last night?

THEAGES: Of course I did.

SOCRATES: Now, Theages, let us be very precise: Did you see the whole vase last night?

THEAGES: I would have to say that I did and that I did not.

SOCRATES: You did and you did not?

THEAGES: I saw a dark round object with my eyes, and I saw my small red vase (with its fine white lines) with my memory.

SOCRATES: You saw an object with your eyes?

THEAGES: Yes.

SOCRATES: And where was that object?

THEAGES: It was on the shelf, in my room.

SOCRATES: In addition, you saw a vase with your memory?

THEAGES: Yes I did.

SOCRATES: And where was *that* vase?

THEAGES: It was on the shelf in my room.

SOCRATES: Is that where you saw it?

THEAGES: I suppose that if we are being precise, then, no—I saw it in my mind.

SOCRATES: And where is your mind located?

THEAGES: It is a part of my soul, of course.

SOCRATES: So you looked within your soul, and you discerned something?

THEAGES: Yes.

SOCRATES: Is this not what we call "remembering"?

THEAGES: Yes. I would say that remembering is peering into one's own soul—distinguishing specific objects and then plucking them out.

SOCRATES: Specific *objects*?

THEAGES: Well, not always objects of course, "specific images" would be a more accurate descriptor.

SOCRATES: Theages, you are well known for your fine memory—especially, your memory of the old verses, like the *Iliad*. Have you thought much about the way in which your mind stores and retrieves memories?

THEAGES: No, Socrates—I have never really analyzed the remembering process.

SOCRATES: Would you agree, though, that you are probably a good source of information about remembering?

THEAGES: Yes, I suppose that I must be.

SOCRATES: From your description, it seems that you picture each memory as a single entity, sitting somewhere within the vast pile of images that you have stored within your soul.

THEAGES: It seems like that to me, Socrates.

SOCRATES: Is each memory just one specific thing?

THEAGES: Yes.

SOCRATES: It is? Consider again your small vase: close your eyes, and remember it.

THEAGES: All right.

SOCRATES: Is it just one memory?

THEAGES: Yes—I have a distinct picture of it.

SOCRATES: Do you also see the picture when you open your eyes?

THEAGES: No, not really.

SOCRATES: Close your eyes, and picture it again. Now, Theages, can you remember what the vase feels like?

THEAGES: Yes, I can. It is quite smooth—well, actually, I remember that there are little sharp edges of glaze along the bottom rim: if you run your finger along that edge then you can almost cut your skin.

SOCRATES: Is that feeling also a part of the memory of your vase?

THEAGES: Definitely.

SOCRATES: Now, Theages, open your eyes—

THEAGES: All right.

SOCRATES: Can you still remember how the vase feels?

THEAGES: Yes.

SOCRATES: Can you still see the vase?

THEAGES: No, the image of the vase is gone.

SOCRATES: Then it seems that memory of its feel is distinct from the memory of its appearance.

THEAGES: You are right.

SOCRATES: How about its smell? Does the vase have a smell?

THEAGES: A smell? . . . Yes, on very damp days, it does get a clayey smell.

SOCRATES: Can you remember that smell with your eyes opened?

THEAGES: Yes.

SOCRATES: How about the sound of your vase?

THEAGES: The sound, Socrates?

SOCRATES: Yes—if you give it a sharp tap with your finger, does your vase make a special sound?

THEAGES: I do not think I ever did that. However, I do

remember setting it down abruptly one morning, and the vase made a fine musical "ping."

SOCRATES: Can you remember that sound with your eyes opened?

THEAGES: Yes . . . You know, Socrates, now that you mention this sound, I remember well that particular day.

SOCRATES: The "ping" day?

THEAGES: Yes—the "ping" day. I had awakened with a special feeling—something about the sunshine was magical. It was the springtime; I was excited about the feel of the air or the sound of the leaves or something in the sky. I got out of bed and picked up the vase, and I tapped it down on the shelf, for no special reason. The vase made a happy "ping"; then I dressed and I was happy all day.

SOCRATES: Are the sight and the feel and the smell and the sound of your vase all memories of the same vase?

THEAGES: They are.

SOCRATES: Is any one of them the more real memory or the more elemental memory?

THEAGES: I suppose not, Socrates. Still, it is the image—the appearance—that I think of first when I think of the vase. The picture always comes first; the other memories follow.

SOCRATES: Theages, we mortals are especially visual creatures. But try this experiment: close your eyes and picture the endless ocean.

THEAGES: The ocean?

SOCRATES: Yes—put everything else out of your mind. Can you see the ocean?

THEAGES: I can.

SOCRATES: Can you hear the regular roll of the surf?

THEAGES: Yes.

SOCRATES: Now imagine a slightly clayey smell.

THEAGES: All right.

SOCRATES: What image does that conjure up?

THEAGES: It brings my vase to mind.

SOCRATES: I see. Now, return to the ocean. You are on board a ship, looking out at the sky. You run your finger along the rail, and you find a round spot like a circle. Why, Theages, it is the rim of something the size of your fist, and it is sharply glazed. What picture comes to mind?

THEAGES: My vase of course.

SOCRATES: So, other memories *can* appear first, and they can lead secondarily to the picture memory?

THEAGES: Obviously—vision can follow smell or touch.

SOCRATES: Now, capture in your mind a picture of the vase from last night.

THEAGES: All right—I see a dark round object.

SOCRATES: Can you also recreate a picture of the vase from the day that you happily tapped it on your self?

THEAGES: Yes.

SOCRATES: Do these two pictures differ?

THEAGES: Yes, they do.

SOCRATES: Could you form pictures of the vase from other nights and from other days?

THEAGES: Yes, I have countless pictures of that vase.

SOCRATES: Do the pictures differ?

THEAGES: I think that each picture may be slightly different.

SOCRATES: But they are all memories of the same vase?

THEAGES: Yes.

SOCRATES: If you think of one picture, then does it let you into the other pictures?

THEAGES: Yes.

SOCRATES: So your memory of this vase is many different but related memories?

THEAGES: My remembered vase—my ''vase memory''—

seems to be a great many slightly different things. There are many memories; there are pictures, sounds, smells, and feels all tied together somewhere inside my soul.

SOCRATES: They are all interconnected?

THEAGES: Yes, Socrates—clearly memories are all interlinked.

SOCRATES: When you say that the memories are all interlinked, do you mean that you can get to *any* memory from any other?

THEAGES: That sounds too broad, Socrates. I do not think that *every* memory can be reached from a given starting post—at least, not directly.

SOCRATES: Does this mean that your memories are arranged in some order?

THEAGES: I imagine so.

SOCRATES: Tell me, Theges: What is this order?

THEAGES: I am not certain that I know.

SOCRATES: This memory order intrigues me: I would like to explore it, Theages.

THEAGES: Fine.

SOCRATES: We have already decided that some memories come in the form of pictures. Would you say that some memories also come in the form of words?

THEAGES: Certainly. Words and names are things that we remember; thus, words can be a form of memory.

SOCRATES: Can word memories be interconnected with picture memories?

THEAGES: Definitely.

SOCRATES: You have talked about an order among memories. Do you imagine that the words and the pictures are interlinked in some rational order? Or are they all knotted together in one large indecipherable tangle?

THEAGES: Clearly there must be some sense among the interconnections: there must be some natural rational order.

SOCRATES: Then let us understand this order among words and images, Theages. Suppose that I give you a word, like "diota." What does that mean?

THEAGES: Diota? It is a two-handled vase; it is a "two-eared" amphora.

SOCRATES: Does the word "diota" conjure up a *picture* of a two-eared amphora?

THEAGES: Yes it does.

SOCRATES: Does "diota" bring to mind a Thracian foxskin cap?

THEAGES: Do you mean an alopeke?

SOCRATES: Yes.

THEAGES: No—"diota" is in no way connected with the picture of an alopeke.

SOCRATES: It is not? But, Theages, can you not picture a Thracian horseman charging fiercely down upon the enemy and wearing a foxskin helmet topped with a two-handled wine jug, upside-down?

THEAGES: Frankly, no.

SOCRATES: Hmm, I can see it quite clearly. Ah well . . . Now, Theages, when picturing a two-eared amphora, do you immediately conjure up the word "diota"?

THEAGES: Certainly.

SOCRATES: So, the word evokes the picture, and the picture evokes the word. Would you say that all memories are interconnected bi-directionally?

THEAGES: Bi-directionally?

SOCRATES: Yes. Do you find that if you can remember one way, then you can also remember the other way? For example, if a word evokes a picture, then will the picture always evoke the word?

THEAGES: Of course, Socrates—how could you imagine any other thing?

SOCRATES: Theages, an old man like me has seen many things—some of them I never would have imagined. Therefore, I try to set my imagination aside: I simply inquire of the world, in order to find what wonders and surprises the gods have set for us.

THEAGES: Be that as it may, Socrates—it seems to me that if two memories are really interconnected, then either one will always evoke the other.

SOCRATES: You may be right, Theages. Let us try a test.

Although you have lived only in Athens, you know many foreign words. Tell me: What is the name of the waxy substance that floats in the Indian Sea? (It is that stuff with an unearthly sweet smell and with magical healing properties.)

THEAGES: Ambergris of course, Socrates.

SOCRATES: That seems to have been too easy for you, Theages.

THEAGES: I have always liked that that word, Socrates. The name ''ambergris'' is Syrian, and it is related to the word ''ambrosia.''

SOCRATES: Then let me ask you to recall a more difficult name. I am thinking of an Egyptian boat. It has a long overhang at its forward end, it has a wide open waist at its middle, and it has a huge triangular sail that is hung at an angle from a short mast. (You may not have seen one of these vessels, but undoubtedly you have heard them described—you may have seen drawings of them.)

THEAGES: Yes yes—I know the boat you mean.

SOCRATES: Do you recall its name?

THEAGES: Not at the moment. I can picture the ship: it carries a tremendous amount of cargo. But I cannot remember the name. The word is on the tip of my tongue; it is something like ''prow'' or ''scow'' or ''drought.'' No, I just cannot remember it exactly.

SOCRATES: You have the definition and the picture, but you cannot go from the visual description to the name?

THEAGES: It is frustrating, Socrates, but I cannot make that last leap.

SOCRATES: I wonder if you can go the other way?

THEAGES: What do you mean?

SOCRATES: If I tell you the name, then do you think that you can immediately form the picture? If you begin with the word, then can you recall the visual image of the ship?

THEAGES: Probably.

SOCRATES: All right, let us see: close your eyes and picture a blank wall . . . Now—the name is "dhow"—

THEAGES: Dhow! Of course—the image is crisp and sharp. You know, I did see a dhow once, in the harbor at Peiraeus when I was a boy. The boat was filled with briny ropes and smelly bails, and it creaked constantly in the tide. I can remember that day very well: it was another of those magical mornings. My father carried me around on his shoulders (because I tired so easily); it was a rare treat to travel with him, and I was tall and I felt quite safe, far above the boots of all the noisy strangers.

SOCRATES: Theages, I see that this name has unleashed a whole Panathenaic procession of memories. Apparently, between some memories it *is* easier to go in one direction than in the other direction.

THEAGES: I guess you are correct—but that surprises me. I would have imagined that these memory connections are the natural links between concepts, and surely natural links are unbiased and unpolarized. If you have a bee hive then you have honey, and if you have honey then you have a bee hive.

SOCRATES: "Natural links," Theages?

THEAGES: Yes, Socrates, natural links—linkages and interconnections that are determined by the natural associations of things. There must be some natural order to the world, which was set up initially by the gods.

SOCRATES: Are all memories interconnected in this natural way?

THEAGES: I would think so, Socrates.

SOCRATES: Let me try another test: If I say "diota," then what image does *that* conjure up?

THEAGES: A two-eared wine jug.

SOCRATES: If I say "alopeke," what images does that conjure up?

THEAGES: It is the same image as before—a Thracian fur helmet. (Well, now I also see your silly vision of a mad Thracian horseman charging down the plains with a wine jug upside down on his head.)

SOCRATES: "Alopeke" is linked to a mad Thracian wearing an inverted wine jug?

THEAGES: Now it is.

SOCRATES: Is that a natural linkage?

THEAGES: Of course not—it is only because you fabricated a crazed picture, earlier in our conversation.

SOCRATES: Nonetheless, the linkage now exists in your memory?

THEAGES: Yes, I suppose that it does—but I doubt if such an unnatural linkage will last long.

SOCRATES: Oh? Now, Theages, would you consider a connection between "eeps" and meat scraps to be a natural linkage?

THEAGES: "Eeps"? What is "eeps"?

SOCRATES: "Eeps" is a nonsense word.

THEAGES: Then the answer is "no"—there is no natural linkage between "eeps" and meat scraps.

SOCRATES: When I was young, we had a dog named Ginger. At first, my little brother—

THEAGES: Are we still talking about natural linkages, Socrates?

SOCRATES: Yes.

At first, my little brother could not pronounce properly the word "meat": he used to say "eeeps." Soon, everyone in the family began to call meat scraps "eeeps." Our dog, Ginger, learned to come running when we said "eeeps"; she would drool and pant and wag her tail and jump up, hoping for a bit of meat. Ginger and my brother were about the same age. Ginger died when she was thirteen years old, and because my brother was only three years old when he invented "eeeps," I would say that Ginger probably retained this unnatural link between "eeeps" and meat scraps for at least ten years.

THEAGES: All right, Socrates—I concede that unnatural links can persist for long periods in our memories. Nonetheless, it is probable that many unnatural links fade quickly.

SOCRATES: Undoubtedly, Theages—nonetheless, I wonder: Exactly how long is "quickly"?

THEAGES: Oh, I do not know—perhaps a few days.

SOCRATES: Let us do an experiment to see if we can discover how long these unnatural links might last. However, my young mnemonist, we had best try to find out from someone with a normal memory—yours is much better than that of the average man.

Hermogenes, are you still awake?

HERMOGENES: Yes yes, Socrates—I was just resting my eyes a moment.

SOCRATES: Hermogenes, old friend, we need your help.

HERMOGENES: Certainly, Socrates.

SOCRATES: We need to create an unnatural linkage in your soul; then we would like to see how long the linkage lasts.

HERMOGENES: An "unnatural linkage"? This sounds painful.

SOCRATES: Fear not, old man.

Now, Hermogenes, repeat after me: 275 435 698 0010.

HERMOGENES: All right. 275 435 698 0010.

SOCRATES: Again please: 275 435 698 0010.

HERMOGENES: 275 435 698 0010.

SOCRATES: Again, Hermogenes.

HERMOGENES: Again?

SOCRATES: Yes.

HERMOGENES: 275 435 695 0010.

SOCRATES: No no, Hermogenes: 698.

HERMOGENES: Oh yes: 275 435 698 0010.

SOCRATES: One final time, Hermogenes—and chant it in rhythm.

HERMOGENES: All right: 275
                           435
                           698
                           0010.

SOCRATES: Good. Now, Theages, would you say that the associations between these numbers are unnatural.

THEAGES: I am not certain whether "unnatural" is the best descriptor. The linkages between these numbers are indifferent or arbitrary or even nonsensical.

SOCRATES: Very well. Let us see how long these arbitrary linkages last: Hermogenes, would you repeat the list again?

HERMOGENES: Certainly: 275
                           435
                           698
                           0010.

SOCRATES: How about you, Theages—can you repeat the list.

THEAGES: Yes: 275
                435
                698
                0010.

SOCRATES: Perfect. Now let us all wait a moment quietly . . .

   A few minutes have passed—Hermogenes, the list again, please.

HERMOGENES: Let me see: 275
                           435
                           698
                           0010.

SOCRATES: Perfect. What were you doing while we waited, Hermogenes?

HERMOGENES: I was chanting the numbers to myself, so as not to forget them.

SOCRATES: How long would the list last if you did not chant it to yourself?

HERMOGENES: Well, Theages thought that an unnatural connection might last a few days.

THEAGES: (That was just a guess.)

SOCRATES: Let us find out: Hermogenes, do you have a favorite nursery rhyme?

HERMOGENES: No.

SOCRATES: Then I will teach you a favorite of mine.

HERMOGENES: All right.

SOCRATES: It goes:

> One-ery, two-ery, ziccary zen;
> Hollowbone, crack-a-bone, nine-ery, ten.
> Spit-ery spot: it must be done—
> Twiddle-um, twaddle-um, twenty-one.

Can you repeat that?

HERMOGENES: You had better say it once again, Socrates.

SOCRATES:

> One-ery, two-ery, ziccary zen;
> Hollowbone, crack-a-bone, nine-ery, ten.
> Spit-ery spot: it must be done—
> Twiddle-um, twaddle-um, twenty-one.

HERMOGENES: Once more, Socrates. (This time I will repeat it line by line after you.)

SOCRATES: Very well: One-ery, two-ery, ziccary zen.

HERMOGENES: One-ery, two-ery, ziccary zen.

SOCRATES: Hollowbone, crack-a-bone, nine-ery, ten.

HERMOGENES: Hollowbone, crack-a-bone, nine-ery, ten.

SOCRATES: Spit-ery spot: it must be done.

HERMOGENES: Spit-ery spot: it must be done.

SOCRATES: Twiddle-um, twaddle-um, twenty-one.

HERMOGENES: Twiddle-um, twaddle-um, twenty-one.

SOCRATES: Can you repeat it yourself?

HERMOGENES:

> One-ery, two-ery, ziccary zen;
> Hollowbone, cracker-bone—

SOCRATES: Crack-*a*-bone.

HERMOGENES: Yes, yes—crack-a-bone, nine-ery, ten.

> Spit-ery spot: it must be done—
> Twiddle-um, twaddle-um, twenty-one.

SOCRATES: Again.

HERMOGENES:

> One-ery, two-ery, ziccary zen;
> Hollowbone, crack-a-bone, nine-ery, ten.
> Spit-ery spot: it must be done—
> Twiddle-um, twaddle-um, twenty-one.

SOCRATES: Perfect, Hermogenes. Can you repeat it, Theages.

THEAGES: Certainly:

> One-ery, two-ery, ziccary zen;
> Hollowbone, crack-a-bone, nine-ery, ten.
> Spit-ery spot: it must be done—
> Twiddle-um, twaddle-um, twenty-one.

SOCRATES: Now, Hermogenes—can you repeat our list of numbers?

HERMOGENES: The numbers? Well—295 475 045 . . . I do not remember them exactly, Socrates. What were they again?

SOCRATES: I do not remember either, Hermogenes. Do you Theages?

THEAGES: Yes, they were: 275 435 698 0010.

SOCRATES: You may be right—I am not certain. You have a special memory, Theages; but for a normal memory, arbitrary memory linkages seem quite ephemeral: unless continually repeated, ideas last a few minutes at best.

THEAGES: The chanting and the continued repetition that Hermogenes used is critical for all of us, Socrates. Everyone (even a mnemonist) depends on stable mental elements for his day to day memories, and it is continued repetition that inevitably transforms transient linkages into permanent linkages. In order to learn the long verses of the *Iliad,* I had to hear them over and over again, and then I needed to repeat them myself for endless hours.

SOCRATES: Then is this the way that we create certain permanent memories?

THEAGES: Yes, and if children only understood this simple fact—why, anyone can learn anything by constant repetition.

SOCRATES: But are things really so simple, Theages?

THEAGES: What do you mean?

SOCRATES: To me, this short-term chanting memory seems quite distinct from our long-term regular memory, and I am not certain that one type of memory leads inevitably to the other.

THEAGES: Of course it is not *inevitable,* Socrates: you must work at repeating the connections in order to transform short-term memories into long-term memories. It takes effort to solidify a memory; it takes energy to make it firm and fixed and unshakeable. All the links must be indelibly engraved. The short-term chanting memory is just the first stage in consolidating long-term memories. Chanting memories are the children memories that grow up to be adult, persistant memories: they are both different phases of the same thing.

SOCRATES: Is repetition always necessary to create a persistant adult memory, Theages?

THEAGES: I think so.

SOCRATES: Oh? Then tell me, young friend: Do you remember what you had for breakfast yesterday morning?

THEAGES: Yesterday? I had poached eggs with sauce—one of my favorite dishes.

SOCRATES: And you, Hermogenes? What did you have for breakfast yesterday morning?

HERMOGENES: Let me see . . . I had bread and milk, with some honey and cheese.

SOCRATES: Have either of you been asked about yesterday's breakfast, before now?

THEAGES: No.

HERMOGENES: No, certainly not.

SOCRATES: Have either of you thought about yesterday's breakfast or have you reviewed your menus before I just asked you?

THEAGES: No.

HERMOGENES: No.

SOCRATES: But you remember yesterday's breakfast perfectly?

THEAGES: Certainly.

HERMOGENES: Yes—there are some things that we remember naturally, even for a long time.

SOCRATES: Do you think that this differs from the short-term chanting memory, Theges?

THEAGES: I must admit that it does differ: the breakfast menu has remained clear in my mind for more than a day, but I have done no chanting in order to remember it.

HERMOGENES: It is the same with me: I have not thought of my breakfast since yesterday morning.

SOCRATES: Yes, some things, like your breakfasts, seem to take up a firm residence on their own within your memory. Other things, like the *Iliad,* you must work at to remember: you must chant them repeatedly, and you must struggle and sweat over them in order to afix them in your memory. What is the difference between those two types of things?

THEAGES: Well, Socrates, my breakfasts are fairly simple: they consist of only a few items. But the *Iliad* is very complex: the *Iliad* has a great many diverse words, it has innumerable intricate verses, and it has endless ornate convolutions.

Perhaps simple things stick in your soul with no effort because they take so little room. On the other hand, complex things require work to affix because each complex thing is really an assemblage of many many simple things.

SOCRATES: I see. So the difference is that complex things take up a great many spaces in your soul?

THEAGES: Yes, complex things occupy many spaces, and these many spaces must all be interconnected in order to retain them as a full, coherent, usable memory.

SOCRATES: Then let me see if I can repeat your argument. (It is complex, and by chanting it back to you, I may be able to afix it in my memory.)

THEAGES: Very well.

SOCRATES: Simple things—

THEAGES: Like a breakfast—

SOCRATES: Simple things, like a breakfast, comprise only a few interconnected items. Therefore, simple things need only a few ties in order to consolidate them within our mental storehouses. In contrast, complex things—

THEAGES: Like the *Iliad*—

SOCRATES: Complex things, like the *Iliad,* comprise manifold elements and myriad interconnections. Therefore, complex things need a great many separate consolidations in order to fit usefully within our mental storehouses.

THEAGES: Correct.

SOCRATES: So, to remember complex things, we must set to

work firming up a vast number of interattachments and building many, many tethers?

THEAGES: Exactly. The process of strengthening and of making substantial the tethers is the aging process of a memory. Aging and consolidation are why I said earlier that the chanting memories are just young and weak and tentative phases of the other, persistant, solid grownup memories.

SOCRATES: They are different stages of one and the same type of memory?

THEAGES: Yes they are.

SOCRATES: I wonder, Theages—you may be right, but then again you may be wrong.

THEAGES: Socrates, why would you think that short-term memories are really any different from long-term memories?

SOCRATES: Theages, do you know Ariphron and his father Socias?

THEAGES: I only know Ariphron by name—we have never spoken.

SOCRATES: Did you ever know Socias?

THEAGES: No.

SOCRATES: Old Socias (who has been dead now for many years) was quite fond of wine.

HERMOGENES: Fond, Socrates? Old Sosias was always drunk. He rarely ate any normal food. He would sit in the marketplace all day everyday, singing and laughing, and when he walked, he stumbled constantly.

When we were little, Theages, we teased Socias quite a bit. He was afraid of fish, and we could make him believe that sharks were crawling up his legs. Or spiders—Socias often claimed that great hairy spiders followed him everywhere.

SOCRATES: Yes, that was old Socias. Now, there is an interesting fact about Socias: he was a surprisingly good mimic. Socias could copy anything that anyone said.

HERMOGENES: He certainly could.

SOCRATES: But Socias could never remember things for longer than a few minutes. At one moment, he was maddeningly repeating every word that you said—and he was chanting them back exactly in your tone of voice.

HERMOGENES: But later if you asked him a question about that same thing, he would give you a blank stare.

SOCRATES: Often Socias could not, for the life of him, recount what you had just been talking about.

Once, I actually tested his recall. I listed all the members of my family by name. Twice, he repeated a list of seven or eight individuals. Nonetheless, a little later I asked him the name of my son, and he could not give me the name of *anyone* to whom I am related. He could not remember one single correct name.

THEAGES: So, you think that Socias had chanting memory but that he did not have a long-term memory?

SOCRATES: If he had any long-term memory, then it certainly was not the regular, full type of long-term memory like Hermogenes or I have.

THEAGES: He had no long-term memory? That is a strange state in which to live—it would be an endless foreign land.

SOCRATES: Or it would be like walking in a fog.

THEAGES: Yes. You could see immediate things clearly: it would be easy to recognize your hands, your clothes, and nearby people. In contrast, distant things would be vague and misty, and voices from far off would be a quiet blur.

SOCRATES: But once again it was not quite so simple, Theages. Socias had some memory—but what did he really know? He always made up stories, and he would talk on and on, and in order to put some organization into his foggy world, he invented names and places and events. Often, his tales seemed real. Then to complicate matters, he could dredge up a few things from his distant past—specifically, he knew names from when he had served in the army and had been a hoplite in the attacks on Scyros and Pamphylia. For instance, he frequently spoke of general Cimon who had led the invasion of Scyros.

HERMOGENES: I am surprised to hear that Socias remembered even those few details; he seemed to know nothing at all about his entire adult life.

THEAGES: From your descriptions, it seems that Socias was all clothes and no man. His talk had all the dressings and the trappings of speech, but his talk had no content: Socias had nothing to say.

SOCRATES: And that is a strange situation, Theages. It makes me think that besides having a long-term memory for specific facts, we must also have another separate long-term memory—this one for operations and procedures.

THEAGES: What are "operations and procedures"?

SOCRATES: By "operations and procedures," I mean our ordinary behavior. Let me show you what I am thinking. You have a cup beside you. Is there any wine in it?

THEAGES: No, it is water.

SOCRATES: Very well. Take the cup, and while looking at me, take a sip of water. Then set the cup down again.

THEAGES: All right . . .

SOCRATES: You did that with no problem.

THEAGES: Of course.

SOCRATES: You put the cup to your lips, you sipped some water, you swallowed, you removed the cup from your lips, and you set it down neatly on the bench. You did all this smoothly and quickly, with no special thought or effort and without spilling a drop.

THEAGES: Certainly, we do this tens of times each day of our lives.

SOCRATES: Each day of our entire lives?

THEAGES: Of course.

SOCRATES: Can a baby do that?

THEAGES: Not until he learns how to manipulate a cup.

SOCRATES: And afterwards, he remembers these behaviors?

THEAGES: Yes.

SOCRATES: These are examples of the behaviors that I refer to as remembered ''operations and procedures.'' These are things that we learn to do; then we must remember them, so that subsequently we can carry them out without thinking about them.

THEAGES: Do you think that these operational and procedural memories are different from other long-term memories? Are they stored in a different place? Do they reside separate from other long-term memories, such as the memories of specific facts?

SOCRATES: Think back to old Socias. He drank from a cup. He talked, and his talk was quite smooth; if you did not listen carefully, then you would imagine that he actually was making sense. Socias certainly remembered words, and he strung them together efficiently. Socias walked about. He could move his hands just the right way during a conversation, and he would emphasize a point with his eyebrows up and with his head tilted.

How could he do all of this, if he could remember nothing? He had forgotten most of his detailed knowledge. Nonetheless, he must have remembered his myriad daily operations—he remembered his procedures and his behaviors. Therefore, these long-term behavior memories cannot be the same as our memories of specific facts: there must be distinct repositories of operations and procedures, repositories that are in addition to and separate from the storehouses of specific facts.

THEAGES: So, not only are there short-term and long-term memories—there are also various types of long-term memories?

SOCRATES: Yes, I think that is the case, Theages.

THEAGES: And which type of memory did you draw upon when you told us of Pan's visit to Olympos?

SOCRATES: All these memories, and many more.

THEAGES: In your fairy tales of Pan, I suspect that you discovered some memories that had not yet been formed.

SOCRATES: It is possible, my friend. Who can know, where Pan is concerned?

THEAGES: You seem to have a fond spot in your heart for the old god Pan, Socrates.

SOCRATES: Yes—of all the gods, he remains closest to the earth, and he is the least pretentious.

THEAGES: I remember your little Pan poem, old friend.

SOCRATES: My "Pan poem"?

THEAGES: It was your prayer to Pan—the one that you told to Phaedrus.

SOCRATES: To Phaedrus? When was that?

THEAGES: It was just after you had returned from your trip to Larissa.

SOCRATES: Theages, if you can repeat that little poem, then you do have an incredible memory—that was more than five years ago.

THEAGES: Oh I remember it exactly, Socrates. It was rather brief; you said:

> Dear Pan, grant that I grow to be
> Deep-rooted and confident as an old oak tree,
> And cool and clean and fresh, ablaze
> Like a clear stream on bright spring days.
> And if I'm wise, I'll also be rich
> And won't even prize those few coins which
> A baby can hold in one tiny hand.
> Instead, good Pan, godling of the land,
> Give me a halo—a little child's glow
> At holding a turtle's tail-o or tickling his tiny turtley toe.

September 30: AGATHARCUS

CLEITON: Hello, Socrates—do you know the painter Agatharcus?

SOCRATES: I certainly do; Agatharcus and I have been friends for years and years. (Although, Agatharcus is not exactly a full-time friend; I would have to call him more of an afternoon friend.) Agatharcus, what brings you into the marketplace this morning?

AGATHARCUS: Yes, Socrates, it is a bit early for me to be up and about.

SOCRATES: A bit early? You are never awake until well after the midday meal. Yet suddenly today, here you are in the early morning, blinking and unsteady on your feet. Let me give you a hand, Agatharcus . . . Sit down—we will get you a cup of wine.

AGATHARCUS: No, no, thank you—I am fine; I am just a little slow to awaken.

SOCRATES: It is the foreignness of the experience that confuses you, old friend. You are probably unfamiliar with all these many things around you: women shopping for the day, servants carrying empty baskets. And then seeing Helios the sun in the East—this must make you feel as if you are in some alien land.

AGATHARCUS: Listen here, Socrates: believe it or not, I have actually seen the Dawn before—complete with her fresh rosy fingers, her pink toes, and her flowing golden robes.

SOCRATES: Undoubtedly she has aged a bit since those days. But you are looking rosy-cheeked yourself. Are you ill?

AGATHARCUS: It is just paint powder: we are preparing the scenery for *Prometheus*.

SOCRATES: Ah, a work of the master playwright Aeschylus. Are you setting up in the Temple of Dionysius?

AGATHARCUS: Yes—I am building the backdrops. I am painting a landscape (or perhaps I should call it a skyscape) of the mountain on which Prometheus was nailed to the Scythian rock.

SOCRATES: I have never seen Aeschylus's *Prometheus,* Agatharcus.

AGATHARCUS: It is a finely-wrought tragedy, Socrates.

SOCRATES: Is it not part of a trilogy?

AGATHARCUS: *Prometheus* itself is the trilogy that you mean: it comprises *Prometheus the Fire-bringer, Prometheus Bound,* and *Prometheus Unbound.* This trilogy won the annual Tragedian Prize, over fifty years ago.

CLEITON: Aeschylus won that prize twelve times.

SOCRATES: Twelve? That is remarkable!

AGATHARCUS: During one five year span, he won each year (except for when young Sophocles suddenly appeared and won with his great play, *Triptolemus*).

SOCRATES: Sophocles—what a gentle man he was. I miss him, Agatharcus.

AGATHARCUS: Sophocles was a wonderful playwright. Nonetheless, Aeschylus completely dominated Greek drama when he was alive; even today he towers above all other playwrights.

SOCRATES: Yes, he seems still to be much in demand.

AGATHARCUS: Much in demand?! Listen, Socrates: you know that Theognis wrote a play called *Agamemnon.*

SOCRATES: Yes.

AGATHARCUS: Well, we produced it recently, but when the audience discovered that it was Theognis' *Agamemnon* and not Aeschylus's *Agamemnon* some men rose in a fury. They threw stones, they shouted, and they demanded that we immediately begin the "true" play. For a moment, I feared for the chorus's life.

SOCRATES: So, you have returned to producing plays of the master?

AGATHARCUS: We have—and *Prometheus* is definitely a masterpiece.

SOCRATES: What is the plot?

AGATHARCUS: As usual, the plot is crime and punishment— the hero suffers the inexorable results of his impiety; this is like most of Aeschylus's work.

SOCRATES: Is it the traditional Prometheus story?

AGATHARCUS: In many ways it is the same. You know the background: Prometheus, the foresighted, was the son of the Titan Iapetus and the sea nymph Clymene. When he grew up, Prometheus created mankind out of clay—

CLEITON: And then Athena set all the earthen mortals alive by breathing into them.

AGATHARCUS: Later, headstrong Prometheus stole Fire from the forge of Hephaistos; he brought it to earth hidden in a hollow fennel stalk, and he gave it to men. This was against all the decrees of Zeus, sombre and stern "god above the world who directs all, who is the cause of all." Bringing Fire to man was Prometheus's great sin.

SOCRATES: In those old tales, Zeus is cold and unloving to mankind.

AGATHARCUS: Yes, and eventually, Zeus captures and punishes Prometheus: he has Hephaistos, Kratos, and Bia chain Prometheus to the Scythian rock, atop Mount Caucasus.

SOCRATES: Is this the substance of Aeschylus's drama?

AGATHARCUS: Actually, that is only the background. Aeschylus's entire trilogy takes place during the long ages that Prometheus passed on the mountain top.

During those centuries, poor tortured Prometheus is visited by all manner of divine gods and heroes and shades. First, the Oceanic Nymphs float in on a winged car to console him. Bumbling old Oceanus himself appears, riding a griffin—he advises Prometheus to beg Zeus in order to be released. Next, Io (a distracted wanderer and a victim of Zeus's love and of Hera's jealousy) comes in, and she learns Prometheus's mystical prophesy of further long and sad wanderings for her.

Finally, Hermes arrives. He is an insolent messenger of the gods, and he comes to extort Prometheus's secret knowledge. Hermes wants especially to learn the identity of the goddess who is destined to bear a formidable son—

SOCRATES: Is this the goddess Thetis?

AGATHARCUS: Exactly, Socrates. (You have the advantage of hindsight, but at the time, of course, Hermes leaves without discovering her name.) To Aeschylus, "Death always lurks behind the wall." Prometheus remains impious and unrepentant to the last, and in the final crashing fate, he and his chains and the rock and the mountain are all destroyed in one vast engulfing earthquake.

SOCRATES: Prometheus is destroyed in an earthquake?

AGATHARCUS: Yes.

SOCRATES: That differs from the old stories. In the legends, Prometheus is finally released by Heracles, during his quest for the apples of the Hesperides—as Hesiod wrote:

> Prometheus, the crafty son
> Of the Titan Iapetus,
> Stole heavenly Fire. Whereupon
> Zeus had him cruelly trussed
> With seamless bonds and magic craft
> With chains and metal rope,
> And through his middle drove a shaft
> Into the mountain slope.
> Then from Zeus an eagle flew
> To eat his liver day by day;
> But late at night the liver grew
> As much as had been gnawed away.
> And ages later, Heracles
> Released the rope and chain
> And in his hands he quickly seized
> The bird—the long-winged bane—
> And broke its neck, to finally ease
> Prometheus's endless pain.

AGATHARCUS: You remember those verses well, Socrates.

SOCRATES: Things that we learn when young remain imprinted in our minds forever.

AGATHARCUS: True enough, my friend.

SOCRATES: So, Aeschylus changed the end of the old tale?

AGATHARCUS: Yes. Aeschylus believed that once a sin is committed, the Fates inexorably carry its consequences far into the future. You cannot escape your actions: there is no reprieve.

SOCRATES: Even at the hands of the gods?

AGATHARCUS: Even at the hands of the gods. The strong gods, like Zeus, are strong precisely because they have the will to follow out any road, regardless of where it leads. The strong gods walk steadily; they walk with an even pace, both uphill and down.

SOCRATES: Would Aeschylus say that man should behave like a strong god?

AGATHARCUS: I am not certain of the answer, Socrates—Aeschylus is now dead.

SOCRATES: Yes he is, but—just a moment, Agatharcus . . . I think that I hear Aeschylus's quiet voice here.

AGATHARCUS: You are hearing voices? And what do they say?

SOCRATES: It is not "voices": it is a single voice; I think that it is Aeschylus.

AGATHARCUS: Oh? Well he is speaking too softly for me. What does he say?

SOCRATES: He says: "Yes, my friends, man *should* behave heroically like a strong god."

AGATHARCUS: Is that what he says?

SOCRATES: It is.

AGARTHARCUS: Does Aeschylus mean that man should hold

tenaciously to a course of action, regardless of the consequences?

SOCRATES: Exactly.

AGATHARCUS: Aeschylus was a wise man, and this principle sounds good. Nonetheless, it would seem to me that we must all change direction sometimes.

SOCRATES: True, we all detour: we step aside, we even turn back at times. But the heroic ideal—the goal to which we must aspire—is persistance over the long term.

AGATHARCUS: Is this Aeschylus speaking? Or is it Socrates?

SOCRATES: It is the voice of Socrates, but it is the spirit of Aeschylus.

AGATHARCUS: What gives you confidence that Aeschylus can speak to you, my friend?

SOCRATES: I have seen many of Aeschylus's tragedies, and they all set well with me. But it is more than that, Agatharcus: Aeschylus's plays resound warmly in my soul. Aeschylus's words sound true and clear. I can easily picture the man, and now Aeschylus seems to speak quietly to me from somewhere just around the corner.

AGATHARCUS: You know, Socrates, I have probably heard as much of Aeschylus's work as has any man alive.

It began almost fifty years ago, when I painted a small dais for the head of the chorus in Aeschylus's *Supplices*; I was just an apprentice in those days. Since then, I have designed, painted, and arranged the sets for most of his plays—well over eighty in all. Seeing those dramas and hearing their words day after day, year in and year out, well-spoken and poorly, with mistakes, corrections, and revisions—well, I see what you mean: this has etched his voice into my soul. It is just as you told me earlier (about the Hesiod verse that you quoted): those words with which we grow up are most strongly imprinted in our minds.

SOCRATES: There is no doubt that Aeschylus still lives in you and in me and in countless others.

AGATHARCUS: That is true, Socrates . . . So, old man, you believe that Aeschylus sets dogged persistance above all else?

SOCRATES: I believe that is what he would say, Agatharcus. Listen: Do you not hear him defending this view also?

AGATHARCUS: No, I cannot hear Aeschylus now; furthermore, Socrates, I am not convinced that this statement that you report is actually a practical view.

SOCRATES: It is not practical? Well we can put it to the test: let us try out a practical example.

AGATHARCUS: Very well. Shall I propose one?

SOCRATES: Please do.

AGATHARCUS: It is best to take a very simple case first. Let me suggest this one: Do you own a dog, Socrates?

SOCRATES: No—but when I was a boy we had a dog.

AGATHARCUS: What was his name?

SOCRATES: *Her* name, Agatharcus—it was Ginger.

AGATHARCUS: Fine. Did Ginger like meat scraps?

SOCRATES: She loved them; she would nose about for hours in any garbage pile, looking for the least bit of meat.

AGATHARCUS: Now, imagine that you awaken one morning, and you find that Ginger has disappeared. Off you go in search of her, down the market road because you know that Ginger loves to root among the leftover scraps by the sausage stalls.

(Does this sound like a practical and realistic scenario, Socrates?)

SOCRATES: I can easily picture it, Agatharcus; please continue.

AGATHARCUS: Along the way, you run into a friend—say, Cleiton.

"Good morning, Cleiton," you call out. "Have you been here long?"

"Unfortunately, I have been here for hours," answers Cleiton. "I have been waiting for Euthydemus since dawn, and he has not showed up yet."

"Ah, Euthydemus has always been here just a moment ago, or he is just about to be here soon. But Euthydemus is never actually here," you say. "On his tombstone they will write *He was here a moment ago . . .* But, Cleiton, have you seen my dog, Ginger, running by here recently?"

"No," says Cleiton, "no dogs, no children, few men, and no Euthydemuses have passed here this morning."

CLEITON: (That story is a fairy tale, Agatharcus. Few men would wait for Euthydemus—certainly no one would wait for any length of time.)

AGATHARCUS: (It is a purely hypothetical situation, Cleiton.)

Now, Socrates, what will you do? Will you persist on the road to the marketplace? Or will you go back and search in some other direction?

SOCRATES: Undoubtedly I will search somewhere else, Agatharcus.

AGATHARCUS: I see. Now tell me, Socrates: Do you believe—along with Aeschylus—that you should live your life consistently? Do you think that you should apply all of your best ideals in each realm? Should you always live by your principles?

SOCRATES: Absolutely.

AGATHARCUS: And this persistence is regardless of whether your behavior is in court, in council, in the marketplace, or in searching for your dog?

SOCRATES: Yes.

AGATHARCUS: But, Socrates, in your search for Ginger, you changed direction; you turned about face. Are you not abandoning the highest ideals of behavior?

CLEITON: Yes, Socrates—you have abandoned your principles.

AGATHARCUS: So, Socrates, why have you changed your course? Why not persist fixedly, stubbornly, and obstinately on your way—mistaken though that way may be? Initially, you set out on a clear and determined course of action. How can you reverse yourself and still remain true to your heroic standard of action?

SOCRATES: Did you say "mistaken," Agatharcus?

AGATHARCUS: I did.

SOCRATES: By "mistaken," do you mean "contrary to the best evidence that you possess"?

AGATHARCUS: Yes.

SOCRATES: Then you have answered your own questions, Agatharcus.

AGATHARCUS: Oh? How is that, my friend?

SOCRATES: Aeschylus says that persistence is the ultimate criterion for heroic behavior.

AGATHARCUS: Yes I understand that, Socrates.

SOCRATES: However, there is a qualifier, Agatharcus.

AGATHARCUS: What is that?

SOCRATES: This heroic persistence is persistence in a behavior in which one truly *believes*. But, Agatharcus, in your example you have created a situation containing "mistaken behavior." When you say "mistaken behavior," you are saying "behavior that is contrary to available evidence." Now, Agatharcus, can a man truly believe in behavior that is incompatible with other realistic information?

AGATHARCUS: This definition is getting a bit complex, Socrates. Let me see if I understand exactly what you have in mind. Are you saying that one can only truly believe in behavior that accords with other realistic information.

SOCRATES: Yes.

AGATHARCUS: I see. Then would you say: one can only believe truly in things that do not contradict other information known to be true?

SOCRATES: Well, not exactly, Agatharcus.

AGATHARCUS: What is wrong with that statement?

SOCRATES: Let me show you by example. Consider the

following situation. One day, my son comes home, and he tells me that he has bought part of a trading vessel; now he plans to set off for Egypt, with a load of wine, cloth, and figs.

AGATHARCUS: Is this a true story?

SOCRATES: No, it is imaginary. (However, the characters do resemble certain persons I know well.) Now, suppose that my son is impetuous and also that he tends to be a poor businessman.

AGATHARCUS: All right.

SOCRATES: Moreover, what if my son had always depended on me for his living money? Suppose that he had never before shown any inclination to take up an independent living. My son is a novice in business, he has no experience in seamanship, and previously he has shown poor judgement. Should I encourage him in his sea-faring commerce? Do I give him my blessing?

AGATHARCUS: It is a difficult question, Socrates, with no simple answer.

SOCRATES: Give me your best reply.

AGATHARCUS: Well, on the whole this trading adventure sounds like a step in the right direction. Assure yourself that your son's partner is an honest man; then encourage your son, and hope for the best.

SOCRATES: Would you have reservations? Would you doubt that this endeavor will end satisfactorily?

AGATHARCUS: Obviously, as you have set up the situation, the history does not bode well for the future. Still, we must always be hopeful. Besides, some effort is better than none.

SOCRATES: I agree, Agatharcus—and Aeschylus agrees too.

This is a complex world; it has manifold interactions, and it has unpredictable quiddities. We cannot talk in absolute, complete, and exhaustive terms. Therefore, I would not say (as you did earlier): "One can only believe truly in things that do not contradict other information known to be true."

That statement is too simple. Instead I would rather say: "One should hold fast to those things which least contradict other information known to be true.''

AGATHARCUS: That is a fine qualification: one should always do one's best—even when one's best is not perfect.

CLEITON: Let me interrupt here, Socrates.

SOCRATES: Certainly.

CLEITON: Socrates, I always smile when you speak of the difficulties of living comfortably in an inherently complex world. This is an issue to which you return tirelessly. ''Pockets of the world are thick tangles of incondensable complexity''—this rich complexity is your own special god.

SOCRATES: An incondensably complex world is a *mortal* world, Cleiton. In the divine realm, the great gods aspire to purity and to simplicity. Remember: the great gods are perfect, it is we mortals who are imperfect.

AGATHARCUS: We are imperfect—yet we must try our best.

SOCRATES: Exactly, Agatharcus. We lay out the best possible plan of attack—and then we *persist* in that course. Aeschylus does not require blind persistence; he does not ask us to carry out arbitrary courses of action thoughtlessly. No, Aeschylus exhorts *heroic* persistence. Aeschylus asks for persistance in those ideals and through those behaviors that are the best truths we mortals can find.

AGATHARCUS: I can only remain silent at such fine sentiments, Socrates.

SOCRATES: Ah, I appreciate your silence, but my Muse drives me ever on, Agatharcus—so I will give you another example.

AGATHARCUS: Fine.

SOCRATES: Let us consider Prometheus again. And here we should return to the very origins of his dilemma, to the time when Zeus first hears that one of his sons will rise up and threaten him. Was that not the true beginning?

AGATHARCUS: Yes, it was.

SOCRATES: Of course Zeus was worried. Zeus well knew the

parallel precedents: he had been the undoing of his father, Kronos, and Kronos had overthrown his own father, Uranos. Zeus understood that one of his sons would inevitably threaten him.

AGATHARCUS: True.

SOCRATES: Poor Prometheus, he was prescient, and he knew who it was that was destined to be the mother of this fearsome child.

AGATHARCUS: It was not prescience, Socrates: Prometheus had learned the secret from his mother, Themis. (Themis was an elder Titan, older and wiser than Zeus himself.)

SOCRATES: Ah yes, Agatharcus, you are right.

CLEITON: Exactly.

SOCRATES: Later, it was Prometheus's refusal to reveal the name of the fateful mother that drove Zeus to imprison him.

AGATHARCUS: That was not the full reason, Socrates; Zeus had also been angered by Prometheus's theft of heavenly Fire.

SOCRATES: Then was Fire the main cause?

AGATHARCUS: This bravura—this defiance—was added to a long list of irritants. You see, Prometheus had often championed mankind against the god's wishes; in truth, Zeus was none too fond of the human race. Eventually, Prometheus's constant support of us poor mortals drove the Thundergod to wreak a vengance on the young Titan.

SOCRATES: I see. Now, as I recall the original tale, all the gods knew how Prometheus could secure his release: Prometheus must simply tell Zeus the name of the mother of the vengeful son.

AGATHARCUS: That is correct, Socrates—and many deities came to plead with Prometheus, especially Hermes. But Prometheus refused to reveal the secret.

SOCRATES: Nonetheless, Prometheus *was* eventually released.

AGATHARCUS: After long ages, Heracles (on his way to

retrieve the golden apples of the Hesperides) set Prometheus free.

SOCRATES: Was this after Prometheus finally relented and told Zeus the fateful name—that is, the name of the mother of the avenging son?

AGATHARCUS: The tales go both ways, Socrates. Somehow Zeus did eventually learn the mother's name—that is, Thetis—and often it is said that he actually discovered her name from Prometheus. Whatever the truth, Heracles was Zeus's son, and it was only with Zeus's tacit approval that Heracles could release Prometheus from his eternal agony.

SOCRATES: I see: so, in the old versions of the tale, Zeus relents, and in some of these versions, Prometheus has given in also.

AGATHARCUS: Yes, many of the old legends have both gods giving ground.

SOCRATES: Zeus and Prometheus both turned aside from the path of heroic principles?

AGATHARCUS: Apparently they did.

SOCRATES: Why would the great god Zeus alter his stance?

AGATHARCUS: He may have finally learned Thetis' identity.

CLEITON: Or he may have taken pity on Prometheus.

AGATHARCUS: Then again, Heracles may have made the decision himself; in this case, Zeus gave way simply to be tolerant of his son, Heracles', willful behavior.

SOCRATES: These are all possibilities. And what about Prometheus? Why would he relent?

AGATHARCUS: Clearly he wished to avoid endless suffering.

SOCRATES: Clearly?

AGATHARCUS: Of course, Socrates, who would want to endure torment or, worse yet, death for the sake of a purely intellectual principle?

CLEITON: Yes—what person would knowingly choose to suffer?

SOCRATES: Who would be willing to suffer? Why, the great heroes of history, those men who persisted doggedly and who followed the heroic principles of honor at any cost.

Listen to brave Achilles, gentlemen. In the *Iliad*, Achilles' mother had warned him:

> Beware, my son, if you repay
>   The death of Patroclus, your friend,
> If you persist, and Hektor slay,
>   Then bleak Death too is *your* fated end.

Then she looked at him; she saw his unwavering resolve, and she wept quietly, saying:

> I see I must lose you to Death,
>   My child, now full-grown;
> The Fates have decreed your last breath
>   Will follow Hektor's own.

But the great Achilles answered back:

> My death the gods preordain.
> But I will not e'er desert
> My companion as he is slain;
> I cannot stand inert,
> A useless lump in the noontime light,
> Far from my home and hall.
> Here shall I stay and furious fight,
> And here I too shall fall.
>
> Oh how I wish that evil all
> Would vanish now from sight
> Among the gods and men. Vile gall,
> Envy, and evil spite,
> Which grow bleak hate inside
> And blacken hearts once red,
> Will one day turn to quiet pride
> Or turn to joy instead—
> But it shall not be this day, I know;
> So if Dark Deaths intone
> My name, then I shall gladly go
> In heroic robes, alone.

And when your tears are wiped aside
You will recall your own
Sweet child who'd never hide,
Who'd never yield, who'd never flee
From all acts that were best—
And then you too will smile for me.
And then, both mother and son shall rest.

Agatharcus, can this sentiment be tossed aside lightly? Should one who is dedicated to greatness waste time attempting to anticipate the Fates? Should we ever temporize? Can we balance our actions against fleeting pleasures or against ephemeral and insubstantial gain? If a man is really worth anything, then how can he waste time weighing up the prospects of life and death?

No, my friend—there is only one question to ask in performing any action, in carrying out any course of behavior, in persisting on our chosen path: Do we act rightly, or do we act wrongly— like a good man or a bad? Have we done the heroic?

AGATHARCUS: Are you speaking for Aeschylus too, Socrates?

SOCRATES: I am, old friend. For, why do you think that he changed the ending of his *Prometheus* from the standard ending of the old tales? In Aeschylus's version, Prometheus never relents, and in his fury, Zeus crashes down the mountain top, destroying the young Titan forever.

AGATHARCUS: Actually, Socrates, I had supposed that Aeschylus was emphasizing our powerlessness at the hands of the Fates.

SOCRATES: No no, Agatharcus—Aeschylus's *Prometheus* is written in the tradition of the great Achilles. Aeschylus was a student of Homer, and Aeschylus made Prometheus live up to Homer's heroic ideal: persist in right behavior, in the face of all odds.

AGATHARCUS: That is the *Iliad*, Socrates; it is from heroic days long gone. These ideals hold only for the most trying of situations. That is all well and good as a standard towards which we may aspire, but is such extreme and heroic behavior really necessary in everyday life?

SOCRATES: My good Agatharcus, can there be any other behavior? Should we behave heroically in one realm and not in another?

AGATHARCUS: But, Socrates, we must compromise a bit; we must be flexible with our wives and our children and with the shopkeepers and with our servants. Think of politics—it is the supreme realm of compromise.

SOCRATES: Can we be heroic in battle but not in politics? Dare we limit the highest standards to art and not carry them into daily life? No—in all we do, we take stands and we make choices. And we are obliged to stand and to choose heroically.

AGATHARCUS: True, but—

SOCRATES: Even when we do not admit it aloud, we have chosen quietly, Agatharcus. And where a man has once taken his stand, there he is bound to remain and to face danger.

AGATHARCUS: Danger, Socrates—in the marketplace, among friends, with our petty daily decisions? You are getting carried away.

SOCRATES: You are right, Agatharcus: I was carried away. It is not danger that we must face, it is ourselves. We must face ourselves, in the dead of night. At the late and final hour of reckoning there is no fear of ridicule or of torment or of death.

AGATHARCUS: Death? You continue to present a rather extreme and dramatic picture, Socrates.

SOCRATES: Yes, *death*, Agatharcus—for as long as he draws a breath and eats and speaks and walks upon the land, for as long as he has grateful charge of his faculties, a man should never veer from the path in which he truly believes.

AGATHARCUS: But death, Socrates? This is not merely one of the possible grim alternatives: it is the final alternative. Furthermore, Socrates, death contradicts your elemental principle—

when you are dead, then you can no longer persist in any action, let alone in heroic actions.

SOCRATES: If one cannot persist by living, then death is the only choice—for at least death is not an acquiesence.

But, Agatharcus, I suspect that you misunderstand death.

AGATHARCUS: Misunderstand death? What do you mean, Socrates?

SOCRATES: Agatharcus, there are two possibilities. On the one hand, death may be an endless, sound, and dreamless sleep; it may be the final wonderful rest. In this case, we should welcome it, with no fear.

AGATHARCUS: There would be no fear, but would we welcome such a death, Socrates?

SOCRATES: Agatharcus, pick out a night on which you slept so soundly as not even to dream. Then compare this with all the other nights and days of your life. Have you had any better or happier days or nights?

AGATHARCUS: Well—

SOCRATES: Why, were death like this, then even the Great King himself (to say nothing of any of us common folk) would have to admit that it would be the finest and most gracious of ends.

AGATHARCUS: Perhaps—but on the other hand—

SOCRATES: On the other hand, Agatharcus, perhaps one *can* persist in death. Perhaps one *can* continue to follow out one's heroic tasks among the shades of those wonderful people who passed before us, in a gentle rolling Elysian land.

Remember, good friend, we all must have our turns at death. It is an inevitable phase. And in death we must persist heroically, just as we did in the preceding phases of our life. Death is fated for us all, and I myself will welcome death at its appointed hour, in whatever guise; for I always remember warmly the prophecy of Teiresias, prince of Thebes, when he spoke to Odysseus in the Land of the Shades:

After weathering sore trials more
(And after death you put
To two score suitors at your door)
Go overland on foot,
And on your shoulder place an oar.
Walk to a far community
Where men still live with saltless meat,
Never having known the sea
Nor seen red bows of a golden fleet
With gleaming hulls that grace

The seas in swift and foam-sprayed flight.
You'll recognize the place,
For a passerby will soon recite:
"Ho!—what sort of winnowing fan
Is that you carry in your hand?"
Halt there, by that old sea-less man,
And plant your ship's oar deep inland

In the dirt, among the plants.
Then turn around again,
Without a backward glance
At man or oar or earthy glen;
Return home peacefully
To Ithaca, a home-worn breath

Floating on the deep-waved sea.
And then, fair friend, a sea-borne death
Awaits for you like mist—
Quiet, gentle, soft like tears,
Drifting in, to assist

When you are tired with seventy years.
Then all your children's children's race
Will be forever blessed with grace
And gentle winds will them embrace;
While soft rains you'll forever taste
Upon your peaceful, sleeping face.

I remember that prophecy, Agatharcus, because now I too am
seventy.

September 30: SOCRATES

SOCRATES: Hello, Socrates—with no moonlight tonight I hardly recognized you.

SOCRATES: What a silly thing to say, my friend. But I suppose that we old men can be allowed a bit of foolish talk.

SOCRATES: True. And I talk because it is so quiet here: there is not a soul stirring in the marketplace so late at night. Why are you out?

SOCRATES: When you get as old as I am, you sometimes have trouble sleeping. In the early evening I can barely keep my eyes opened. Then I awaken in the dead of night, and I cannot fall back asleep.

SOCRATES: So you walk through the empty streets?

SOCRATES: Yes, I walk about—and I talk to myself.

SOCRATES: With no one around, this city could be a dream . . . Yes, it could be a dream or some far off, peopleless land.

SOCRATES: Peopleless, perhaps, but there is still the warmth of spirits in the streets and the buildings.

SOCRATES: I feel that also.

SOCRATES: I suppose that it would be different in the wilds or in the bare desolation at the edge of the world.

SOCRATES: You and I will never see those stange lands, old man.

SOCRATES: You know, Socrates, it no longer matters. Adding one new sensation—a strange touch, a new color, a different sound, a smell, a twisted branch, a curled leaf—where would I store these oddities? I am a stretched out wineskin; I am filled to the brim. If I drop in a stone, then some of the wine will overflow. If I float a leaf on top, then undoubtedly it will roll over the edge and onto the dirt.

I would rather just sit and sag in the warm sun nowadays. Ah, I suppose that it is the accumulated tiredness of seventy years.

SOCRATES: Old age? No my friend, this is simply your laziness coming through again. You have never really wanted to do new things. Do you remember your first trip to Scyros?

SOCRATES: Of course I do.

SOCRATES: You certainly resisted going.

SOCRATES: I suppose that I did.

SOCRATES: You arose early in the morning.

SOCRATES: I had not slept well, and there was an ache in the back of my neck. Was I coming down with a cold?

SOCRATES: The sky was bright and blue, with only a touch of cloud on the horizon. You walked down the dirt road to the water, with your sack of sea-clothes on your shoulder.

SOCRATES: Everything seemed damp. The birds were too loud, and the sun was too bright. If only I had not agreed to travel, then I would still be in bed. With a leisurely stretch, I would have dressed in my old tunic instead of in the stiff canvas sailing-shirt. I would have eaten an extra slice of oatbread—then the accustomed morning greetings, as I walked to the market-place. Certainly there would have been plenty of time to think about unresolved problems from the night before.

SOCRATES: What was it you were working on?

SOCRATES: I have forgotten now, Socrates.

SOCRATES: Was it virtue?

SOCRATES: Or venality—

SOCRATES: Nemophily—

SOCRATES: Or mnemonics?

SOCRATES: Who remembers? It could as easily have been thirty years ago or last week or yesterday—you are still the same philosopher.

SOCRATES: I am? I wonder, old man.

SOCRATES: Do you recall the leaving?

SOCRATES: No, I cannot remember debarking, but I do remember arriving.

It was the morning of the next day. The island of Scyros rose from the sea. It was a line of rocks; then suddenly it was a sharp full island, treeless and green and brown. A few other ships lay about unmoving. We rolled in with the waves, and we rocked alongside the pier. Everyone climbed out, damp from the sea, salty from the spray. The buildings were low—at first they looked like piles of rocks. Children were far off. Crabs skittered along the stones. We all looked up, because much of the town towered on a steep hill. The Temple of Achilles was a rough slab house to the left, at the top of a cliff. I was far from home.

SOCRATES: I remember the clouds.

SOCRATES: The clouds—yes, they *were* striking. The sky was bright.

SOCRATES: The day was cool.

SOCRATES: And the clouds were thick and deep.

SOCRATES: They were grey-bottomed—

SOCRATES: White along the edges.

SOCRATES: Like frozen white smoke.

SOCRATES: Like white smoke.

SOCRATES: In mass after mass, they flew across the sky, past the tops of the Scyros rock peaks.

SOCRATES: The clouds arose white in the far eastern Ocean, without a thought or a care and without a glance at you or at me.

SOCRATES: They plowed steadily on, toward those fair lands beyond sight in the West.

SOCRATES: Like those clouds up there?

SOCRATES: Clouds? Where? I see only the black sky tonight, black with faint starry stripes.

SOCRATES: There are clouds above those hills, my friend,

clouds with white tops and blue outlines and dark hollow bottoms.

SOCRATES: Socrates, you have your eyes closed.

SOCRATES: Yes I do, old friend. And do you know what else I see?

SOCRATES: No—what do you see?

SOCRATES: I see a horn, in the faroff vineyards. I smell the woodlands beyond. I hear the river Cephissus, shallow and bubbling and sparkling, green and gold, with a slippery black stoney bed.

SOCRATES: Socrates, you crazed old man, the Cephissus is deep and muddy and old and slow.

SOCRATES: No no, my friend—not the Cephissus here in Attica. I hear the Cephissus that we found hiking back on Scyros.

SOCRATES: The Scyrosian mountain stream Cephissus?

SOCRATES: Exactly. It was cold and shining. Rocks stuck up along the edge, and black stones lined the bottom. A fish flashed by—a dragonfly stopped for a moment. There was no place to sit, do you remember?

SOCRATES: I certainly do: dried brush and sticks and broken stone were everywhere.

SOCRATES: That world was empty and at ease.

SOCRATES: The sky was far, far away.

SOCRATES: You know, I can still feel the ground where we finally sat down for a meal. It was rocky and scratchy; dried twigs and scrabble rock were scattered about. That wine we had was bitter—a fine balance to the cheese.

SOCRATES: Wine and cheese—ah, Socrates, the gods are making me hungry.

SOCRATES: Where would you find a bite to eat here, in the dead of night? Old man, sit down a moment and let us talk of other things.

SOCRATES: Very well. I suppose that it is too much bother to return home and to root up a snack?

SOCRATES: Of course it is too late now. (And Xanthippe would be furious if we awakened her.) It is best to stick with food for the mind, Socrates.

SOCRATES: Very well . . . (silence)

SOCRATES: It is cool tonight; the wind is chilling the hair on my arms.

SOCRATES: How can you notice? You have only a few wisps of old man's hair.

SOCRATES: Ah, but those wisps are as sensitive as a baby's hairs.

SOCRATES: Babies have no hair.

SOCRATES: You are mistaken, my friend. Some babies are born with full rich hair.

SOCRATES: Perhaps a few babies.

SOCRATES: More than a few, Socrates—have you ever seen babies that are born too early?

SOCRATES: Do you mean babies who are born too small?

SOCRATES: Yes.

SOCRATES: All right, then—I admit that the tiniest babies have some fuzz on their shoulders.

SOCRATES: Fuzz? It is hair, Socrates, and it covers their shoulders and their backs.

SOCRATES: It is not hair: it is down. The little baby's fuzz is more like the down on tiny ducks than it is like hair.

SOCRATES: Socrates, it is hair—it is baby hair—and you well know it.

SOCRATES: You know, Socrates, quibbling over words like this irritates people. I am afraid that you are not well liked.

SOCRATES: Yes, I know.

SOCRATES: What will people say after you are dead and gone? I see you walking the streets of Athens as a vague mist, as an empty shade. Will you hear: "Ah, finally old Socrates has left us in peace"?

SOCRATES: Undoubtedly.

SOCRATES: And will the man in the marketplace say this?

"When I was a boy, I could not wait to grow up. I thought: 'My parents are constantly correcting everything that I do. Let me become a man so that finally I will be free of this badgering.'

"Then finally I was a man, but I did not gain any freedom. Unfortunately, there was old Father Socrates. Socrates chided me about my language and my logic; he questioned my reasoning, my thinking, and my morals. Did we not have enough troubles, enough worries, and enough petty bothers? But cranky old Socrates insisted on setting dogstones on our thoughts and on our talk and on our habits. By the good gods, finally Socrates has left us. Now we can all rest quietly again in the peace of a parentless adulthood."

SOCRATES: Yes, Athenians will breathe more easily.

SOCRATES: Then was your life worth living, Socrates?

SOCRATES: Certainly it was. I lived up to my principles, as best I could.

SOCRATES: Yes yes, I have heard you say that repeatedly. But—badgering your poor countrymen day in and day out? Was that really a good life?

SOCRATES: What other life is there?

SOCRATES: Do not answer me with your Socratic questions, old man. You tell me: What other life is there?

SOCRATES: Ah, you yourself are badgering an old man, Socrates. Still, I suppose that at this late stage in your life, you are too old to change. Very well, I had best face your question: What is it that you would like to know?

SOCRATES: Has your life been worthwhile?

SOCRATES: Was it worthwhile? In truth, I am not certain—I suppose that if I have educated even a few of my fellow men, then I—

SOCRATES: Hold a moment, Socrates. Is that really it? This is a rather arrogant stand. Do you presume that you were so essential to this world? Would other men actually have been *less* well informed without you?

SOCRATES: Well—

SOCRATES: And, Socrates, let us even concede that dubious fact. Suppose that Plato *does* know a bit more today than he would have known had he been born in Syracuse. Does this matter? Is it worth even one fig?

SOCRATES: You are hard on an old man, my friend—but of course you are right. Have I made the world a better place? How can I really know? What would the world have been like without me?

Why, imagine that I were a river. Of course I would water the land around me, and I would cool the peoples on my shore. But what if there had been no River Socrates? Instead, there might just as well have been a woodland in my place. Or there could have been rich plowlands or craggy mountains or the teeming sea. These would have been fine alternatives, and there is no way to pretend that I was an irreplaceable part of the landscape.

Moreover, what if the River Socrates did exist but it flooded too often? Or what if it had too many stagnant pools or if it provided too easy an access for enemy ships. In fact, the surrounding peoples may well have been better off with almost *any* other natural landscape. Who can say whether the River Socrates was really of any value. No, I am afraid that I cannot rest confidently on my conceit that I have been a real contributor to humankind.

SOCRATES: You cannot rest on this conceit, Socrates—and this is because you can never know your contribution to others for certain.

SOCRATES: It is true, friend: we only rest on certainties. In the final night, the only acceptable truths are the unconditional truths. "Undoubtedly" or "probably,""if this" or "suppose that"or "it seems likely"—these conditionals simply will not permit an everlasting, peaceful sleep.

SOCRATES: Then how will you finally judge, in the deep of a night like tonight? Will you ever rest in peace? Where, Socrates, can you find true, unconditional certainties?

SOCRATES: True unconditional certainties?

SOCRATES: Yes.

SOCRATES: Where can I find true certainties? There is only one place to find them.

SOCRATES: And where is that?

SOCRATES: Well answer me this, old friend: If you had a cup of wine and if you told me that it tasted bitter, should I believe you?

SOCRATES: I would hope so, Socrates.

SOCRATES: But what if I tasted the wine myself and found it to be sweet?

SOCRATES: How could that be?

SOCRATES: Perhaps you had been joking with me.

SOCRATES: Remember, Socrates, you know me as well as you know yourself.

SOCRATES: Sometimes, old friend, I am surprised even at what I myself do.

SOCRATES: All right. Then what if I solemnly swore by the gods—by your favorite god, Pan—that the wine tastes bitter. Would you not believe me then?

SOCRATES: I would believe you as well as I would believe any man, but—

SOCRATES: But?

SOCRATES: But, Socrates, suppose that I tasted the wine again and that I still found it to be sweet.

SOCRATES: Then you must be mistaken.

SOCRATES: Oh? How should I know that?

SOCRATES: Socrates, why would I lie to you?

SOCRATES: I do not know.

SOCRATES: Furthermore, Socrates, I will go out into the

streets of Athens and I will find ten other honest men—ten or fifty or one hundred—and I will have them all taste the wine. Now listen to us all, Socrates: we all proclaim the wine to be bitter. Will you now realize that you have been mistaken?

SOCRATES: I would certainly wonder. Nonetheless, how can *I* be mistaken?

SOCRATES: You must admit, old man: we all make errors at times.

SOCRATES: I mean something different, Socrates. In the final analysis, if the wine tastes sweet to me, then the all the testimony of Athens cannot change that fact.

SOCRATES: Then is this the ultimate criterion?

SOCRATES: Testimony is always a conditional thing, old man. Consider this possibility: suppose that my ears are at fault.

SOCRATES: You drink with your ears, Socrates?

SOCRATES: You know very well what I mean. Perhaps I am mishearing the testimony of Athens. What if all men proclaim the wine to be sweet, but by some trick of the gods, my ears hear the word "sweet" as the word "bitter"?

SOCRATES: So, you propose that the wine actually is sweet and that it tastes sweet to you?

SOCRATES: Yes.

SOCRATES: And everyone else agrees that the wine is sweet?

SOCRATES: Correct.

SOCRATES: Yet it sounds (to you) as if everyone says that the wine is bitter?

SOCRATES: Exactly.

SOCRATES: Then all of our testimony is correct, and it agrees with your own personal perception.

SOCRATES: But the testimony that I *hear* tells me that the wine is bitter. Now, how can I decide what is correct?

SOCRATES: Socrates, you can only go by what you most strongly and deeply know to be true.

SOCRATES: And what do I know most strongly and deeply?

SOCRATES: It is what you experience personally.

SOCRATES: I agree: therefore, old man, I shall decide that the wine is sweet. I must always fall back on my own direct and personal sensations. I cannot rely on any indirect judgments, and there can be no intermediaries.

SOCRATES: Yes, in the end, our most solid certainties are those things that we have touched and tasted and smelled and heard and seen ourselves, from the inside and in our innermost selves.

SOCRATES: So, my friend, are you now satisfied?

SOCRATES: What do you mean?

SOCRATES: Well, old man, you have badgered me until I cannot ignore your question. You ask: Have I lived a worthwhile existence? But I must answer you honestly. If I say "Yes" then I must be absolutely confident that I have done my best in this world. I must be truly certain.

SOCRATES: Then what is your answer, Socrates?

SOCRATES: Clearly, I cannot decide by popular acclaim, and I cannot judge from hearsay. It is not by the opinion or the assessment or the judgment of anyone other than *myself* that I can ever truly be certain. The final criterion with which I can close my eyes—

SOCRATES: And rest—

SOCRATES: Yes—with which I can close my eyes and rest, at peace—this final surety can only come from me and from me alone.

SOCRATES: Very well, Socrates, then I will ask you again. Tell me from you and from you alone: Has your life been worthwhile?

SOCRATES: In the dead of the night, my friend, there seems to be no escaping you. Here, there are no other men whose conversations I can interrupt, there are no women bargaining for grain and cloth, and there are no children to distract me with their stones and bones and singing play tones.

SOCRATES: There are no men, no women, no children.

SOCRATES: I see . . .

So, you wish to know whether I have lived a satisfactory life?

SOCRATES: Yes.

SOCRATES: I do not know.

SOCRATES: Come now, Socrates, you cannot push me away. You of all men know that if the answer is not at hand, then you must never give up until you find the answer. Now, how are you going to decide whether you have wasted your days?

SOCRATES: All right, all right, my friend—let me see. We have discovered that the only lasting criteria are personal criteria: we cannot compare ourselves to others.

SOCRATES: True.

SOCRATES: We can only make these judgments directly, from inside of ourselves; we can only decide from our own personal experience. Have I really led a good, dutiful, righteous, and satisfactory life? Only if I personally feel that I have—I must believe it in my innermost soul.

SOCRATES: Very well. And do you, in your innermost soul, feel it to be true, Socrates? Have you led a satisfactory life?

SOCRATES: I do not always think so, Socrates.

SOCRATES: But sometimes?

SOCRATES: Yes, sometimes—there are times when I am quite content. Actually, I would have to say that there are times when I am more than content: there are times when I am very happy.

SOCRATES: Then tell me, Socrates: What is it that makes you happy?

SOCRATES: Well, let me think of a happy time . . . Yes, I know one. A few days ago I was walking with Plato. We were talking idly, about this and that, and after a while we sat down on the steps outside the little Temple of Apollo. The shade of the columns had kept the stone steps cool. (At that hour the sun had not yet heated all of the marble, and when you sat, your legs became cold.) I looked at my Plato. He was so young; nonetheless, there were wrinkles on his face and his skin was worn. For a moment, he was suddenly far away and old; his hands were cold. And did you ever notice how his bottom teeth are jagged and the edge of his lip sags? But his eyes are always bright, and he is so fine and so confident, Socrates. He is hard and tough. Were an archer to shoot at me, Plato would step in front and take the arrow in his chest—I have no doubt. I looked at him, my friend; he smiled, and he was young and near and I was happy.

September 31: SARPEDON

SARPEDON: Why, Socrates—with no moonlight tonight I hardly recognized you.

SOCRATES: Sarpedon? Is it you?

SARPEDON: Yes, good friend, but why are you out and about now? There is not a soul stirring here in the marketplace.

SOCRATES: When you get as old as I am, you sometimes have trouble sleeping. In the early evening, I can barely keep my eyes opened; then I awaken in the dead of night and I cannot fall back asleep.

SARPEDON: So you walk through the empty streets?

SOCRATES: I do.

SARPEDON: With no one about, this city could easily be a dream . . . Yes—it could be a dream or some far off peopleless land.

SOCRATES: Peopleless, perhaps, but there is still the warmth of spirits in the streets and the buildings.

SARPEDON: I feel that also.

SOCRATES: I suppose that it would be different in the wilds or in the bare desolation at the edges of the world.

SARPEDON: The edges of the world? . . . You know, Socrates, that reminds me of a story that my father used to tell. It was a tale about a wee bit of a god who lived off at the far corner of the world—I have not thought of that story for years and years and years.

SOCRATES: I did not know that you had ever seen your father.

SARPEDON: Oh yes. When I was quite young, Zeus would

visit my mother Laodameia and I—and when I could not fall asleep, then he would tell me tales of the gods.

SOCRATES: Well Sarpedon, here I am, awake in the dead of night and talking to myself, so perhaps you will tell me that old story.

SARPEDON: All right, Socrates. It begins long ago, when there once was a god, a very small god, and he lived on the edge of the world:

There once was a god, a very small god, and he lived on the edge of the world. He lived alone in a tiny hut, and he gardened quietly for his food. The garden plot was bordered in jipijapa plants. And this garden was in front of the little god's house, because the back wall of the house was right along the high cliff of the astral universe. In the mornings when he ate breakfast, the godling looked out and down into the deepest blue, where the clouds floated below as far as eye could see. When he looked up, it was a golden gray. And straight out there was no horizon, but the stars and the moon and the planets rolled along in the waves of the deep blue, far beyond.

The little god never talked, of course, for there was no one with whom to talk. He grew yams and he grew peas. And the days were all cool and fair, and his life was all ordered and fine. Each evening was like the early spring. A damp wind would come from a marsh not far away; it would roll over the fields and it was warmed by the grasses, the stackburs, and the field cedar. Growing so fast on a May night, the plants heated the dirt around them and you could walk barefoot for miles and miles and miles.

Nightly, the very small god would sit on his porch, in front of the house. He would look out at his garden. He would watch the yams grow and he would follow the peas as they gently twisted about on the vines, under the patient jipijapa plants. The olive trees were old, and they grew slowly and quietly.

The little god had a chair and a rail for his feet, and he sat back and rocked gently. Late one night, along by the turn of the path, down as far as he could see in that cool misty light in the back glow of the edge of the world, past the black oaks, came a young man walking along. The small god rocked quietly. The young man wore a brown tunic and he carried a cloth sack. He walked up to the porch, and without a word, he set the sack down on the ground. Then he turned, and he left. The young man passed the weathered wood fence at the far edge of the garden plot, rimmed with jipijapas, and he went up beyond the olive trees, along the beginning of the forest that rimmed the edge of the world. And then, he disappeared, through the black oaks.

Nothing stirred. No wind blew, no insects moved, the stars were frozen and watchful. The small god stopped rocking; the peas stopped growing. The night deepened, and the sack sat silently.

Now, after a while a bit of mist accumulated at the corner of the world, there along the rim of the newborn world. Undoubtedly it was some damp stardust, blown in with the universal tides as the planets swept by; it was some wispy cosmic wind from the edge of the Heavens, a bit of galactic foam. The mist curled slowly, fraying and dissolving. Then it rolled up at the tip, and it flowed, ever so gently, toward the hut and the porch and the god and the garden and the jipijapa plants and the sack.

You would not have noticed that mist, if you had not been sitting for hours, if your eyes had not been accustomed to everything else. The mist was so fine that it was like the lightest foggy rain on a rainy day. It misted and it twisted slowly, past the house and the porch, past the god and along the garden, through the jipijapa leaves. It touched the sack almost by accident. The mist curled slowly, fraying and dissolving and settling, and it slid and it sank, and the sack was misty for a moment.

A little breeze arose. The insects cricked a bit. The stars marched. The godling rocked, and the peas grew and the night deepened. The wind rustled the sack—and out of the sack rolled a smooth round stone, no bigger than your fist.

Out rolled a rock no bigger than your fist. It was just a rock, smooth and round and creased and old and worn, and it rolled with a limp.

SOCRATES: With a "limp", Sarpedon?

SARPEDON: Well, Socrates, it rolled slowly and unevenly, bumping along—not uncomfortably, mind you, but not quite smoothly. It rolled out of the sack. Now, there in front of the rock, was a small pebble; so the smooth old rock, rolling out from within the sack, opened its mouth and—

SOCRATES: Its mouth?

SARPEDON: Yes, its mouth—please do not interrupt, Socrates.

SOCRATES: I am sorry, Sarpedon; continue your tale.

SARPEDON: Very well, my friend.

The rock opened its mouth, and it swallowed that little pebble. Then it rolled on, slowly and unevenly, bumping along until it had reached the border of the garden with its neat grey fence and with the jipijapas peeking through, watching the old worn rock.

That old black rock was worn and creased through and through. It stopped at the edge of the garden, and then it opened its mouth and it swallowed the fence, post by post. It inhaled the neat grey fence, post by post by post, and then it rolled on into the garden. The peas were gently growing and twisting on the vines. The peppers were getting fat and thick. The old black rock just swallowed the peas and the vines and the peppers and the leaves and the stems and all. And then, the old black rock began to grow bigger and bigger.

The wee small god sat back, still and silent. His eyes grew wide. And the black rock rolled on and on. It opened its black rocky mouth, and it swallowed an olive tree. It gaped its stony jaws, and the forest of black oaks slid down its craggy gullet. Its canyon chasm swallowed fields and grasses and stackburs and cedar; it swallowed knotroot grasses and rutabaga fields and crabapples and tangleberries. The old black rock was round and swollen—it looked like a great black hill. It sipped and it sucked the river beyond; it drank and it gulped the marshes, the lowlands, and all the wet places that lined the old foresty woodlands, down past the hills on the edge of the world. That old black rock, from within the sack, had become a giant; it was stone-crushing, bone-breaking, and mountain-devouring. Relentlessly it ate, and it tore away at the lands and the towns and the great grey granite cliffs afar. The wee small god sat very still indeed.

SOCRATES: Yes, very still, indeed.

SARPEDON: With a ravenous intake of all that was around it, the rock devoured the earth; the oceans sank into its bottomless throat. As the waters poured down in a murky whirlpool, a small island floated toward the black maw. On the island was a tiny yellow flower—a buttercup. In the daylight it would be a bit of golden sun, with five round petals newly painted, happy and bright. In the center of the buttercup was a little puff of yellow. It would be smiling there, that buttercup, standing on its one spindly leg with a few green shavings on its toes. That would have been in the day of course. But now it was night, and the black rock swallowed the island, buttercup and all, clover fields and honey hives and gulls nests and crab caves and all.

Insatiable, the enormous rock devoured the islands and the seas. It ate the earth, and it ate the Ocean's roaring streams. As the waters poured down its bottomless throat, an old ship was swept along. On its mast was a torn sail, on the sail was a frayed rope, and on the rope was a black bug. In the daylight the bug would be a glistening beetle; it would be a soldier dressed in glints and gleams, with shining wings and neat clicking feet. It would be standing there at attention on its sharp legs, with not one speck of beetle dust, not one smudge of beetle dirt. That would have been in the day of course. But now it was night, and the black rock blindly swallowed the ship, sail, rope, beetle and all, planks and flags, sailors and rigging and rudder and all.

With boundless appetite, the vast rock sucked in the seas; it drained the rivers, it emptied the lakes and the ponds and the bays, it dispatched the brown hills and the gray cliffs. And as the land broke away and crumbled into the grim gaping pit, a thatched home teetered on one of the massive rock teeth. In this home was a baby, just one month old. In the daylight that child would be opened-eyed, rosy-cheeked, and tousled haired; it would wave its fists and it would roll its wrinkly neck. The tiny child would raise its eyebrows, surprised at every thing around it—its crib and its mother and its blankets and its fist. The little baby would blink and flip its tongue and hit its eye with its tight hand and twist its lumpy pink potatoe of a tummy around. That would have been in the day of course. But now it was night, and the black rock could not see and it could not hear and it could not smell or feel or taste—and it did not care. The home fell in, and the thick black mountain of a rock swallowed the home, baby and all, crib and blankets and mother and father and cupboards and all, and grandmothers and grandfathers and grandchildren and all.

SOCRATES: And all.

SARPEDON: Now the only thing that the little god could see was a massive black shape, as tall as the sky and as wide as the earth. It was the back of the old black hungry rock.

From within this rock, there came a deep rumbling and drumming sound, as the blocks and the chunks of the world fell upon one another. Inside of the great rock, thunder echoed back and forth and waves crashed. The massive black shape grew larger and larger and larger. On the far side, the whole mortal earth was fast disappearing, and the wee small god sat there, on the last remaining rim of the world, with the clouds and stars and vast cosmic spaces falling endlessly away behind him, with the deep blue sea of the Heavens rolling forever back. And the old black rock devoured the entire earth—and then it began to turn around.

SOCRATES: It began to turn around?

SARPEDON: Yes, the old black rock—worn and creased, massive, swollen, mountainy, and thick—it stopped, and it turned around. It turned back toward the wee small god. The cold black breath of its chasm and gullet chilled the air, as it rolled back toward the house at the edge of the world. Its stone jaws were wide; its stone mouth was empty.

The wee small god sat still as stone himself. There was no marsh, no woods, no garden, no jipijapa plants. There was only the wee small god on his rocking chair and porch, with blackness before him and with endless Night behind. The old black rock was full in front and as wide as forever. It was as cold as Death, and it moved and it rumbled and it drummed and it echoed, and the wee small god just sat still. The wee small god sat still as stone—and then, Socrates, then the little baby godling jumped.

The wee small god—this little god at the edge of the world, living on the rim of the fresh, clean, old world of before—he jumped. He jumped a little baby godling's leap, as only a little god can jump. He bounced up, and he leaped around, and he tipped and he topped and he flipped right up and over that massive black mountain hole. The wee little god jumped higher than the knotroot grasses; he jumped higher than the appletrees. The wee small god jimped and he jumped, and he tickled the nose of the old black rock, the old worn nose, past the creased crevice and up around. And that hungry rock stretched its black chasm of Death, its gloomy black jaws, to snap and to gobble the last little god from all this mortal earth—and then it cracked.

The old stone rock cracked and it split. The old black rock stretched and it gaped, and it cracked, and great thundering fjords broke along its old worn face. Great thundering jagged rips of stone rent its sides, and in powdering spumes of dust and scrabbling skree, it dissolved—like a curtain of harsh rain at the end of a storm, when it is suddenly ripped and blown away by the wind. Then the world tumbled forth again, and as the clouds and the rocks and the trees and the lands suddenly fell into place, there was blank silence once more across the world.

SOCRATES: A silence across the world.

SARPEDON: For a moment, the wee small god was lost—he found himself on the grass, in the corner of a woods. The godling looked around, and he saw the old oak trees and the low spicebush brush. He picked up two brown leaves and crumbled them and cracked them, and he kicked a little pebble.

Then the little one walked back, slowly, to his hcuse on the edge of the world. The little godling walked down the path, in the cool misty light, and he passed the sack sitting in front of his porch. A hint of mist curled about the brown canvas flap of that old sack. The little god climbed onto his porch; he sat on his chair, and he watched the peas growing again on their summer-pea vines.

The wee small god sat back, and he gently rocked. The ancient olive trees continued to grow, slowly and quietly. And after a while, along by the turn of the path, down as far as you could see in that cool misty just-before-morning light, in the back glow of the edge of the world, past the black oaks, came the young man walking along. The small god rocked quietly. The young man walked up to the porch. Without a word, he took the sack; and then without a backward glance, he turned and he left.

The young man passed the weathered wood fence—now grey in the early light—at the far edge of the garden plot. The garden was rimmed with jipijapa plants, and the young man went up beyond the jipijapas and beyond the olive trees along the beginning of the black oak forest that rimmed the edge of the world. The very small god looked away and then he looked back again, and he rocked a bit. The grass was a misty sea. The first streams of sunlight from the great and rosy-fingered Dawn rolled across the marsh, the field, the hills, and the trees. And soon, even in the morning glow, I could not tell whether it was a young man in brown tunic. Or was it just one of the oaks that had stepped out into the dirt road—an oak that had decided to dig its rooty toes into a fine cool spring morning road.

SOCRATES: *You* could not tell, Sarpedon?

SARPEDON: Yes *I*, Socrates—for my father would say that it was a story about me, when I was just a very small god, once long ago when I lived on the far edge of my bright, fresh, baby godling world.